MERCHANT FLEETS

First published 1992

British Library Publication Data

HAWS. Duncan,
    Merchant Fleets 23
    Canadian Pacific
    1. Merchant Marine History.
    1. Title.

ISBN 0 946378 20 7

Printed in 9 on 10 point Times by
The Starling Press Ltd., Rogerstone, Newport, Gwent NP1 9FQ
for TCL Publications, 1 Meadow Bank, Hereford HR1 2ST, England.

CONTENTS

ILLUSTRATIONS BY DUNCAN HAWS
Scale 1: 1200 ie 1 inch = 100 ft

INTRODUCTION

CANADIAN PACIFIC

Originally this book formed a part of volume 3 of the earlier 1979 much more condensed Merchant Fleets in Profile quartet. I have expanded that section to full book length, re-drawn the profiles to the larger scale now regularly used and brought the whole work up to date.

The short unadorned name of this book is chosen deliberately because it is about the ships owned by a very great railway company which helped to weld Canada into a unified country and, geographically, linked Great Britain via the 'All Red Route' to Hong Kong and Australia. The vessels which it owned within the group were diverse: ranging from sternwheelers on the lakes and rivers of British Columbia to giant passenger liners epitomised by the lovely and tragic *Empress of Britain* (201).

Sadly, yet again, the shipowning activities have been divested entirely – although investment in some vessels ans ship management remains. So, once again, this volume becomes the recounting of a historical saga rather than the story of a burgeoning shipowner.

In compiling the book I have again used all the many times praised sources: Lloyd's Register (the base document), Sea Breezes, Syren & Shipping, Motor Ships, the invaluable Marine News, Ships Monthly, Alan Tennent on U-boats and the World Ship Society Photo Library. Nancy Williate-Battet of CP, Montreal has kindly ended the story at Dec. 1991.

The books consulted for snippets are legion and too numerous usefully to list; however mention must be made of those books majoring all or in part on C.P.R.: Noel Bonsor's *North Atlantic Seaway*, George Musk's classic *Canadian Pacific*, Newell & Williamson's *Pacific Coastal Liners* and *Pacific Steamboats*, George Newell's *Ships of the Inland Sea*, Harold Innis's *History of the Canadian Pacific Railway*, Art Down's *Paddlewheels on the Frontier*, Richard Benson's *Steamships and Motorships of the West Coast*, G & P Bannerman's *Ships of British Columbia* and George Hilton's *Great Lakes Ferries*, plus my own C.P.R. files going back to a Liverpool childhood.

DUNCAN HAWS

Hereford
December 1991

EXPLANATORY NOTES

Research: The details are repeated in such a way that individual ships or dates can be looked up without the need for further study.

Tonnage: These frequently changed during the lifetime of a ship. Those recorded applied when the ship entered service or was acquired. Minor changes are not included.

Dimensions: Are 'Between Perpendiculars' unless otherwise stated.

Limited: Except where applicable in the text the word is omitted.

ABBREVIATIONS

To assist international readers as few as possible have been used. Short cuts to reduce printing have been avoided.

aux	auxiliary		kts	knots
B	Built		lp	low pressure
bhp	brake horse power		Ltd	Limited
blr	boiler		m	metre
C:	Cargo		M/v	Maiden voyage
CP	Canadian Pacific		min	minute
CPOS	Canadian Pacific Ocean Services		mp	medium pressure
CPR	Canadian Pacific Railway		max	maximum
CPS	Canadian Pacific Ships Ltd.		n	net tons
CPSS	Canadian Pacific Steamships Ltd.		nhp	nominal horse power
Co	Company		oa	overall
comp	compound		obb	over bulbous bow
cu	cubic		**P**	Passengers
cyl	cylinder		P.O.W.	Prisoner of War
dbl	double		psi	pounds per square inch
drg	double reduction geared		Q	Quarter deck
dft	draught		quad	quadruple
dk	deck		ref	refrigerated
D	Dimensions		r	registered tons
DD	Dry Dock		rhp	registered horse power
disp	displacement		r/n	renamed
dwt	deadweight		rpm	revolutions per minute
E	Eng/Engine		SB	Shipbuilding
Eng'g	Engineering		Shg	Shipping
exp	expansion		S.N.	Steam Navigation
F/Fcsle	Forecastle		srg	single reduction geared
ft	foot		SS Co	Steamship Company
furn	furnace		S.S.Co	Steam Ship Company
g	gross tons		scr	screw
gp	goal post masts		stm	steam
H	Hull		**T**	Tonnage
hp	horse power		tpd	tons per day
hp	high pressure		tpl	triple
hrs	hours		Tst	Tourist
in	inch		turb	turbine
inv	inverted		tw	twin
ihp	indicated horse power		Wks	Works.
km	kilometres			

5

CANADIAN PACIFIC

Chronological History

1873 The story of the Canadian Pacific Railway Company's connection with the sea began when Sir Hugh Allan, founder of the Allan Line, which was itself finally to become a part of Canadian Pacific, was made president of a company formed to construct a railway extending across Canada to the Pacific Ocean. It was, however, to be some years before the construction actually began.

1880 Oct 21: The contract for the construction of the CPR railroad was signed.

1881 Feb 1: Letters Patent creating the Canadian Pacific Railway Company were issued thereby fulfilling the promise given to British Columbia, when back in 1871, the Province joined the Dominion of Canada. Feb 16: The Company was incorporated.
May 2: The first sod was cut at Montreal, marking the beginning of the main construction. However, financial troubles caused several delays and it was not until the intervention of the energetic Donald A.Smith (later Lord Strathcona) and his financial partner George Stephen (later Lord Mount Stephen) that matters were brought under control and progress made. In fact George Stephen became the first President of the Company.

These two men, and their associates, negotiated to receive from the Dominion Government of Canada the sum of £5 million to complete the construction, 25 million acres of land for railway use and development (some of which was later returned to the Government) together with the 713 miles of track already laid.

The company appointed as its chief engineer and surveyor Sandford Fleming whilst construction was placed in the hands of William Van Horne, a man of dynamic thrust, tenacity and ingenuity.

1882 Jan 1: W.C. Van Horne, then the manager of the Chicago, Milwaukee & St Paul Railway Co., joined CPR as General manager. In October he was joined, from his former company, by T.G. Shaughnessy who became CPR's Purchasing Agent. At the same time Henry Beatty, a partner in North West Transportation, became head of CPR's Lake Transportation Services.

1883 By this date CPR's issued shares totalled 550,000 held by 525 stockholders. Not all were Canadian. Citizens of New York State held 290,000 shares, those of Quebec Province over 100,000, Great Britain in excess of 90,000, with the Netherlands holding 57,000 and France 15,000. The largest numbers were thus concentrated in New York and Montreal. Among the men prominent in CPR George Stephen (later Lord Mount Stephen) held 31,000, Donald Smith (later Lord Strathcona) 23,000, Duncan MacIntyre (manager of the Canada Central Railway) 20,000, R.B. Angus 15,000 and Messrs J.S. Kennedy and J.J. Hill 10,000 each. A further 60,000 were held by solicitors on behalf of funding banks - such as the Bank of Montreal - who were advancing loan money on behalf of the Canadian Government to cover railway construction in the 'wilderness areas' of British Columbia, etc.

There was muted concern that voting control could pass into the hands of the United States whose own transcontinental railways were in competition with those of CPR. There were already signs of a possible conflict of interests because the Canadian route along the Great Lakes northern shore was pretty inhospitable whereas the southern US perimeters were, by comparison, thriving.

To develop steamship services, along the Pacific coastline of both the United States of America and Canada, Captain John Irving (he later styled himself Commodore) and some associates formed a syndicate which took over the Hudson Bay Company's marine division and its services from Vancouver to Alaska and set about expanding them. To do this they formed the **Canadian Pacific Navigation Company** - known as CPN - in which, at this stage CPR had no interest. Their ships had buff funnels with black tops.

In addition to the inherited services CPN commenced the important task of introducing freight and passenger services to many of the small townships which dotted the coastline of British Columbia. To the States they established routes into Puget Sound to serve places like Seattle and Olympia.

CPN was well aware of the progress of the transcontinental railway and planned to meet the boom in trade that would follow the linking of the Pacific coast to the remainder of the Canadian centres of trade.

At this stage CPN owned ten ships but, as trade warranted, they purchased a miscellany of vessels, 11 of them small and sturdy craft.

1884 The Canadian Pacific Railway Company entered ship owning. Their charter, in Appendix 'B' thereto, contained the following comprehensive clause No 26:

"The Company shall have the power and authority to erect and maintain docks, shipyards, wharves, slips and piers at any point on or in connection with the said Canadian Pacific Railway and at the termini thereof on navigable water, for the convenience and accommodation of vessels and elevators; and also to acquire and work elevators and to acquire, own, hold, charter work and run steam and other vessels for cargo and passenger upon any navigable water which the Canadian Pacific Railway may reach or connect with".

By now the construction of the line was spreading along the north shore of Lake Superior and grain storage elevators were being built to receive prairie grain for onward shipment. To assist in the task three steamers were built on the Clyde, these being *Algoma*, *Alberta* and *Athabasca*. The vessels made their own way across the Atlantic but, being too large for the existing St Lawrence river locks, were built so that they could be cut in half at Montreal and towed from there to Buffalo where they were re-joined. These three then ferried construction workers and material along the lake to the expanding railhead. In the time left over they introduced the Company's Great Lake services.

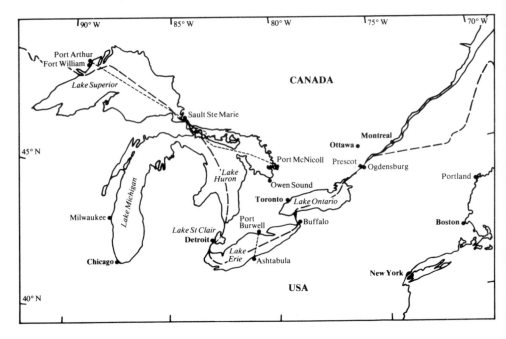

1885 Oct: The Imperial Government in London advertised for offers to open a steamship service Vancouver-Hong Kong. CPR offered two sailings per month in return for a ten year subsidy of £100,000 per annum. This was refused as too high a sum and too long a duration. Nor was the amount of mail between the two ports high enough. CPR pointed out that the Far East mail would reach London quicker via Canada than by the existing P & O service.

On November 7, the transcontinental railway was completed when Lord Strathcona drove in the last sleeper spike at Craigallachie, midway between Calgary and Vancouver. The next day the first through train left Montreal for Port Moody, on the Burrard Inlet, near Vancouver. But signalling and the introduction of extra rolling stock took a further six months to implement.

Tragically on the very same day CPR suffered its first shipwreck when *Algoma* sank in a storm off Isle Royale with the loss of 48 of the 63 aboard.

1886 June 28: Regular passenger services were inaugurated between Montreal and Port Moody, Vancouver, with a journey time of five and a half days. A steamer service, by Canadian Pacific Navigation Co., from Vancouver to Victoria was introduced to connect.

The main CPR problem was that the rail trucks were returned empty westwards from Vancouver. The Board had to encourage Orient shippers to send their Europe bound goods via Canada. In readiness for trade with the Orient, CPR appointed Everett, Frazer & Co., Hong Kong, as their Far East Freight Agents. A number of sailing vessels were chartered the first being *W.B. Flint* which arrived at Port Moody, on July 27, with a cargo of tea for New York. Her crossing had taken a month.

Other charters followed with sailings taken by *Bylgia, Carrie Delap, Eudora, Flora P, Frieda Gramph, Stafford* and *Zoroya*.

1887 CPR's first British Columbian vessel was the chartered *Skuzzy* (I) which was used by the construction engineer Andrew Onderdonk for Fraser River work. In fact they never owned this vessel.

May 23: Vancouver's Granville Street Station became the Pacific terminus. The first train to complete the 2,900 miles from Montreal arrived four days later.

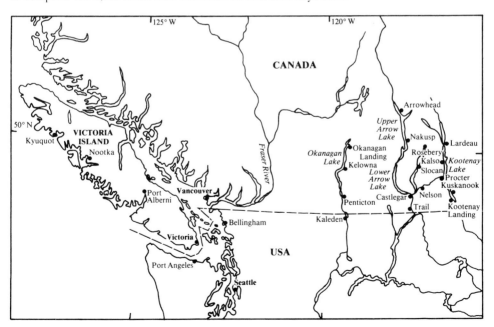

Plans to link the Orient with Canada had been dependent upon the introduction of a regular rail service for both passengers and freight into Vancouver. With this service now in being the introduction of a transpacific steamship service could really commence. At Hong Kong Adamson & Bell were appointed managers by CPR to inaugurate the route for them. Three of the Guion Line's ex-Cunard passenger steamers, *Abyssinia* (5), *(Milburn), Port Fairy* (Milburn), *Straits of Belle Isle* (N. MacLean & Co.), *Sussex* (Money, Wigram) and *Zambesi* (P & O) were chartered; mainly for single voyages Hong Kong-Japan-Vancouver prior to their inbound to UK China tea service.

In July CPR made another offer to run monthly from Vancouver to Hong Kong via Shanghai. This time the Canadian Government agreed to subscribe £15,000 per annum for a monthly sailing and £25,000 for twice monthly departures subject to there being through connections across the Atlantic to London and provided the London authorities met their share. The agreement, modified, was duly signed in 1889 (q.v.).

1888 The flow of Chinese workers bound for the United States, to which no suitable service then existed, necessitated a Vancouver-USA service and this led to a close working relationship with the Canadian Pacific Navigation Co., of Vancouver.

1889 The Canadian built *Manitoba* replaced the lost *Algoma*. She was powered by *Algoma*'s machinery.

July: CPR signed the ten year Canadian Transpacific Mail Contract with the Government of UK which carried a subsidy of £60,000 per annum of which the Canadian share was £15,000. The mail route was to be rail Halifax-Vancouver, ship Vancouver-Yokohama-Shanghai-Hong Kong and to be accomplished in 684 hours April-November and 732 hours in winter. A penalty of £500 was payable for a late departure and £100 per 24 hours, or part of, for delays. In addition the Admiralty could hire the ships at 20 shillings per gross ton at any time of their choosing (the other terms being suspended for the period) and during the contract term troops should be carried at cost price. In effect the CPR ships were to be available not only in time of war but also if the British Pacific Fleet's cruiser squadron fell below strength. The contract thus demanded an all weathers average service speed of 16 knots with 17½ knots for emergencies. Furthermore the mail vessels had to be built to satisfy the British Admiralty requirements for subsidised steamers to act as armed merchant cruisers in the Pacific or to serve as troopships.

To meet these requirements for their planned three vessels CPR went to the Naval Construction and Armament Co., Barrow-in-Furness, whose skills were entirely suited to just such specifications. In fact in making their proposals the firm guaranteed not 17½ knots but a service speed, if necessary, of 18 knots. (Presciently, this actually was put forward with Royal Naval duties in mind.) On Oct 12 the three ships were ordered as *Empress of India* (9), *Empress of Japan* (10) and *Empress of China* (11).

With the completion in 1887 of the link to the Pacific, eastern Canada was served almost entirely by the Grand Trunk Railway. The Government of Canada then encouraged CPR to expand their activities into Ontario, Quebec and the Maritime Provinces. (This policy has been criticised because the Grand Trunk Railway was thereby so weakened financially that it had to be taken into Government ownership and is today's Canadian National Railway.) Thus by 1889 (July 22) CPR had extended its railhead to Saint John, New Brunswick (known as the 'Short Line'; Halifax was the 'Long Line'). This led to a Government offer of £110,000 per annum for a twice monthly transatlantic service - but the arrangement failed to materialise; mainly because of the supremacy of New York. It was pointed out that European shipowners carried the mass of the traffic and a Canadian based company serving St John stood little chance against such competition.

In July Anderson, Anderson & Co., managers of the Orient Line, announced the likelihood of a weekly contract on the Canadian route but it failed to be implemented for much the same reason.

1890 CPR constructed a branch line from London, Ontario, to Detroit. This 112 mile stretch ran parallel, and indeed, in sight of the Grand Trunk Railway. To complete the rail link to Detroit, where the service would be handled at the Wabash Railway Co's slips, a ferry service was needed across the Detroit River. CPR now took delivery of the two ferries *Michigan* (12) and *Ontario* (13) which were the longest and largest paddle ferries ever to serve on the Great Lakes (but not the largest paddlers, of course).

June: Passenger services were started from Toronto-Chicago and Montreal-Chicago using *Alberta* (2) and *Athabasca* (1) which were no longer needed for railway construction support.

In late 1890, in readiness for the introduction of their three new Empress liners CPR announced three delivery voyage 'Round the World' cruises. The itinerary was Liverpool-Gibraltar-Naples-Port Said-Suez-Colombo-Penang-Singapore-Hong Kong-Woosung-Nagasaki-Kobe-Yokohama-Vancouver-CPR to Montreal thence any Atlantic sailing back to Europe. At prices starting from £120 there was a quick demand - especially for the first cruise which was a sell out.

1891 Feb 8: *Empress of India* (9) was commissioned and sailed from Liverpool. In order to run in her engines she proceeded to Hong Kong at only 10 kts. Apr 16: The vessel arrived at Yokohama. Her first crossing to Vancouver in a little over 10½ days established a record; better still the mails from Yokohama reached Montreal in only 14 days 22 hours. Apr 11 saw the introduction into service of *Empress of Japan* (10) and the third of the trio followed on July 15. With the entry of the new ships *Abyssinia*, *Batavia* and *Parthia* were released from passenger service.

Aug 19: On her second voyage *Empress of Japan* beat the transpacific record arriving at Vancouver on Aug 31. The connecting boat train enabled both passengers and mail to arrive in New York in time to catch the Inman liner *City of New York* bound for Liverpool. The Yokohama mail reached London on Sept 9, in a time of less than three weeks and, incidentally, ten days below the contract time. This event was hailed with near incredulity and aroused world wide comment and praise.

1896 The Crow's Nest branch of CPR was completed and added southern British Columbia to the steamer network as well as opening up the line into Montana State, USA.

1897 For the planned 'All Canadian Route' to the Yukon, up the Stikine River to Telegraph Creek then 150 miles by rail to Lake Teslin and thence, again, by steamer to Dawson City, CPR planned a fleet of no fewer than 20 vessels. Politics killed the 150 miles of rail and the four ships so far built were redundant. See *Hamlin* (35).

CPR purchased the **Columbia & Kootenay Steam Navigation Company** for $200,000 and with this acquisition entered into the sternwheeler traffic of the lakes and rivers of the Canadian Rockies.

Following the strike at Bonanza (giving a word to the English language) the second Klondyke Gold Rush also began, bringing many thousands of prospectors to the area - as well as a host of elderly steam ships. CPR reacted by buying *Athenian* (34) and *Tartar* (33) from the Union Steam Ship Co. For their delivery voyage from Southampton each was loaded with every conceivable item of equipment that a gold prospector could possibly want.

1898 Feb 8: *Tartar* left Southampton carrying the first batch of prospectors. *Athenian* followed a few days later. Both vessels carried 'Round Trip' passengers for £65. Out to Vancouver and back by rail and a choice of transatlantic steamer. The single fare to Vancouver was £230 1st and £20 2nd class. After the Gold Rush subsided both vessels served on secondary transpacific routes.

In the December *Athenian* made CPR's first call at Honolulu.

1901 March 5: The ships and coastal services of the **Canadian Pacific Navigation Company** were acquired. the vessels taken over were (48-61): *Amur*, *Beaver (I)*, *Charmer*, *Danube*, *Islander*, *Maude*, *Otter (I)*, *Princess Louise (I)*, *Queen City*, *R.P. Rithet*, *Tees*, *Transfer*, *Willapa* and

Yosemite. Unfortunately the largest ship, *Islander* was lost before actually entering CPR service. To replace her the China coastal packet *Ningchow* was bought and renamed *Princess May* and she thereby commenced the practice of 'Princess' names which have been applied to the passenger ships of the Pacific coast ever since. As part of the deal Captain Irving was given a free CPR ship pass for life and he spent much of his later life on the ships which he had once owned.

1902 Following the formation of Pierpont Morgan's International Mercantile Marine Company, the Canadian Government again called upon CPR to institute transatlantic services and offered a financial guarantee in respect of the monies needed to acquire the necessary ships. Half the Canadian mail contract was included in the deal; to become effective as soon as the new tonnage was introduced.

1903 Feb 23: The 1902 deal was announced. Mar 27: As a result of the negotiations (George M. Bosworth was Vice President in charge of negotiations) CPR purchased for £1,417,000 the route interests and fleet of fifteen vessels (book value £1,120,000) which comprised the North Atlantic activities of **Elder, Dempster & Co Ltd.** This included their subsidiary the **Beaver Line** (formerly the Canadian Steamship Company Elder, Dempster acquired in 1898). The ships taken over were *Lake Manitoba, Lake Michigan, Lake Champlain* and *Lake Erie* from the Beaver Line and *Milwaukee, Montreal (I), Montcalm (I), Montfort, Monterey, Monteagle, Montrose (I), Monmouth, Montezuma (I), Mount Royal* and *Mount Temple* from Elder, Dempster. This introduced CPR services from Liverpool, London and Avonmouth. On March 31 *Lake Manitoba* took the final advertised 'Beaver Line' sailing. CPR's first North Atlantic loss soon followed when, on July 10, *Monterey* was lost on Miquelon Island in the St Lawrence estuary. Incidentally the sale was one which Alfred Jones soon bitterly regretted. CPR paid in cash and, to raise it, issued debenture stock of £1.5 million. It was heavily oversubscribed and immediately exchanged hands at a premium. CPR had bought a bargain.

1904 Jan 20: *Princess Beatrice* inaugurated the year round service between Seattle and the British Columbian capital of Victoria. From the summer of that year Vancouver was added to her schedule and she was joined by CPR's first three-funneller *Princess Victoria* - known affectionately as the *Princess Vic.* The new ship kept an immaculate schedule being easily capable of over 20 knots when required. The main competition which CPR faced came from the American Puget Sound Navigation Co. whose vessels *Chippiwa* and *Iroquois* were both fast steamers. *Princess Vic* boasted a resplendently uniformed bugler who announced all meal times and the story is told of how he would stand at the stern of his ship and deliver a fanfare as the *Vic* sped past one of her rivals.

Antwerp was added to the London service. *Montrose (I), Montreal (I), Mount Temple* and *Montfort* were placed on the route.

1905 June 11: *Princess Victoria* established the record for the 70-mile run Seattle-Victoria. This was claimed as the fastest steamship route in North America. The publicity pointed out that if the transpacific ships were capable of such a speed then a whole 24-hours would be clipped off the voyage.

1906 On the Great Lakes CPR was now ferrying 200 rail freight cars a day across the Detroit River. This was, however, below the full capacity of the two paddlers on the route and at various times *Michigan* was chartered to the Grand Trunk and Pere Marquette railway companies.

May: The first of two new Atlantic liners *Empress of Britain* (I) entered service between Liverpool and Quebec. She and her sister, *Empress of Ireland* soon captured both the westbound and eastbound records and were consistently better than the Allan Line's crack ships *Victorian* and *Virginian*. With the advent of these two new ships Canadian Pacific was awarded the promised half mail contract with Allan holding the remainder. The joint contract necessitated a planned collaboration between the two organisations which grew steadily closer and was eventually to lead to their amalgamation - a step long devised by the Government. With the advent of the two new ships the Beaver Line four were relegated to the secondary service with intermediate calls.

For the Bay of Fundy service between Saint John, NB and Digby the *St George* arrived from the Great Western Rly Co.

1907 The two old ships *Tartar* and *Athenian* were sold for scrapping and to replace them *Monteagle* had been transferred to the Pacific.

The CPR British Columbia fleet was increased by the delivery of *Princess Ena* and *Princess Royal* commenced the Alaska route.

On the Great Lakes *Assiniboia* replaced *Athabasca* and *Keewatin* took over from *Alberta*.

1908 *Princess Charlotte* was added to the triangular Seattle-Victoria-Vancouver route.

The North Atlantic Conference was formed.

1909 July 6: Allan Line's chairman Sir Montague Allan received a solicitor's letter confirming discussions that 'my clients' (no name mentioned) are ready to buy the Allan Line for £1,609,000 + £100,000 for goodwill. The un-named clients were the Royal Trust Co of Montreal. On Sept 8 the agreement came into being. A new man joined the Allan Board. He was H. Maitland Kersey and he was a Canadian Pacific appointee; having assisted them on the Oriental routes. It became secretly clear that the Royal Trust had been acting for CPR and that they now actually owned the Allan organisation.

1910 The private Haley owned Detroit River Tunnel was opened and this commenced the decline in the transriver ferries.

On the BC coast the Vancouver-Chilliwack electric railway was opened and the stern-wheeler services ceased.

Montrose (I) achieved the distinction of being the first vessel to use wireless in assisting the police. Dr. Crippen, the wife-murderer, and his mistress Ethel le Neve were detected aboard. The information was radioed back to England; two detectives immediately took passage on the express service and effected an arrest before Dr Crippen, an American by birth, could move out of British jurisdiction.

1911 July 26: The *Empress of China (I)* was wrecked near Yokohama. This was also the year when the Japanese company Toyo Kisen introduced their three new express steamers on the transpacific routes. To counteract this CPR ordered two new ships with which to offset this serious competition.

1912 Jan 1: The Dominion Atlantic Railway Co. was leased to CPR for 999 years and with it came six ships (111-16). However CPR did not wish to serve the Canada-USA route and all but *Prince Rupert* were sold.

Nov: The shipping fraternity noted with raised eyebrows that, following the withdrawal of the Glasgow resident shareholders, the control of Allan moved to Montreal and the new chairman was none other than Sir Thomas Skinner - a CPR director.

1913 The collaboration between CPR and Allan intensified when the two set up joint victualling and stores depots in Liverpool. Arthur Piers, Allan's general manager, retired and his successor was H. Maitland Kersey whom CPR had appointed to the Allan Board in 1909. Within weeks CPR men were in several key positions. The holding of the shares at this time was: UK 62.88%, Canada 13.64% and the USA 10.39%.

On the Pacific the two ships ordered were delivered; they were the three-funnellers *Empress of Russia* and *Empress of Asia*. The pair were easily the finest vessels on the route and well justified the decision to out-build the Japanese.

With the blessing of the Austro-Hungarian Government, and the opposition of the German and Italian shipping concerns, a passenger and freight service was instituted between Trieste and Canada. *Lake Erie*, renamed *Tyrolia*, and *Lake Champlain*, renamed *Ruthenia* were placed on the route - which only lasted until the outbreak of war in 1914.

1914 On the Atlantic the Allan Line introduced their two fine new 18,000 ton express steamers *Alsatian* and *Calgarian*; these two ships had the first cruiser sterns on the Atlantic and effectively moved Allan ahead of all its competitors.

Tragedy struck on May 29 when, off Father Point, *Empress of Ireland* was run down, keeled over and sank in a swift fifteen minutes. The accident happened in the early hours when most passengers were asleep in their cabins and as a result a horrific 1,053 persons were drowned. The loss dramatically overshadowed the May 30 maiden voyage of Cunard's magnificent *Aquitania*.

Aug 4: World War I began. Most of CPR's fleet was requisitioned for war service. The two brand new Pacific coast vessels *Princess Irene* and *Princess Margaret* were converted into naval minelayers and neither survived to reach Vancouver.

Of the Atlantic fleet the Admiralty took six for an assortment of duties. They were: *Montezuma*, *Montcalm*, *Mount Royal*, *Tyrolia*, *Ruthenia* and *Montrose*. The situation was ameliorated by the arrival of two new intermediate liners named *Missanabie* and *Metagama* - the latter entering service in 1915. The two new ships were the first to introduce, onto the Atlantic, Cabin Class accommodation for 520 passengers and with 1,100 in Third Class. They were planned to replace the two remaining and inadequate 'Lakes' - *Lake Manitoba* and *Lake Michigan* - although, because of the war, neither was released. The Cabin Class concept caused a good deal of comment among the competition. It was felt that it constituted a cut price First Class which would affect ships of a similar size and destabilise the market. War blanketed the debate and the outcome was left for peace time normality to decide.(Incidentally the fears were to be proved correct but chronologically 'historians' should never, God like, jump ahead of time.)

1915 March 16: The Ottawa Government granted CPR the right to operate ships independently of the railway undertaking. The company registered Canadian Pacific Steamships Ltd to own such vessels and to work through a new set of accounts a new subsidiary of this was at once planned to cover both the Canadian Pacific and Allan Line ships.

May 27: The minelayer *Princess Irene* was destroyed by internal explosion at Sheerness accompanied with heavy loss of life.

CANADIAN PACIFIC OCEAN SERVICES LIMITED

Oct 1: The new concern **Canadian Pacific Ocean Services Ltd** was formed to manage the North Atlantic fleet. It was known, then, that the title was to include Allan Line ships. Mr G.M. Bosworth, Vice-president of CPR, was Chairman with, as managing director, Major H. Maitland Kersey.

1916 Jan 10: The long expected fusion of Allan Line with CPR was implemented. Seventeen Allan ships were integrated. They were: *Alsatian, Calgarian, Corinthian (II), Corsican, Grampian, Ionian, Mongolian, Pomeranian, Pretorian, Sardinian, Scandinavian (II), Scotian, Sicilian, Tunisian, Victorian* and *Virginian*. The tonnage of the 39 vessel combined fleet was almost 400,000grt comprising 239,000 CPR and 155,000 Allan.

July 16: Vesting day saw the whole staff and assets of Allan incorporated into CPR with Head Office at 8 Waterloo Place, London. Press comment was not unfavourable and saw it as 'the big ally absorbing its little brother'. Because of the war and grey painted ships the take over went almost unnoticed; indeed some ships on Government charter service did not transfer into Canadian Pacific Ocean Services until towards the end of the war. As a deliberate policy CP allowed all the Allan ships to retain their names. They had a fine reputation which would have been forfeited if new and unfamiliar names had been bestowed.

1918 CPOS took over two Cabin Class ships from the Liner Requisition Scheme. Both had been ordered before the war by a British offshoot planned by the Hamburg America Line for a Liverpool-Canada service. They were completed as *Melita* and *Minnedosa* and commenced the practice of giving cabin class vessels names begining with 'M'.

The year proved somewhat calamitous for CPOS. No fewer than nine ships were lost and replacement tonnage had to be acquired.

In January *Montreal* (I) was rammed by White Star's *Cedric* and sank within sight of safety.

Six ships, *Calgarian* (which because of her war-time duties never really became part of CPOS), *Pomeranian*, *Medora*, *Milwaukee*, *Missanabie* and *Montfort* were torpedoed.

In the Pacific *Princess Sophia* was lost in bizarre circumstances when, high and dry and seemingly safe, she was swept off a reef by mountainous seas with the loss of all 343 persons aboard.

The final loss was that of *Corinthian* by marine hazard.

Four war loss replacement cargo ships were acquired from Harris & Dixon. The four, *Batsford*, *Dundrige*, *Holbrook* and *Mottisfont* brought the fleet back to 26 vessels.

1919 *Lake Manitoba* was severely damaged by fire at Montreal. Although repaired and made ready for service she was sold out of the fleet.

1920 Aug: *Empress of France* (I) set up a new passage record between Liverpool and Quebec with a time of 5 days, 20 hours, 6 minutes at an average speed of 18.8 knots.

On the BC coast the price of oil was fluctuating and delivery erratic. As a precaution CPR converted its Pacific ships back to coal.

The mail contract came up for revision. Because of war inflation CPR's cost had risen, like everyone else's, but their request that the subsidy be increased from $350,000 pa to $450,000 was refused. The Dominion Government even transferred mail from *Empress of Asia* to a Nippon Yusen sailing. However the US authorities found it much cheaper to use CPR and diverted their mails via Vancouver. This led to the strange situation of Canadians sending their mail by rail to Seattle so that it could come back to Vancouver for shipment. The press outcry at this nonsense rectified the situation and the CPR contract renewed at a higher figure.

CANADIAN PACIFIC STEAMSHIPS LTD

1921 Sept 8: The title of the operating company for the North Atlantic and Pacific routes became Canadian Pacific Steamships Ltd - known familiarly as CPS. The funnels reverted to plain buff and a white band was added to the hulls. The CP Railway vessels on the Pacific and Bay of Fundy were unchanged.

The record passage time was again reduced. This time to 5 days, 9 hours, 30 minutes by *Empress of Britain* (I).

Three splendid German liners were also added to the passenger fleet: *Empress of India* (II) (171), the classically beautiful *Empress of Australia* (I) (172), for the Pacific service to replace *Empress of India* (I)(9), and the rather top heavy looking *Empress of Scotland* (I) (173) - once the largest ship in the world.

1922 Chairman George M. Bosworth died in London after an emergency appendix removal.

The Empresses transferred their base from Liverpool to Southampton. *Metagama* joined *Tunisian*, *Corsican* and *Scotian* on the joint CPS-Anchor service from the Clyde to Canada.

Stemming from Elder, Dempster days Atlantic vessels had names beginning with 'M' which developed into names commencing with 'Mont' (or Mount) now the new 'Mont' class entered service *Montcalm* (III), *Montrose* (the best loved of the three) and *Montclare*. The three were to replace some of the older and slower Allan ships. They extended the capacity of CPS in the Cabin class market with a noticeable improvement in comfort and cabin space.

Empress of Canada (I)(177) was delivered for service across the Pacific. Her coming released the now thoroughly outclassed *Empress of Japan* (I) (10) of 1891. This brought the Pacific passenger fleet up to the required four.

When fighting broke out between the Greeks and the Turks British troops were carried by *Empress of India* and *Corsican* to the scene where they acted as a buffer between the opposing sides. During the winter *Empress of Scotland* made her first post war cruise of 79 days to the Mediterranean for the Frank C. Clarke Travel Agency, New York. *Empress of France* followed a few weeks later.

1923 *Montcalm* (I) was sold to Norway for conversion into a whale factory ship while *Scandinavian* was scrapped.

Sept 1: *Empress of Australia (I)* was just casting off her moorings at Yokohama when the earthquake struck and after anxious minutes - dealt with under her fleet listing - she remained to give valuable assistance.

In British Columbia the sternwheeler fleet was reduced to five. *Nasookin* (125), *Kuskanook* (92) and *Moyie* (40) on Lake Kootenay and *Bonnington* (117) and *Minto* (39) on Arrow Lake. The twelve cargo ships were all given names commencing with the letter 'B'.

1924 Belfast was added to the Clyde-Canada route.

1925 Feb 27: Sir Thomas Fisher, General Manager of CPS, died and was succeeded by Captain James Gillies, the fleet commodore. On the shipping scene, taking into account the wartime standard constructions, there were now too many vessels and the overtonnage drove down freight rates. The post-war surge of immigrants from Europe was also flattening out so that load factors on the passenger ships were in decline. This was compounded by the restrictions placed on immigration by the United States. To counter all this the Canadian Government introduced a scheme whereby for the ensuing two years emigrants to Canada paid only £2 to CPS and the Government made up the balance.

Many of the pre-war ships were becoming worn out and much of the wartime construction was already obsolescent. Companies with adequate reserves planned to introduce new generation ships with which to replace their older units. CPS was one of these.

1926 The Clyde-Canada service was reduced to two vessels - *Metagama* and *Montnairn*. Three former Allan liners were sold for breaking up - *Pretorian*, *Scotian* and *Grampian*.

1927 Five new express cargo steamers were introduced into service. They were given 'Beaver' names to commemorate the defunct Beaver Line: *Beaverburn* (I), *Beaverford* (I), *Beaverdale*, *Beaverhill* and *Beaverbrae* (I) (184-187). *Bawtry* (ex *Mottisfont*) was sold.

On the North Atlantic competition was so fierce and the argument over what constituted 'Cabin Class' so intense that CPS threatened to leave the conference.

1928 In the spring the experiment was tried of landing registered mail at Father Point, near the mouth of the St Lawrence, and flying it to Quebec and Montreal.

Now that Southampton was the home of the 'Empresses' the traditional Liverpool berth, which always drew support from a large area of the country, had to be strengthened. Four new 'Duchess' ships were built, *Duchess of Bedford* (193) being the first to enter service on June 1. The quartet again catered for Cabin class which, by now, had become the mainstay of the Liverpool passenger market. The new 'Beavers' displaced some of the older ships and *Balfour*, *Berwyn*, *Brecon* and *Brandon* were all sold for further trading.

Back in Canada a number of vessels owned by the United States Shipping Board were operated on their behalf, by CPS. The USSB were not interested (nor did their remit permit it) in developing trade out of Canadian ports and were thus no threat to CPS activities.

1929 *Metagama* (129) was transferred to the Antwerp-Quebec-Montreal route with a call at Southampton and Cherbourg. During this year CPS made 127 Atlantic crossings which was a record that was never bettered.

1930 The big event of the year was the introduction into service of the new Queen of the Pacific,

Empress of Japan (II) (197). In June she left Liverpool for Quebec before proceeding to Vancouver to take up station and at once took the Pacific Blue Riband. She was the largest, fastest and most luxurious ship ever on the service. Normally there would have had to have been a balancing pair of sisters but the world depression was affecting thinking and with the coming of their new transatlantic flagship CPS had enough to occupy them. *Empress of Australia* (I)(172) came back to the UK for a refit and then took up her place on the Atlantic.

In British Columbia the completion of the Kettle Valley Railway diverted traffic from the 134 mile long Upper and Lower Arrow Lake service maintained by CPR's sternwheeler fleet. This led to the retirement of a lake fleet that had provided the CPR connection, via Trail, west of Calgary into the USA at Washington State.

Mountroyal, ex *Empress of Britain* (I)(86) was broken up.

1931 Jan 28: A notice of dissolution of the Allan Line was finally lodged in Edinburgh some 15 years after it had become only a legal entity. The surprise was that even at this late date $8.4 million reserves were transferred to the Canadian Pacific Replacement Fund.

The 'Great Depression' bit hard. A number of CPS cargo ships were temporarily out of service while passenger liners deployed onto inexpensive £1-per day type cruises. Even so, some of these were also dock-bound for periods although, unlike many, they avoided care and maintenance lay up.

In July the **Canadian-Australasian Line Ltd** was formed jointly with the Union Steam Ship Company of New Zealand.

But the year saw the delivery of the largest passenger ship ever owned by CPS - the magnificent *Empress of Britain* (II)(201).

In the Rockies April saw the ending of the Lake Okanagan sternwheeler services although local demand led to *Sicamous* (130) being kept.

1932 An indication of the effects of the depression can be seen in that only 6,882 emigrants were landed in Canada - this compared with 133,141 in 1929.

1934 In August *Empress of Britain* (201) made her fastest crossing from Father Point-Cherbourg in 4 days, 6 hours, 56 minutes.

The fleet was reduced during the year by the scrapping of both *Metagama* (129) and, rather sadly, the former Allan liner *Alsatian* now *Empress of France* (I)(136); an elegantly distinguished looker all her life and, especially, with a white hull. She was the last Allan liner to survive with CPS although *Drottningholm* ex-*Virginian* (151) was afloat.

1935 Italy was embroiled in a war of conquest in Abyssinia. *Melita* (156) and *Minnedosa* (157) both found their way into troopship service, with Lloyd Triestino, after being sold to Italy for scrap and being requisitioned by that Government for further service.

1939 In the spring King George VI and Queen Elizabeth visited Canada. The outward voyage was aboard *Empress of Australia* (172) with a June homeward passage in *Empress of Britain* (201) which, upon seeing her spotlessly resplendent, the King aptly said 'was the most magnificent ship he had ever seen'.

Sept 3: Great Britain, the Commonwealth and France entered World War II against Germany following upon their invasion of Poland. Canadian Pacific placed all their ships at the service of the Government. Two of the British Columbia coastal liners, *Princess Marguerite* (I) and *Princess Kathleen* (180/81) were transferred to European waters as short haul troopships.

1940 The majority of CPS passenger ships were now either trooping or had gone to the Royal Navy for repair ship duties. The most grievous loss occurred, Oct 26, when *Empress of Britain* (201) was set on fire by a long range bomber and crippled. Despite being taken in tow she was caught by two torpedoes from *U-32* and CPS's finest liner was lost. Chairman Edward Beatty called it 'the saddest day of my life'.

Nov: *Beaverford* (185) sunk; she was a member of the convoy, guarded by *Jervis Bay*, (Aberdeen & Commonwealth) which was attacked by the German 'pocket battleship' *Admiral Scheer*. Her sister *Beaverburn* (184) had already been sunk by *U-41* back in February.

1941 *Beaverbrae* (188) was sunk by air attack and *Beaverdale* (186) was torpedoed by *U-58*.

Dec 7: The United States entered the war when, without warning, Pearl Harbor was attacked by 'planes from Japanese carriers. In fulfilment of his undertaking Adolf Hitler, incredibly unwisely, immediately declared war on America. Japan knew she could only win a short naval war (US war production capacity was five times that of her assailant).

1942 During the war British registered vessels were forbidden to change their names. An exception was made with the *Empress of Japan* (197) which was permitted to become *Empress of Scotland* (II). Feb: At the time of the fall of Singapore *Empress of Asia* (120) was sunk by Japanese aircraft.

A major loss was that of *Duchess of Atholl* (194), torpedoed west of Ascension by *U-178*.

1943 In July *Duchess of York* (196) was lost after being set on fire by long range German bombers.

1944 The final 'Beaver' cargo vessel and the last wartime casualty, *Beaverhill*, was wrecked outside Saint John, NB. All five had now been lost.

1945 On September 2 (Six years and one day after Germany invaded Poland) the war ended with the surrender of the Japanese aboard the battleship USS *Missouri* in Tokio Bay. Within the week *Empress of Russia* (119), refitting at Barrow-in-Furness was burnt out and had to be scrapped.

1946 The return to peace was slow. In May *Duchess of Richmond* (195) was the first trooper to be released for refurbishing. She emerged from this as *Empress of Canada* (II). One change was the the CPR houseflag was now worn on the funnels. The first three of the four replacement cargo ships were delivered: *Beaverdell*, *Beaverglen* and *Beaverlake* (203/05). In addition three wartime fast standard ships joined the fleet (207/09).

1947 When the final cargo ship, *Beavercove* (206) entered service the freighter fleet stood at seven.

1948 To meet the requirements for immigrants from war-torn Europe *Beaverbrae* (II) (211), the former H.A.P.A.G. *Huascaran*, entered service from Germany with 700 austerity berths.

1949 The Pacific coast ships had also had a hard war and some of the elderly ones had already been disposed of. During the next eighteen months three, *Princess Patricia* (II), *Princess Marguerite* (213/14) and *Princess of Nanaimo* (216) were completed.

1951 Nov: Princess Elizabeth and the Duke of Edinburgh travelled home from Newfoundland in *Empress of Scotland* (197).

Somewhat ignominiously the revered *Princess Victoria* (66), doyen of the Pacific coast, was sold and reduced to a timber barge.

1952 A bizarre fate befell *Princess Kathleen* (180) when she grounded on steeply inclined rocks and the rising tide swamped her stern with the result that she slid off into deep water. The ensuing legal case, much resented, was fought on the basis that the liability of the owner was restricted to the value of the ship at the end of her voyage - which in this case was zero. The year also saw the end of the still trooping, immaculately profiled *Empress of Australia* (172).

1953 Jan: *Empress of Canada* (II) (195) caught fire in Gladstone Dock and capsized inwards, jammed up against the quayside. Her costly salvage took until the following March and it was August before she left the Mersey in tow for Italian breakers. The problem for CPS was that the ship was fully booked with visitors for the coronation of Queen Elizabeth II. To honour these obligations *De Grasse* was bought from the French Line and renamed *Empress of Australia* (II) (219). Once she had done a two year stint she was sold. In fact CPS were already well ahead with plans to replace *Empress of Canada*.

1954 The German emigrant traffic to Canada had now declined to negligible proportions and *Beaverbrae* (211) was sold for an Italian service to Australia.

1956 Apr: The first of two sisters, *Empress of Britain* (III), entered service to be followed a year later by *Empress of England* (221/22). Oddly the first in the fleet to bear the name. It might have been expected, over the years, that another ship bore the name thereby excluding duplication but this had not been so.

1958 *Empress of Scotland* (II) (197) had never returned to the Pacific post war and she was now sold, out of lay up, to the Hamburg Atlantic Line for rebuilding and further service.

1959 *Princess Elizabeth* and *Princess Joan* (198/99), the last Vancouver CPR three funnellers, were sold to Epirotiki of Piraeus. They were 29 years old.

April: That magnificent engineering feat the St Lawrence Seaway was opened to give deep sea access from the Atlantic to the Great Lakes. The American and Canadian mid-west could now be reached by sea. CPS naturally made plans to use their Great Lake rail heads. While ships were planned chartered tonnage was used. Mainly *Elise Schulte* and *Hermann Schulte* (Schulte & Bruns), both of which were in CPS black livery.

Summer: On the Atlantic three ships maintained the weekly Montreal service: *Empress of Britain* (221), *Empress of England* (222) and *Empress of France* (193). Apr 3 (Friday): *Empress of Britain* sailed first: Liverpool-Greenock-Quebec (Apr 9)-Montreal (Apr 10). They made, respectively, 12, 11 and 11 sailings = 34 in all.

1961 The last CPS passenger ship for deep sea service was completed. Named *Empress of Canada* (III) (223) entered service on April 24 with a scheduled sailing from Liverpool.

The first ship acquired for the St Lawrence Seaway-Great Lakes route was bought on the stocks. Renamed *Beaverfir* (224) she left Antwerp on July 7 for her maiden voyage. She introduced white livery, with Canadian Pacific in black on her flanks, for the service and was the forerunner of a fleet of five (plus charters) employed on a weekly service.

In August Canadian Pacific Airways (CPA) was granted a licence to operate across the Atlantic but the refusal of the British licencing authorities to accede to landing rights (British Overseas Airways appealed against the dilution of its traffic) caused the cancellation of the concept.

1962 *Beaverpine* (225) and *Beaverelm* (226) joined the Great Lakers followed in the next year by *Beaverash* (227).

The North Atlantic fleet was pruned by the sale of three of the immediate post war additions: *Beaverdell* (203), *Beaverlake* (205) and the 'Empire' ship *Beaverford* (II) (208). It marked the run down of conventional cargo as CPS planned to switch to a more specialist fleet. The white liveried *Beaverpine* and *Beaverelm* (225/226) joined the Great Lakes fleet.

1963 Max Wilson's Travel Savings Association chartered *Empress of Britain* (III) (221) and *Empress of England* (222) for his inexpensive cruise programme. His members paid regular monthly subscriptions and enjoyed 'no frills' cruising. The scheme was backed by three shipping companies, Canadian Pacific, Royal Mail (who owned P.S.N.C) and Union-Castle but gradually faded until only P.S.N.C's *Reina del Mar*, operated by Union-Castle, remained for a final decade but mostly under their ownership and management, not Travel Savings. The problem was simple: TSA could fill a five month summer season. There were a few attempts at a winter market in white South Africa but this was small. The remaining seven months ruined the economics of TSA which could not maintain their annual charters.

1964 Passenger shipping continued to show a marked and sustained loss of profit not helped by the vigour of the North Atlantic airlines with the latest jet aircraft - the Boeing 707. CPS declared its intention to reduce its involvement in this and *Empress of Britain* (III) (221) was sold to the Greeks. Only two CPS Atlantic passenger ships now remained.

CANADIAN PACIFIC (BERMUDA) LIMITED

Nov 11: Canadian Pacific (Bermuda) Ltd., Hamilton, Bermuda, known as CP Bermuda, was formed to operate the diversified fleet of bulkers and tankers.

1965 The final, and largest, CPS Great Laker was *Beaveroak*. The ship was instantly recognisable by her unique, to the fleet, ice breaker bow. She also marked the end of 'Beaver' names - except for one or two renamed charters. Canadian Pacific started to name their new ships after persons prominent in the history of the company - although not all worked for the Company. The first of the new breed was *R.B Angus* (229) purchased from Saguenay Terminals for Pacific cargo service.

C P Air had its London operating rights transferred to the Government owned Air Canada which operated Canada-Amsterdam.

1966 In times when funds are available and depreciation tax allowances make it worth while shipping companies can build ships for long term charter to others. They receive a good return on the capital employed without the need to market the vessels themselves. CPS now built two tankers for just such a role: *Lord Mount Stephen* and *Lord Strathcona* (230/31). At Vancouver passenger carryings were declining as air made local movement so much faster. However road and rail freight continued to expand. The post-war converted *Trailer Princess* (232) entered service across to Schwartz Bay, Vancouver Island.

1967 Cunard withdrew from all the Canadian routes.

CP SHIPS

1968 Canadian Pacific, sea, land and air, introduced a new two tone corporate livery (see front cover) which was regarded as too modern at the time but which grew in popularity as it came to be recognised as a brilliant piece of branding which no one (except possibly Carnival Cruise Lines) was able to copy. The theme was that the circle and incut triangle represented a modern letter 'C', although it was not seen this way by the uninitiated. In addition their ships were to be known as CP Ships and this was to be painted on their hulls. It was added, unattractively, to the passenger ships, in green, but soon popularly removed. Three paper product carriers were the next and natural diversification for a country covered in vast swards of forest. The client was MacMillan Bloedel and the ships, on wet charter (ie crewed by CPS) were *H.R. MacMillan*, named after their chairman, *J.V. Clyne* and *N.R. Crump* (233/35). These carried the MacMillan funnel.

1969 The Japanese paper making firm of C. Itoh needed logs not pulp and the result was a ten year charter for *Pacific Logger* (236) - a one off member of what was becoming a fleet of classes of ship.

CPS also entered the thriving bulk carriage market, again for term charters on a wet boat basis. *T. Akasaka* and *W.C. van Horne* (237/38) were delivered for this activity.

1970 The new Point Tupper Refinery in Nova Scotia led to another contract and to supply the site with oil three massive 250,000dwt VLCC (Very Large Crude Carriers) tankers were constructed: *Port Hawkesbury*, *T.G. Shaughnessy* and *I.D. Sinclair* (239/41).

Containerisation was sweeping all before it and the revolution in cargo handling which this brought affected every major shipping company - driving a goodly number into group consortium operations and an even larger number out of business altogether. CP Ships moved into the field with a group of vessels bearing the initial 'C P'. The first of these was *C P Voyageur* (242) which inaugurated a new weekly container service from Europe to Canada. She was followed by *C P Trader* and *C P Discoverer* (243/44). The Great Lakes fleet was selling off those ships which were incapable of economic conversion. Two ships, however, were converted and emerged as *C P Ambassador* (228) and *C P Explorer* (225).

The next move out of passenger shipping occurred when Shaw Savill & Albion took *Empress of England* (222) and renamed her *Ocean Monarch* for their Australia service - a route already dying from the effects of air competition '26 hours versus 26 days'.

CANADIAN PACIFIC LIMITED

1971 July 3: The name of the firm became Canadian Pacific Ltd.

The Bay of Fundy service had been operated by *Princess of Acadia* (I) (215) since the departure of *Princess Helene* (200) in 1963. But vehicular traffic had outgrown the ship's capacity. A new *Princess of Acadia* (245) was delivered. One innovation was that she was powered by sets of standard locomotive engines which could be lifted out and replaced without in-ship maintenance.

The Atlantic passenger service ceased at the end of the summer season.

1972 The end of Atlantic passenger ownership came with the sale of *Empress of Canada* (III) (223) to Carnival Cruise Lines who renamed her *Mardi Gras*. They chose their two tone red funnel merely by turning the incut triangle into a circle to produce a letter 'C'.

1973 *G.A. Walker, W.A. Mather* and *R.A. Emerson* (246/248) introduced a Dutch built series of oil product tankers which were delivered over a period of three years to end as a group of seven. To augment the rail/road traffic between Vancouver and Vancouver island the new *Carrier Princess* (254) was delivered.

INCAN MARINE LIMITED (See separate entry)

Incan Marine Ltd was formed by Canadian Pacific (40%) and Inchcape's Inchcape (Canada) Ltd (60%). The new company was a market research unit. In turn this company founded, May, Incan Ships Ltd, a $6 million joint venture with CP Ships holding 43% and Incan Marine Ltd 57%. A contract was vested in the company for a road and rail transport vessel across Lake Superior. A sister was later planned.

Bulk carriers were still in demand – especially those with OBO (ore-bulk-oil) capability which enabled them to move two types of cargo during one round voyage. This compared with the oil tanker's defect of one direction loaded with the other in ballast. Three such ships were now delivered: *E.W. Beatty, D.C. Coleman* and *W.M. Neal* (255/257). They were the last ships to carry the names of men connected with CP's history.

1974 The fourth of the product tankers was delivered as *Fort Macleod* (249) and she set another trend. The use of 'Fort' became predominant, although with two 'Port' exceptions.

Incan Superior inaugurated the service from McKellar Island, Thunder Bay, Ontario to Superior, Wisconsin, with a round trip time of 36 hours. The principal cargo being newsprint and wood pulp from the Great Lakes Paper Co., Thunder Bay.

1975 Seven sistership bulk carriers were building at the Japanese yard of Sanyosan for delivery over two years. They were of a common Japanese profile with prominent deck cranes and hull strengthening for heavy cargo. In addition containers could be carried on deck.The first of the class was *Fort Nelson* (258). She was followed by a confusingly named vessel: *Leda* (259). This ship started as *Leda*, was registered as *Fort St John*. Left on her maiden voyage as *Leda*, for the subsidiary Atalanta Ship Management Services Ltd, and was eventually to become *Fort Nanaimo* - thus even occurring in some fleet lists twice.

At Vancouver *Princess Marguerite* (212) was taken over by the Province of British Columbia Ferries.

1977 Denmark's Burmeister & Wain supplied the next two 'gearless' (ie no cargo handling gear) bulk carriers: *Port Vancouver* and *Port Quebec* (264/65). These were, like others, used world wide on voyage or short term charter.

1978 Sanyosan Dockyard now produced another group of ships which were very similar indeed to, but slightly shorter than, the *Fort Nelson* (258) class. They could be recognised by having one set of deck cranes paired. The first of these was *Fort Walsh* (266) and she was followed by the sisters *Fort Carleton* and *Fort Hamilton* (267/68).

1980 Jan 31: Canadian Pacific Ltd (C P Rail) ceased its Northland tug-barge operation between Vancouver and B.C. ports. RivTow Straits Ltd took over most of it.

A rare event for Canadian Pacific was the purchase, solely to meet current commitments, of three second hand bulk carriers: *Fort Fraser, Fort Douglas* and *Fort Erie* (270/72). Their careers were modest. *Fort Erie* lasted a year and *Fort Fraser* five.

The missing category of ship within the now specialist fleet was rectified with the building by Sanoyasu Dockyard of four chemical tankers. They had the capability of carrying four differing types of liquid each being dischargeable by a separate pump. All four were launched during the year. Three, *Fort Assiniboine, Fort Garry* and *Fort Rouge* (273/275) being delivered by the year end with the fourth, *Fort Toronto* (276), appearing early in 1981. To augment the 'C P' container ship fleet the Belgian *E.R. Brussel* was chartered and renamed *C P Hunter*.

1981 Another container ship came on charter, she became *C P Ambassador* (II) (278) having formerly been *Dart Atlantic*.

1982 The last four ships to be built for C P Ships were all bulk carriers but with container capacity for some 800 TEU's on deck. *Fort Providence* and *Fort Resolution* (279/80) were the first pair, the second being delivered in 1983.

1983 Burmeister & Wain were the builders of what will probably be the last ocean going ships to be built for Canadian Pacific. *Fort Dufferin* and *Fort Frontenac* (281/82) being near sisters of the *Fort Providence* pair.

During the year the Canadian Pacific Railway group made a profit of £12,759,297 but with a less than adequate contribution of £233,605 from the heavy capital intensive C P Ships Ltd. Against fully allocated costs, including interest on the funding of the ships, a loss of £74,293 was recorded. On sea trading this was a 33% loss. This pattern had been growing over the previous years and the forward prognosis looked no better.

1984 The operation of the fleet was by now spread over a number of separate concerns. Canadian Pacific Bermuda looked after 32 bulk and oil carriers. Canadian Pacific Bulkship Services Ltd. operated three for Centennial Shipping. They were *Andes Trader* (ex *C P Trader*, (243), *Andes Voyageur* (ex *C P Voyageur*, 242) and, for the Dart Consortium, *Dart Atlantica* (not to be confused with *Dart Atlantic*) built in 1979. Next there was Canadian Pacific Ltd with three Vancouver based vessels, *Carrier Princess* (254) and *Trailer Princess* (232) plus the much loved *Princess Patricia* (213). Finally comes Canadian Pacific Steamships Ltd., the London based end of the system, with 8 ships, five 'Forts' plus *C P Ambassador* (II)(278), *Dart Americana* – a sister of *Dart Atlantica* – and *Andes Discoverer* ex *C P Discoverer* (244). A total of 46 ships of which three and the 'Andes' trio were owned outside of the group and were managed as part of consortium type operations.

But this was at a time when profits were slumping in parallel with freight rates which were being compressed by low wage competition. There was also the growing feeling that Canadian Pacific was fundamentally a railway concern which had spilled over into shipping (and air, hotels, road haulage etc). The view took hold that if maritime activities could not be self supporting then they should be disposed of. The shedding process began.

1985 On the coast of British Columbia the remaining commercial ferry services were Vancouver-Nanaimo and Vancouver-Schwartz Bay, on Vancouver Island, operated by *Carrier Princess* (254) and *Trailer Princess* (232).

1986 Aug: A CP move into ' Flags of Convenience' occurred when Boele's yard at Dordrecht commenced converting the purchased *Canada Maritime* into a china clay and paper carrier to be renamed *Repap Enterprise* for the Liberian Ozmillion Shipping Corporation, Monrovia. Like so many such companies their ownership is not apparent.

1987 *Trailer Princess* was taken over by the British Columbia Department of Ferries to leave only one ship, *Carrier Princess*, to carry the C P livery in coastal waters.

1988 A significant move out of shipowning occurred when Canadian Pacific (Bermuda) Ltd sold its bulk carrier fleet for US $149,100,000 to B & H Bulkships Acquisition Corporation. A subsidiary of Bergvall & Hudner, Bermuda. These in turn were re-registered with single ship companies. The profit to Canadian Pacific (Bermuda) Ltd was over $100 million.

CP (Bermuda) retained only six speciality tankers (carrying caustic soda, chemicals and vegetable oils) and one ro-ro vessel. The tankers, all on time-charter, were then moved into a new division **Canadian Pacific Tankers Ltd.**

1989 June 30: The six remaining tankers plus all contracts, commitments and goodwill were sold to Ceres Hellenic Shipping Enterprises and placed under the ownership of single ship companies within the group. The sale price was US $100 million. The ships themselves were handed over during July and August as their current voyages ended. At the time Ceres already owned seven IMO class 2 chemical tankers.

1990 The move out of ship owning was, by now, virtually complete and after tidying up yet another great shipping name disappears from public view. The remaining ships being looked after by the recently formed **BCP** (= Barber Canadian Pacific) **Ship Management Ltd.** with branch offices in London and Hong Kong, thereby utilising the skills of long serving shipbroking and operating staff as well as providing continuity for C.P. vessels which had been siphoned off to purely financial investing groups. The effect of this move is to free Canadian Pacific from the cost of owning ships while leaving them with the earnings from their ship management capability.

Future involvement in the maritime trade may well be only along these lines but thankfully the Canadian Pacific name remains active in rail, air and hotel form and may, one day, return to carry at sea their own livery and houseflag. One fervently hopes so.

LIVERY

Houseflag	1883-1968	Red and white check. See cover.
	1968-1990	New style. See cover
Funnel:	1883-1968	Coastal steamers: yellow black top.
	1890-1906	Transpacific: yellow.
	1897	The Kootenay River Nav Co. retained their black funnels for some years after being taken over.
	1903-1906	Elder Dempster purchases: Buff, including Beaver ships.
	1906-1921	Buff yellow with black top.
	1921-1946	Canadian Pacific Ocean Services: Buff yellow. Coastal and river craft retained their black tops.
	1946-1968	The houseflag was superimposed on the funnnels excepting the B.C. ships. This followed at a date after 1955 and before 1963.
	1968-1990	Green, white semicircle, dark green triangle for Ocean going with red, white semicircle, black triangle for coastal steamers (See front cover).

Hull	1883-1990	Black with the following variants:.
	1890-1922	Transpacific: white, green waterline. A buff strake along the bridge deck also occurred 1919-1922.
	1921-1927	Black, white band, white castles.
	1927-1972	Empresses: White with yellow band; from 1961 dark green band. Note *Princess Marguerite* (212) had a white hull from 1966.
	1961-1972	Refrigerated Beavers had white hulls, no band. Later with the words **Canadian Pacific** in black.
	1945-1990	Cargo vessels, other than reefers, had black hulls, no band. About 1965 Canadian Pacific added in white **C P Ships** added just forward of the bridge.
Waterline	1883-1975	Coastal: Red. Post 1945 there were some cases of a white dividing line in the passenger vessels.
	1890-1968	Ocean going: Green.
	1968-1990	Black hulled vessels: red (with the new funnel). The change over was not instant.
Uppers	White	Note the Dominion Altantic Rly Co, retained their brown uppers until 1911.
Masts	Funnel buff.	From 1956 white on white hulled vessels, 1968-1990 White.
Boats		White.
	1921-1927	CPOS; Brown boats.
	1974-1990	Cargo ships had orange lifeboats;.

ROUTES

Ports in brackets were occasional calls

1884–1886	Great Lakes railhead supply service.
1886–1968	Owen Sound/Port McNicoll–Port Arthur/Fort William.
1890–18??	Toronto–Chicago and Montreal–Chicago.
1887–1891	Transpacific route with chartered ships. Hong Kong–Vancouver.
1891–1941	Vancouver–Yokohama–Kobe–Nagasaki–Shanghai–Hong Kong.
1887	British Columbia river work started.
1897–1930	B.C. lakes and river services.
	Note: CPN routes pre–date the CPR take over.
1891–1903	Victoria–Seattle
1891–1985	Vancouver–Seattle (145 miles).
1904–1974	Vancouver–Victoria–Seattle (Triangular Route).
1891–1974	Vancouver–Victoria (83 miles).
–1989	Vancouver–Nanaimo (40 miles).
–1956	Cargo: Vancouver–British Columbia ports–Alaska.
–1958	Vancouver–Victoria–39 Vancouver Island ports.

1897–1958	(Seattle)–Vancouver–Victoria–Prince Rupert–Ketchikan–Wrangell–(St Petersburgh)–Juneau–Skagway.
1926–1979	Cruises: Vancouver–Wrangell–Glacier Bay–Skagway–Juneau–Tracy Arm–Prince Rupert–Alert Bay–Vancouver.
1966–1991	Vancouver–Schwartz Bay.
1904–1974	Victoria–Seattle.
1901–1942	New Westminster/Sydney–(Lardne)–Steveston and Gulf Islands service.
1901–1919	New Westminster–Fraser River (replaced by motor coaches).
1890–1925	London (Ontario)–Detroit.
1898–1901	Vancouver–Nome (Klondyke gold rush).
1912–1974	Dominion Atlantic: Saint John–Digby.
1912–1940	Kingsport–Parrsboro–Wolfville
1903–1971	Atlantic routes of Elder Dempster.
	The route was: Summer: St Lawrence–Quebec–Montreal.
	Winter: Halifax–Saint John, New Brunswick.
1903–1971	Liverpool–(Greenock 1923)–(Belfast)–(Halifax)–Saint John/Quebec–Montreal
1903–1914	Antwerp–(Halifax)–Saint John/Quebec–Montreal.
1909–1931	Glasgow–(Belfast 1924)–(Halifax)–Saint John/Quebec–Montreal.
1909–1914	London–Le Havre–(Halifax)–Saint John/Quebec–Montreal.
1913–1914	Trieste–Canada.
1919–1922	London–Le Havre–(Halifax)–Saint John/Quebec–Montreal.
1927–1963	London–Panama Canal–US ports–(Victoria)–Vancouver.
1919–1939	Antwerp–Southampton–(Halifax)–Saint John/Quebec–Montreal.
1922–1939	Southampton–Cherbourg–(Halifax)–Saint John/Quebec–Montreal.
1922–1933	Hamburg–Southampton–Cherbourg–(Halifax)–Saint John/Quebec–Montreal.
1948–1954	Hamburg–(Southampton)–Saint John/Montreal.
1959–1973	St Lawrence Seaway route.
	Antwerp/London/Liverpool–Great Lakes–Toronto/Chicago.
1971–1986	Persian Gulf–Point Tupper, Nova Scotia.

CANADIAN PACIFIC RAILWAY

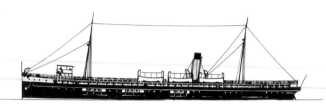

ATHABASCKA / ATHABASCA, ALBERTA, ALGOMA

1 ATHABASCKA / ATHABASCA

B 1883 Aitken & Mansel, Kelvinhaugh, Glasgow. **T** 2,269g, 1,545n.
D 262.8/80.06 x 38.2/11.63 x 23.3/7.09.
E Sgl scr, 2 cyl comp inv, 283 nhp. 8 kts. By D. Rowan, Glasgow.
H Steel. 2 dks. **P** Carried 240 1st class berthed and 1000 deck.
These ships were built with a special bulkhead so that they could be separated into two halves at Montreal and towed through the locks up to Buffalo. There each was re-joined.
1883 July 3: Launched as *Athabascka*. On arrival at Montreal the vessel was renamed *Athabasca*, halved and taken to Buffalo. Nov 2: At Montreal; halving completed.
1884 Jan: Re-joined and laid up awaiting the thaw. May 17: Entered the weekly service Owen Sound-Port Arthur (railhead for Winnipeg); this was before the railway along the north shore of Superior was completed. During this construction many regular delivery calls at shore points were made. The trio were the finest vessels on the Lakes.
1885 The railway was completed and the three became passenger vessels Owen Sound-Port Arthur three times weekly.
1909 Oct 13: Grounded on Flower Pot Island, Owen Sound. Bottom damage, went to Collingwood for rebuilding.
1910 Rebuilt at Collingwood, Ontario by Collingwood SB. Co. **D** 298.8/91.07. **T** 2,784g, 2,349n. New engine by Western DD & SB Co., Port Arthur.
1912 Port McNicoll replaced Owen Sound as the embarkation point.
1937 Cargo only Port McNicoll-Milwaukee-Chicago.
1946 Aug: Sold for use as a pallet loading, via her side doors, fruit carrier in Florida. Actual service doubtful. Still recorded as CPR owned when sold for scrap. **1948** Broken up.

2 ALBERTA
Sister to *Athabasca* except: **B** Chas.Connell & Co., Glasgow. **T** 2,282g, 1,552n.
1883 July 12: Launched; same service as her sisters.
Nov 10: Left Montreal in two halves for Buffalo. **1884** May: Entered service.
1911 Rebuilt by Collingwood SB Co. **D** 309.7/94.39. **T** 2,829g, 2,377n.
1937 Cargo service with her sister.
1946 Aug: Sold with her sister for Florida use. Same comment. **1948** Broken up.

3 ALGOMA

As *Athabasca* except **T** 2,272g, 1,554n.
1883 July 31: Launched. Nov 4: Left Montreal for Buffalo.
1884 May 11: Sunday. Inaugurated the Great Lakes service a day late.
1885 Nov 5: Left Sault Ste Marie. Nov 7: In a severe gale, wrecked, near Port Arthur, on Greenstone, Isle Royale. the ship broke in two. 48 drowned, 15 saved, many by her sister *Athabasca* which left Port Arthur on her schedule and unexpectedly came upon the scene. *Algoma*'s engines were salved and transferred to *Manitoba* (14). The local lake steamer *Campana* (A.M. Smith) was chartered to replace her.

4 GEORGIAN

B 1864 J. Potter, Georgian Bay. **T** 377g. **D** 130/39.62 x 22/6.7 x 11/3.35.
E Sgl scr, 1 cyl, 1 sgl blr, 3 furnaces, 20 psi. 8 kts. By builder. **H** Wood. 1 dk.
1864 Built as *Georgian* for J.C. Graham. Georgian Bay.
1884 Apr 1: Acquired for use as a supply boat to work sites. Carried a doctor and medical dispensary (and presumably hospitalisation facilities). **1888** May 9: Lost in Owen Sound.

THREE SHIPS OPERATED PENDING THE DELIVERY OF
CPR TRANSPACIFIC LINERS

The ships were operated for C.P.R. by Sir William Pearce, owner of the Guion S.S. Co., Liverpool and the John Elder shipyard. Their sailings connected with C.P.R's trans-continental boat trains. The service was referred as the Liverpool-Hong Kong Direct 'All Red' Route.

ABYSSINIA, PARTHIA

5 ABYSSINIA

B 1870 J & G Thomson, Glasgow. **T** 3,376g,2,159n. **D** 367.5/112 x 42.2/12.85 x 34.5/10.52.
E Sgl scr, 2 cyl direct acting, 500 nhp, 4 rectangular blrs, 24 furnaces, 60 psi. 13 kts. By builder. Coal: 1,180 tons at 90 tpd.
H Iron. 2 + spar dk. **C**: 1,600 tons. **P** 200 1st, 1,050 3rd.
1870 Mar 3: Launched for the Cunard Line. Sisters: *Algeria* and *Parthia*. The first of their ships to have bathrooms, one port, one starboard. May 24: M/v Liverpool-New York service.
1871 The trio were outmoded by the new White Star and ongoing Inman competition.
1880 Jan: Sold to her builder to raise money in part payment for *Servia* and *Catalonia*. Placed with Stephen Guion to replace the lost *Montana*. Nov 20: First sailing for them, Liverpool-New York. **1882** Compounded by J. Jones & Co., Liverpool.
1885 Ownership given as Sir William Pearce MP, Guion Line, who also owned the Elder yard.
1887 Feb 11: Placed on CPR's Pacific service while their own ships were being constructed and managed for Sir William by Adamson, Bell & Co. with George B. Dodwell in charge. The ship was not chartered but on the basis of 'All available business'. Buff funnel, black top. May 17: Left Hong Kong for Vancouver. Apr 14: Docked after overnight anchoring.
1891 Jan 28: Made her final and 19th trans-Pacific voyage to Hong Kong. Nov 28: Returned to New York for the Guion service. Dec 12: Left New York for Liverpool. Dec 18: Destroyed by fire 5 days out. All aboard were rescued by Norddeutscher Lloyd's *Spree*.

6 PARTHIA

Sister of *Abyssinia* except: **B** Wm Denny & Bros., Dumbarton. **T** 3,167g, 2,035n.
D 360.5/109.89 x 40.3/12.29. **E** 2 cyl comp inv, direct action, surface condensers, 1,750 ihp, 2 blrs, 60 psi. By builder.
H 4 dks. **C**: 3,139 tons. Coal: 881 tons at 40 tpd (half that of *Abyssinia*).
1870 Feb 2: Keel laid. Sept 10: Launched. Dec 17: M/v Liverpool-New York. Cost £94,970. A slightly smaller but superior version of her sister. Ident: *Parthia* had a thinner funnnel slightly closer to the mainmast.
1883 Nov: Laid up at Liverpool at the end of her 119th voyage.
1884 Taken, with *Batavia*, by John Elder & Co. in part payment for Cunard's *Umbria* and *Etruria*. Fitted with triple expansion engine. Placed on Guion Line service
1887 Joined *Abyssinia*. July 4: First arrival at Vancouver.
1891 Aug 20: Final CPR route sailing, her 20th. Modernised with two masts.
1892 R/n *Victoria* by Guion Line. Transferred to the Tacoma-Hong Kong service of the Northern Pacific Steamship Co. British flag. She was actually now in competition with CPR.
1898 Oct: Entered service with North American Mail SS Co. U.S. flag. Trooped to Manila during the Spanish-American war (1899-1900).
1901 Oct: Reverted to Northern Pacific SS Co. British flag.
1904 Sold to the Northwestern SS Co. Alaska service.
1908 Feb: Northwestern's fleet of eight ships was taken over by the Alaska S.S. Co. Placed on the San Francisco-Seattle-Nome route. **1924** Converted to oil fuel.
1935 Laid up at Lake Union for three years due to the cost of meeting U.S safety and fire precautions. **1940** Reduced to cargo only.
1941-47 Operated by the U.S. War Administration. Made 46 voyages to Alaska.
1952 Owned by Dulien Steel Products for breaking up. Placed in lay up at Houghton, Lake Washington. The hull was sound but the hatchways were too small to take containers.
1954 Purchased by Straits Towing & Salvage Co., Vancouver. Converted into a log carrying barge. R/n *Straits No. 27*.
1956 Sold to Japanese breakers. R/n *Straits Maru* and towed by the tug *Sudbury* (Island Tug & Barge Co.) to Osaka. Oct 16: Arrived and scrapped. Aged 86.

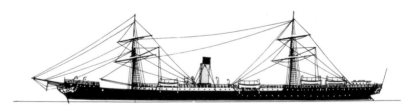

7 BATAVIA

B 1870 Wm. Denny & Bros, Dumbarton. **T** 2,593g, 1,828n. **D** 327.3/99.77 x 39.3/11 x 28.4/8.66.
E Sgl scr, comp inv, direct action, surface condensers, 1,800 ihp, 2 blrs, 12 furn, 60 psi. 12 kts. By builder.
H Iron. 4 dks. **C**: 2,650 tons. Coal: 655 tons. **P** 54 1st, 51 2nd, 624 3rd.
1870 Feb 1: Launched for Cunard, having been purchased on the stocks. She was Denny's first compound engined vessel. Mar 29: Ready for delivery but the boilers delayed completion by six weeks. May 10: M/v Liverpool-New York.
1880 Feb: Made one sailing to Bombay for P & O.
1884 Feb 2: Final Cunard sailing. Taken over by John Elder & Co. in part payment for *Umbria* and *Etruria*. Triple expansion and new boilers fitted. Placed on Guion service.
1887 Placed on the CPR trans-Pacific route.
1891 March: Final sailing to Hong Kong; her 15th.

1893 Returned to Guion service as *Tacoma.*
1898 Sold to the North American Mail S.S. Co. as *Tacoma.* Tacoma-Hong Kong route.
1901 Owned by Northwestern S.S. Co. Same service.
1904 Her owners were North Western Commercial S.S. Co.
1905 Feb 4: During the Russo-Japanese war she sailed for Vladivostok with relief supplies. Mar 15: Taken in an ice field off Hokkaido. R/n *Shikotan Maru.* Owned by R.Yashina, Uraga.
1924 Oct 23: Chinese owned (no name given). Grounded at Shai-wei-shan, 60 miles from Shanghai, inbound from Tsingtao. Taken to Shanghai and scrapped.

8 SKUZZY (II)

B 1885 Savona, British Columbia. **T** 297g. **D** 133/40.54. **E** Machy taken from *Skuzzy* (I) of 1882 which was used by Engineer Andrew Onderdonk on the building of the Fraser River Canyon Line.
1885 Built in 44 days for CPR. Operated from Savona, Kamloops Lake on Thompson River and Shuswap Lake for the delivery of men and construction material for the building of the Shuswap & Okanagan Rly at Eagle River, which was to serve the Coteau region. Once the goods had been landed she stayed and acted as the men's mess hall (they camped ashore) moving with them as the line progressed.
Nov 7: The first train arrived at Kamloops. *Skuzzy's* task was done but she was used to supply settlers along the lake's 600 mile/965 km shoreline.
1890 Sold for local service on Lake Shuswap. Trace lost.

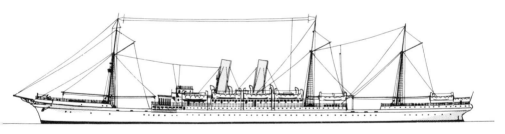

EMPRESS OF INDIA (I), EMPRESS OF JAPAN (I), EMPRESS OF CHINA (I)

9 EMPRESS OF INDIA (I)

B 1890 Naval Construction & Armament Co., Barrow (now Vickers / VSEL). **T** 5,905g, 3,003n. **D** 455.6/138.86 x 51.2/15.6 x 33.1/10.08.
E Tw scr, 2 x tpl exp, 10,000 ihp, 4 dbl blrs, 32 furn, 160 psi. 17½ kts. By builder.
H Steel. 3 dks. **F** 79/24.08. **B** 217/66.14. **P** 65/19.81. Coal: 2,000 tons; radius 11,000 miles/17,702 km. **C**: 1,500 tons, mainly silk. **P** 50 1st, 150 2nd, 400 3rd.
1890 Aug 30: Launched by Lady Louise Egerton. They all managed 19½ knots on trials.
1891 Feb 8: M/v Liverpool-Suez Canal-Hong Kong-Vancouver (arr Apr 28). May: Placed on the trans-Pacific service. Vancouver-Yokohama-Kobe-Nagasaki-Shanghai-Hong Kong and vice versa with coaling in both directions at Nagasaki, done by a chain of chanting women and children using small 15lb bags. Their record was 1,210 tons in 3¼ hours.
1901 Carried the Duke and Duchess of York Victoria-Vancouver during their world cruise.
1903 Aug 17: Hit by the iron Chinese cruiser *Huang Ti* (also spelled *Quang-Ki*) which sank.
1908 The new mail contract demanded 10½ days Vancouver-Yokohama in place of 12. The

built in speed reserves had to be used; the outward sign was that the funnels were lengthened by 10 ft/3.05m. to give a better draught (as drawn). Extra bunker space led to a reduction in 2nd class berths. Kobe was omitted. CPR soon planned replacements which arrived in 1912.

1914 Dec 7: Purchased by the Maharajah of Gwalior and converted into an Indian Army hospital ship. He met all costs, including conversion and operating.

1915 Jan 19: Commissioned and named *Loyalty*. Used Bombay-Mesopotamia with Indian troops.

1919 Mar: Sold at Bombay to Scindia S.N. Co. Started their Bombasy-Marseilles service which made no profit. **1920** Oct: Final sailing Marseilles-Genoa-Bombay.

1921 March: Laid up off Elephanta Island, Bombay.

1923 Feb: Sold and broken up by Maneckchand Jiyray, Bombay.

10 EMPRESS OF JAPAN (I)

As *Empress of India*. **B** 1891.

1890 Dec 13: Saturday. Launched by Lady Alice Stanley.

1891 Apr 11: M/v Liverpool-Suez Canal-Hong Kong-Vancouver. Proved to be the fastest of the three. Held the trans-Pacific record for 22 years at 9 days, 19 hrs, 39 mins.

1892 An electrical fire caused by a wire fusing put her out of service for three months.

1914 Aug 14: Commissioned as an armed merchant cruiser. Based at Hong Kong with Admiral Jerram's Far East Squadron. Nov 10: Recaptured *Exford* (Tatem), taken by the German light cruiser *Emden*, from her German prize crew.

1915 After the destruction of the German East Asiatic Squadron (Admiral Graf von Spee) at the Battle of the Falkland Islands (Dec 7 1915) only *Dresden* was left in the Pacific and when she was eliminated at Mas a Puera Island (Mar 14) *Empress of Japan* was finally released and, Oct 27, returned to her normal run.

1921 Given a black hull with white band (the only one of the three). Placed on an intermediate service.

1922 July 18: After her arrival at Vancouver she was laid up. An Indian prince wished to buy her as his private yacht but it was the running costs which ended the idea.

1925 Sold to V. Lamken, U.S.A., on behalf of Japanese interests. Remained at anchor.

1926 Mar 31: Acquired by scrap merchants R.J. Christian & Co. and demolished at Burrard Inlet, North Vancouver. Her bell hangs in the Merchants Exchange Building, Vancouver, and the figure head is in a public park.

11 EMPRESS OF CHINA (I)

As *Empress of India*. **B** 1891.

1891 Mar 25: Launched by Lady Stafford Northcote. July 15: Delivery voyage to Vancouver.

1911 July 27: Wrecked in thick fog on Mera Reef, Tokyo Bay, some 35 miles from Yokohama. All plus the mails saved. The Court of Enquiry found that swift currents carried the ship landwards and that there was no fog-horn warning to alert her to anchor.

1912 Oct: Refloated, towed to Yokohama, sold for $65,500 and (1912) scrapped there by Sasso Shojiro.

MICHIGAN, ONTARIO

12 MICHIGAN

B 1890 F.W. Wheeler, West Bay City, Michigan. **T** 1,739g, 1,020n.

D 296.5/90.37 x 41.3/12.6 x 15.6/4.75.

E Pad, 2 cyl, 4 Scotch blrs, 8 furn, 80 psi. 8 kts. By S.F. Hodge, Detroit.

H Steel. 1 dk. Rail car carrier, 2, 4, 2 track layout.

1890 Built for the crossing, Windsor-Detroit. The pair were the largest paddle ferries on the Great Lakes (but not the largest paddlers). Black funnels, dark red-brown uppers
1915 Laid up. Carried out some summer work for US operators during the intervening years.
1924 Sold to Newago Timber Co. converted into a wood pulp barge.
1943 Nov 14: Wrecked on Lottie Wood Shoal, Georgian Bay. All the crew were rescued by the tug *Favorite* (Great Lakes Towing Co.).

13 ONTARIO

As *Michigan* except: **B** Polson Iron Works, Owens Sound, Ontario. **T** 1,615g,1,018n. **D** 297/90.53. **E** By builder.
1890 April: Completed. Detroit River ferry. Registered at Windsor, Ont.
1925 Acquired, like her sister, by Newago Timber Co. Wood pulp barge.
1927 Oct 13: After engine failure, foundered in a storm on Lake Ontario near Outer Island.

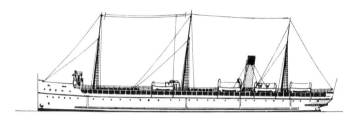

14 MANITOBA

B 1890 Polson Iron Works, Owen Sound, Ont. **T** 2,616g, 1,699n.
D 303.3/92.46 x 38.1/11.61 x 14.7/4.47.
E Sgl scr, 2 cyl comp, 283 nhp. 10 kts. By D. Rowan, Glasgow.
H Steel. 1 dk. **P** Berthed and un-berthed.
1890 May 4: Launched. June: Completed for Great Lakes service to replace the lost *Algoma* (3) on the Owen Sound-Port Arthur run. Released the chartered *Campana*. Her engines were those taken from *Algoma*. Black hull.
1912 Transferred to the new Port McNicoll-Port Arthur service.
1920 The Lakes fleet were given white hulls, as drawn.
1928 Sept 17: Rescued the five crew of the foundered *Manasoo*.
1950 Laid up at Port McNicoll. **1951** Scrapped.

STERNWHEELERS

These very shallow draught wooden vessels (they drew only a few inches/centimetres of water) were spoon bowed with no outside keel so that the long canoe style hull had to be braced with hog-rods and hog-chains attached to upright, centre line, Hog King-posts (usually decorated with brass ball tops) set into the keelson which ran fore and aft within the hull and to which the ribs were affixed. Smaller ones, called hog-posts (seldom decorated), were set upright, or at a fore or aft pointing angle, into the sides of the hull. The connecting wires were kept tight by turn-buckles. They were adjusted to correct any hogging (bow and stern drooping) and swaybacking (twisting). The hull was divided into water tight compartments called snag-rooms - a snag being anything which punctured the hull. These also acted as fresh water tanks. Sternwheelers were all of the same basic design with three decks. The wood fed boiler was forward on the main deck, directly below the wheel house, and the steam was piped to the engine aft. The three or four rudders were forward of the traditionally red-painted paddle wheel. The cargo came in through side or bow doors. Above was the Cabin/Saloon/Promenade deck. Up top was the Upper/Texas/Boat deck. The engine worked just like a non-condensing locomotive with the exhaust steam being shot up the funnel to produce a forced draught. But whereas a steam train blasts it all out at once - the 'puff-puff' sound- a sternwheeler released it progressively so that the noise it made was a hollow 'shuff-shuff' - which in the stillness of the Rockies could be heard miles away. The bow flag staff was used to acknowledge a 'please call' signal or to indicate to those ashore the intention to stop at a landing.

ABERDEEN

COLUMBIA

15 ABERDEEN
B 1893 E.G. McKay, Vernon, British Columbia. **T** 554g, 349n.
D 146.2/44.55 x 29.85/9.09 x 7/2.13.
E Stern-wheeler, 2 cyl horizontal trunk, 17 hp. Wood burner. By British Columbia Ironworks.
H Wood. 1 dk. 4 rudders. 6 snag-rooms. **P** 250 deck. 5 cabins.
1892 June: The railway from the main line at Sicamous to South Okanagan Lake was completed and plans were laid to operate a lake service.
1893 May 22: Launched, CPR's first proper river steamer. June: Delivered. Black hull as drawn. She was the first vessel on Lake Okanagan. Okanagan Landing-Penticton (60 miles). The ship left Okanagan Landing on Monday, Wednesday and Friday at 10.30. At Kelowna 13.00 and Penticton 16.30 to connect with the 17.30 train. She followed the return route next day but leaving at noon, after the train's arrival.
1901 Replaced by *York* (47) as the main-liner.
1902 Converted to coal burning. **1907** Given a part new hull, painted white.
1916 Withdrawn from service when the fruit boom ended.
1919 Sold to B. Johnson. Broken up, parts of her became his houseboat.

**EIGHT STEAMERS (16-21) PURCHASED FROM THE
COLUMBIA & KOOTENAY STEAM NAVIGATION COMPANY**
*These ships had black funnels and red tops; many retained them for
several years after the take over*

16 COLUMBIA (I)
B 1896 at Nakusp. **T** 50g. **D** 77/23.47 x 15/4.57 x 6/1.83.
E Sgl scr, 1 cyl simple direct acting, 1 blr. By builder. **H** Wood. 1 dk.
1896 Tug built for the Columbia & Kootenay Steam Nav. Co. (Known as CKNS). Used for towing barges Nakusp-Kootenay. **1897** Feb 1: Acquired by CPR.
1920 Withdrawn. Machinery transferred to *Columbia* (II) (167).

17 ILLECILLEWAET
B 1892 A. Watson, Revelstoke. **T** 98g. **D** 78/23.77 x 15/4.57 x 4/1.22.
E Taken from a vessel named *Despatch*. Stern-wheeler. 1 cyl horizontal trunk, direct acting. Wood burner. **H** Wood. Copper sheathed to slide over sand banks. 1 dk.
1892 Built as a steam scow under the direction of Captain Troup. Square bow and stern with a steering cabin and the engine aft. She could steam 'in two inches of water'. Oct 30: Launched for the Columbia & Kootenay S.N. Co. Cargo only carrier with iron ore from the Rossland mines to Northport. Also served on Trout Lake services Arrowhead-Beaton.
1897 Feb 1: Acquired by CPR. Same service. **1902** Broken up at Kootenay.

NAKUSP

NELSON

18 NAKUSP

B 1895 T.J. Bulger, Nakusp. **T** 1,083g. **D** 171/52.12 x 34/10.36 x 6/1.83.
E Stern-wheeler, 2 cyl, direct, horizontal trunk. By Iowa Iron Works.
H Wood. 1 dk. **P** 500, deck + 24 berthed.
1895 July 1: Launched for Columbia & Kootenay. Aug 15: M/v on the Lake Arrow service.
The largest vessel on the lake. She replaced their lost *Kootenai.*
1897 Feb 1: Taken over by CPR. Dec 23/4: Destroyed by fire at Arrowhead.

19 NELSON (I)

B 1891 at Nelson, B.C. **T** 496g. **D** 134/40.84 x 27/8.23 x 5/1.52.
E Stern-wheeler, 1 cyl direct horizontal trunk, wood burner. **H** Wood. 1 dk.
1891 June 11: Launched for Columbia & Kootenay S.N. Co., Arrow Lake service, as drawn.
The first on the lake.
1897 Feb 1: Taken over by CPR. **1913** Withdrawn.
1914 July 16: Instead of breaking her up CPR removed her engine and had her burnt, during
a firework display, as a spectacle for the public and was watched by hundreds.

TRAIL   **KOKANEE**

20 TRAIL

B 1896 T.J. Bulger, Nakusp. **T** 633g. **D** 165/50.29 x 31/9.45 x 5/1.52.
E Stern-wheeler, 1 cyl, horizontal trunk, direct acting, wood burner.   **H** Wood 1 dk.
1896 May 9: Launched for Columbia & Kootenay's Arrowhead Lake service. A cargo version
of *Nakusp,* although deck passengers were carried on all lake steamers. Her design enabled
her to push barges. **1897** Feb 1: Taken over by CPR.
1900 Withdrawn from service. **1902** Destroyed by fire at Robson West.

21 KOKANEE

B 1896 T.J. Bulger, Nelson. **T** 1,348g. **D** 143/43.58 x 25/7.62 x 6/1.83.
E Stern-wheeler, 1 cyl, horizontal trunk, direct acting. By Harlan & Hollingsworth,
Wilmington, Del. **H** Wood. 1 dk. **P** 200. 9 in cabins.
1896 Apr 7: Launched for Columbia & Kootenay. **1897** Feb 1: Taken over by CPR.
1923 Machinery taken out. Sold to become a fishing lodge at Deanstown.

22 LYTTON

B 1890 A. Watson, Revelstoke. **T** 452g. **D** 131/39.93 x 25/7.62 x 5/1.52.
E Stern-wheeler, 1 cyl horizontal trunk, direct acting. 17 hp. Wood burner. **H** Wood. 1 dk.
1890 May: Completed for Columbia & Kootenay. Spark catcher funnel top. July 2: M/v
Revelstoke-Little Dalles, Washington State, carrying Sir William Van Horne and other CPR
officials. The Columbia & Kootenay S.N. vessels connected with CPR trains even prior to the
take over. **1897** Feb 1: Taken over with the fleet by CPR. **1903** Scrapped.

NINE STEAMERS (23-31) BUILT FOR THE STIKINE RIVER SERVICES BETWEEN GLENORA, B.C., AND WRANGELL, ALASKA TO CATER FOR GOLD RUSH TRAFFIC. THE SERVICE LASTED ONLY ONE YEAR AND THE GOLD RUSH ENDED BEFORE THE LAST SIX CAME INTO SERVICE

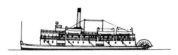

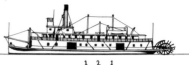

CONSTANTINE, DALTON, SCHWATKA, WALSH   *DAWSON*

23 CONSTANTINE
B 1897 at Port Blakely, Seattle. **T** 337g., **D** 150/45.72 x 30/9.14 x 5/1.52.
E Stern-wheeler, 1 cyl, horizontal trunk, direct acting. **H** Wood. 1 dk.
1897 Built for CPR for the Stikine River, Glenora-Wrangell gold rush traffic. One of four sisters. **1898** Nov: Sold. Taken to Alaska. **1899** July 4: Lost.

24 DALTON
As *Constantine*.
1897 Placed on the Stikine River service.
1901 Jan: Sold out of lay up to the White Pass & Yukon Railway Co. R/n *Capital City*.
1919 Abandoned and finally broken up.

25 SCHWATKA
As *Constantine*.
1897 Completed for CPR's Glenora-Wrangell service.
1904 Aug: Sold out of lay up to the White Pass & Yukon Rly Co. Trace lost.

26 WALSH
Details as *Constantine*.
1897 Built for the Glenora-Wrangell service but this was in its final stages with the ending of the gold rush. Operated on the Stikine River.
1902 Sept: Sold, surplus to requirements.

27 DAWSON
B 1897 T.J. Bulger, False Creek, Vancouver. **T** 779g. **D** 167/50.9 x 34/10.36 x 4/1.22.
E Pad, 2 simple expansion, 1 cyl, vertical blr, direct acting. 192 hp. Each engine worked one paddle. **H** Wood. 1 dk.
1897 Launched for the Stikine river service. Operated on the Wrangell-Petersburg route.
1899 June: Sold to the British Yukon Navigation Co. Same name.
1901 Altered at Dawson to give forward cargo handling when the vessel was nosed ashore at places with no landing. As drawn.
1926 Sept: Wrecked on Tache Reef, Rink Rapids, Yukon River.

---

28 DENVER
B 1896 at New Westminster. **T** 9g. **D** 36/10.97 x 9/2.74 x 4/1.22.
E Sgl scr, 1 cyl, simple exp, direct acting. **H** Wood. 1 dk.
1896 Tug. Built for W.F Wardropper, New Denver, B.C. Esturial and river barge towing services. **1897** Acquired by C.P.R. **1903** Sold.

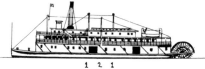

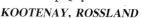

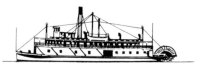

KOOTENAY, ROSSLAND　　　　　　　　　**SLOCAN**

29 KOOTENAY

B 1897 T.J. Bulger, Nakusp. **T** 1,117g. **D** 184/56.08 x 33/10.06 x 6/1.83.
E Stern-wheeler, 1 cyl, horizontal trunk, direct acting, 20 hp. 4 steam powered rudders.
H Wood. 1 dk. **P** 300, 42 cabins.
1897 Bulger's yard were now owned by C.P.R. with son J.M. Bulger in charge.
May 19: M/v Nakusp-Castlegar-Trail. Remained on the route.
1919 Withdrawn. Sold to Capt. Sanderson.
1920 Became his house-boat at Nakusp, complete with front garden. **1942** Destroyed by fire.

30 ROSSLAND

Sister to *Kootenay* except: **T** 884g.
1897 May 2: Launched. Nov 18: M/v Nelson-Trail. Served her career on Arrowhead Lake, Robson-Arrowhead (127 miles). A fast ship which made one round trip per day. Ident: The lifeboat was amidships (as in *Slocan*).
1916 Dec: Sank under the weight of snow on her decks.
1917 Raised and broken up at Nakusp.

31 SLOCAN

B 1897 T.J. Bulger, Rosebery. **T** 578g. **D** 156/47.55 x 25/7.62 x 6/1.83.
E Stern-wheeler, 1 cyl, horizontal trunk, 1 blr, 17 hp. By British Columbia Iron Works, Vancouver. **H** Wood. 1 dk.
1897 May 22: Entered service on Slocan Lake.
1905 Rebuilt with berths for 300 passengers. Engine increased to 2 cyl. trunk. Still direct acting to the stern-wheel. Placed on the Arrowhead-Castlegar route. **1928** broken up.

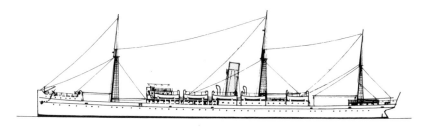

32 TARTAR

B 1883 Aitken & Mansel, Glasgow. **T** 4,425g, 2,768n.
D 376.4/114.73 x 47/14.33 x 30.4/9.25.
E Sgl scr, 2 cyl comp inv, 650 nhp, 90 psi. 12 kts. By J & J Thompson, Glasgow.
H Iron. 3 dks. **F** 44/13.41. **B** 92/28.04. **P** 170 1st, 60 2nd, 50 3rd.
1883 Jan 25: Launched for the Union Steam Ship Co.'s service to South Africa. May: Entered service on the mail route. Electric light throughout.
1886 Took the Plymouth-Cape Town record in 18 days, 2 hrs, 21 mins.
1888 Despite her compound engine still the fastest to the Cape; 17 days, 23 hrs, 37 mins.

1889 Modified to triple expansion by T. Richardson & Sons, West Hartlepool. This was by the addition of a new high pressure cylinder, upgrading the steam pressure and, usually (but not always) new high pressure boilers. For extra draught the funnel was heightened by 10ft/3.05m. Fore mast yards removed. A small promenade deck was added at the base of the mizzen mast (as drawn).

1897 Dec 28: To meet the gold rush traffic two ships were acquired by CPR, *Tartar* and *Athenian* (33), for a new service Vancouver-Wrangel, Stikine River-Skagway. Dec 29: Arrived at Southampton. CPR's first visit to the port.

1898 Feb 5: Delivery voyage. Left Southampton-Teneriffe-Buenos Aires-Valparaiso-Vancouver (Arr Apr 1) with passengers and 250 tons of telegraph cable for the Vancouver-Victoria link. Apr 28: First sailing to Alaska. The lack of a change of name indicated that both ships were to take the traffic while it existed. The Company read the situation correctly. *Tartar* made only six trips before the decline set in. Aug: Laid up. Dec: Placed on the trans-Pacific service. Enroute Hong Kong-Vancouver she made CPR's first call at Honolulu, Oahu, to land 600 Chinese workers for the pineapple plantations.

1899 After the war with Spain (April-July 1898) the U.S.A took over the Philippine Islands. July: Chartered by the U.S. Government for a trooping service U.S.A.-Manila.

1900 May: Reverted to CPR's trans-Pacific service.

1907 Aug: Sold to Japan. Oct 17: Enroute *Tartar* collided with CPR's *Charmer* (50) and had to be beached at English Bay. Laid up locally.

1908 March: Sold out of lay up to K. Kishimoto and broken up at Osaka.

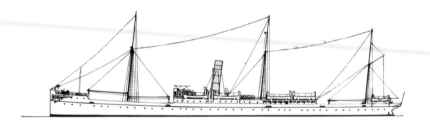

33 **ATHENIAN**

B 1881 Aitken & Mansel, Glasgow. **T** 3,877g, 2,493n. **D** 365/111.25 x 45.8/13.94 x 29/8.84.
E Sgl scr, 2 cyl comp inv, 600 nhp, 90 psi. 12 kts. By J & J Thompson, Glasgow.
H Iron and Steel. 3 dks. **F** 42/12.8. **B** 102/31.09. **P** 120 1st, 90 2nd, 50 3rd.

1881 Dec 7: Launched for the Union Steam Ship Co.

1882 March: Delivered. Mail route to South Africa. Oct 22: On her arrival became the first vessel to enter Cape Town's Robinson Graving Dock.

1886 Converted to triple expansion by the leading conversion specialist, T. Richardson, Hartlepool. 160 psi. Funnel heightened by 10ft/3.05m. Yards removed from foremast. **P** 178 1st, 56 2nd, 130 3rd. **1896** She twice lowered the homeward records.

1897 Dec 28: Acquired, with *Tartar*, by CPR.

1898 Feb 12: Left Southampton well loaded for Vancouver. She too only made six round voyages to Skagway before withdrawal. Laid up for several months. Acted as relief steamer.

1900 Placed on the trans-Pacific route. She made one call at Vladivostok with food. July: Carried troops to China for the relief of the Foreign legations trapped (June-August) in Peking by the Boxer Rebellion.

1904 Chartered to Osaka Shosen K.K. for use as a supply ship after the Russian war.

1905 Jan: Opened the Osaka-Darien service. She was then returned to CPR.

1907 Aug 22: Final trip to Hong Kong. Sept 14: Delivered to K. Kishimoto, Osaka; scrapped.

34 DUCHESNAY

B 1898 T.J. Bulger, False Creek. **T** 277g. **D** 120/36.58 x 21/6.4 x 4/1.29.
E Pad, 1 cyl, vertical direct acting, 10 hp. **H** Wood. 1 dk.
1898 Built for the lower River Stikine service; Wrangell-St Petersburg.
1899 Sold to E.T. Rathbone; same services. Trace lost.

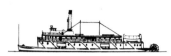

HAMLIN, McCONNELL, OGILVIE, TYRRELL   *MINTO, MOYIE (39/40)*

35 HAMLIN

B 1898 T.J. Bulger, False Creek. **T** 515g. **D** 146/44.5 x 31/9.45 x 5/1.52.
E Pad, 2 x 1 cyl vertical direct acting, one to each paddle, 2 x 17 hp. **H** Wood 1 dk.
1898 Built for the Stikine River service. This group were made redundant by the failure to build the railway between Glenlora, the navigation head on the river, and Lake Teslin which, in turn, occurred due to the decline in the Klondyke gold rush.
1900 The ships were put up for sale. **1901** Mar 28: Sold to British Yukon Nav. Co.
1903 Jan 14: Sold to Wm McCallum, Vancouver. Came down to work in the Vancouver area.
1904 Feb 14: Her owner became T.J. Kickham.
1910 Jun 9: Sold to E.J. Coyle, Victoria. Moved over to Vancouver Island.
1911 Mar 2: Owned by the Hamlin Tug Boat Co., Victoria B.C. **1913** Dec 2: Sold to J.H. Greer.
1917 July 28: Owned by Defiance Packing Co., Vancouver. Lost in the Fraser River.

36 McCONNELL

As *Hamlin* except: **T** 496g. **D** 142/43.28 x 30/9.14 x 5/1.52.
1898 Built for the Sikine River service.
1901 Mar 20: Sold to the British Yukon Nav. Co. Sept 4: After hull damage scrapped at Skagway.

37 OGILVIE

As *Hamlin* except: **T** 541g. **D** 147/44.8.
1898 Built for the Sikine River routes. Ident: No forward loading door, no lifeboat aft and the house extended to the stern.
1901 Mar 20: Sold to British Yukon Nav. Co. Sept 4: Dismantled at Skagway.

38 TYRRELL

As *Hamlin* except: **T** 678g.
1898 Completed for the same service as her sisters. July: Sold to the British American Corporation. Had a deck of passenger cabins added. **1905** Sold to D.W. Davis, Yukon.
1915 Taken over by the British Yukon Nav. Co. **1919** Broken up.

39 MINTO

B 1898 Bertram Iron Works, Toronto, assembled by CPR, Nakusp. **T** 829g.
D 162/49.38 x 30/9.14 x 6/1.83.
E Stern-Wheeler, 2 cyl comp horizontal trunk, double beam direct acting, 225 nhp.
H Wood with steel struts. 1 dk. **P** 225. 40 berths.
1898 Constructed at Toronto, then taken apart and packed in over 1,000 crates. Taken by rail to Vancouver then up to Nakusp where the vesssel was reassembled. The pair were intended for the 'All-Canadian Route' to the Yukon (See History 1897). Nov 19: Launched and named after the Earl of Minto, Governor General of Canada. Entered service between Arrowhead

and West Robson, a distance of 134 miles and a journey time of 12 hours.
1954 Apr 23: Final round voyage West Robson-Arrowhead. She had completed over 2½ million miles. Apr 24: Presented, for $1, to the Nakusp Chamber of Commerce and also used by the Rotary Club.
1956 Apr: Sold for $750 for scrap but John Nelson paid $800 for her 'as is'. The ship was towed to Galena Bay, Upper Arrow Lake, where he intended to restore her but he died on Nov 26, 1967 and the plan went with him. **1968** Aug 1: The hull was burned.

40 MOYIE

As *Minto* except: Re-assembled by T.J. Bulger at CPR, Nelson. **T** 835g. **P** 400.
1898 Oct 22: Ready for service on Lake Kootenay. Nelson-Lardeau, 87 miles in 8 hours including 11 stops.
1957 Apr 27: Withdrawn from service and preserved exactly as she was on her final trip, by the Kootenay Historical Society, on Front St, Kaslo. She was the last British Columbia sternwheeler and the only one still able to steam.

41 SANDON

B 1898 CPR, Rosebery. **T** 97g. **D** 76/23.16 x 17/5.18 x 6/1.83.
E Sgl scr, 1 cyl, vertical, direct acting. 3 hp. 8 kts. Wood burner (like virtually all of the 'lakers').
H Wood. 1 dk.
1898 Tug for barge towing duties on Lake Slocan.

42 WILLIAM HUNTER

B 1893 CPR, Rosebery. **T** 97g. **D** 59/17.98 x 13/3.96 x 3/0.91.
E Sgl scr, 1 cyl vertical, direct acting, 1 blr. 17 hp. **H** Wood 1 dk.
1893 Completed; private steam launch and towboat.
1899 Acquired by CPR for barge docking services at Rosebery on Slocan Lake.
1903 Sold locally.

43 YMIR

B 1898 J.M. Bulger, CPR, Nelson. **T** 90g. **D** 86/26.21 x 17/5.18 x 6/1.83.
E Sgl scr, 1 cyl vertical direct acting, 1 blr. **H** Wood. 1 dk.
1898 Tug on Lake Kootenay. **1928** Broken up.

44 PROCTER

B 1900 J.M. Bulger, CPR, Nelson. **T** 43g. **D** 65/19.81 x 14/4.27 x 5/1.52.
E Sgl scr, 1 cyl, vertical, direct acting, 1 blr. **H** Wood. 1 dk.
1900 Built for the Kootenay Lake service Kalso-Duncan River. This competed with the Great Northern Railway's stern wheeler *Argenta*.
1901 Transferred to the Nelson-Kootenay Landing service.
1904 Transferred to Trout Lake. Based at Gerrard. **1921** Sold.

45 VICTORIA

B 1898 at Victoria, Victoria Island. **T** 107g. **D** 75/22.86 x 15.4.57 x 4/1.22.
E Stern wheeler,1 cyl horizontal direct acting, 14 hp. **H** Wood. 1 dk.
1898 Wooden scow built for Nils Roman, Victoria.
1900 Purchased by CPR. Based Victoria.

1904 Taken to Trout Lake. Her engine was removed and stored (See 100) then she was beached for use as a wharf and freight shed. Remained there until the service finally ended and for some years after that.

VALHALLA, YORK

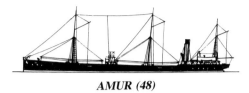

AMUR (48)

46 VALHALLA
B 1901 J.M. Bulger, CPR, Nelson. **T** 153g. **D** 103/31.39 x 21/6.4 x 9/2.74.
E Sgl scr, 2 cyl, comp inv, 36 rhp. 10 kts. By Polson Iron Works, Toronto. **H** Wood. 1 dk.
1901 Tug on Kootenay Lake. Based at Nelson. Towed railway flats to the lakeside railheads at Kootenay Landing, Procter, Lardeau and Kalso. She was later used on the Fraser River.
1931 Sold to R.P. Dill who beached her in a bed of concrete at the spring high water mark and converted her into his home.

47 YORK
B 1901 J.M. Bulger, CPR, Okanagan. **T** 134. **D** 88/26.82 x 16/4.88 x 5/1.52.
E Tw scr, 2 x 1 cyl, direct acting, 1 blr, 13 hp. 8 kts. **H** Steel. 1 dk.
1901 A smaller version of *Valhalla* in appearance but with passenger accommodation below deck aft. Built for the Lake Okanagan service to augment *Aberdeen* (15).
1932 Withdrawn and sold for scrap.

CANADIAN PACIFIC NAVIGATION COMPANY (CPNC)
1901: CPR acquired the company and 14 vessels (48-61)

48 AMUR
B 1890 Strand Slipway Co., Sunderland. **T** 907g, 570n. **D** 216/65.84 x 28.1/8.56 x 11.2/3.4.
E Sgl scr, tpl exp, 170 nhp, 1 dbl blr, 150 psi. 8½ kts. By North East Marine Eng'g Co., Sunderland. **H** Steel. 1 + spar dk.
1890 Apr: Built as *Amur* for the North Sea and Baltic trades by the Governor & Company of the Adventurers of England.
1895 Sold to the Lombard S.S. Co., London. Same name.
1898 Sold to the Klondyke Mining, Trading & Transportation Co. and brought out to Canada.
1899 Acquired by Canadian Pacific Navigation Co., Victoria B.C. Black funnel.
1901 Transferred with the fleet to CPR. Yellow funnel black top.
1911 Sold to the Coastwise Steam Ship & Barge Co.
1924 Feb: Sold to A. Berquist, Vancouver. R/n *Famous*.
1926 Went aground in the Skeena River. Salved. **1929** Broken up.

BEAVER (I)

CHARMER

49 BEAVER (I)
B 1898 CPNC, Victoria, B.C. **T** 545g. **D** 140/42.67 x 28/8.53 x 5/1.52.
E Stern-wheeler, 1 cyl, horizontal direct acting. 13 hp. **H** Steel.

1898 Built for Canadian Pacific Navigation Co.
1901 Taken over with the fleet by CPR. One of four sternwheelers on the Upper Fraser River to Chilliwack (the non-CPR being *Ramona*, *Favorite* and *Defender*). She also made one annual run with stores to Hudson's Bay's Fort Douglas at the head of Lake Harrison.
1919 Sold to the Government of British Columbia. Fitted for passenger work on the Fraser River. **1932** Dismantled.

50 **CHARMER**

B 1887 Union Iron Works, San Francisco. **T** 1,044g, 497n.
D 200/60.96 x 42/12.8 x 12.9/3.91.
E Sgl scr, tpl exp, 186 nhp. 12 kts. By builder.
H Steel. 2 dks. **P** 40 berths, 350 deck passengers.
1887 Completed as *Premier* for CPNC but flew the US flag with E.W. Spencer of Portland, Oregon, as owner.
1892 Oct 8: Collided with the collier *Willamette* off Marowstone Point, Port Angeles. The ship was beached at Bush Point and her passengers taken to Seattle; she was then towed to Victoria. There, to prevent US legal action, she was transferred to the British registry and r/n *Charmer*.
1901 Taken over by CPR.
1907 Oct 17: Collided with CPR's *Tartar* (32).
1933 Withdrawn from service. Became the dressing rooms for bathers at Newcastle Island.
1935 Sold for demolition to Capital Iron & Metals Co., Vancouver.

51 **DANUBE**

B 1869 John Elder & Co., Glasgow. **T** 887g, 561n. **D** 215.6/65.71 x 27.7/8.44 x 20.7/6.3.
E Sgl scr, 2 cyl comp inv, 114 nhp, 9½ kts. By builder. **H** Iron 1 dk.
1869 Built for D.R. MacGregor, Glasgow. Traded to the Mediterranean and Black Sea in the inbound fruit trade with general cargo outwards. **1880** Reboilered.
1884 June 6: Sold to the Scottish Oriental S.S. Co., Glasgow. She does not appear to have served the Far East but remained on the Levant service.
1890 Acquired by Canadian Pacific Navigation Co. Same name.
1901 May 14: Taken over with the CPN fleet.
1905 Oct 20: Sold to British Columbia Salvage Co. R/n *Salvor*. Converted into a salvage vessel with no superstructure aft. **1918** Aug 3: Sold to J.P. Davies, Montreal.
1920 Became *Nervion* of A. Menchaca, Bilbao. Collier duties Cardiff-Bilbao.
1936 Broken up. Her iron hull still being in good condition.

ISLANDER

52 ISLANDER

B 1888 Napier, Shanks & Bell, Glasgow. **T** 1,495g, 478n. **D** 240/73.15 x 42/12.8 x 14/4.27.
E Tw scr, 2 x tpl exp, 324 nhp. 12 kts. By Dunsmuir & Jackson, Glasgow.
H Steel.1 dk. **P** 200. Crew 80.
1888 Sept: Built for Captain J. Irving's Pioneer Line which, since 1883, had been a part of his
Canadian Pacific Navigation Co. but which still operated under the Pioneer Line banner, based
at Victoria. Sept 22: M/v to Victoria. She operated on CPN's Canadian waters Puget Sound
routes and, being based on the design of British cross channel ships (with the addition of the
usual side loading doors), outmoded all the US style ships in the area.
1890 The Pioneer name ceased and she became a fully fledged CPN vessel based at Victoria.
1901 May 15: Taken over with the fleet by CPR. Aug 5: Enroute Skagway-Victoria she collided
with an iceberg in Lynn Channel and sank within 17 minutes with the loss of 65 lives. 107 saved.
1934 Aug: As larger ships commenced to use the Lynn Channel the wreck became a hazard
and it was raised, beached and eventually dismantled.

---

53 MAUDE

B 1872 Burr & Smith, San Juan Island, Washington State. **T** 175g, 54n.
D 113.5/34.59 x 21/6.4 x 9/2.74.
E Pad. 2 x 1 cyl engines. By builder. **H** Wood 1 dk. Passenger ship.
1872 Completed for the East Coast Mail Line, Puget Sound. Fore and aft schooner rig which
indicates two masts. Service Olympia-Tacoma-Seattle.
1885 Converted to single screw by Albion Iron Works, Victoria. Lloyds Register now records
her as an ex-sailing vessel. **1890** Acquire by CPN for coastal work.
1901 May 15: Taken over by CPR. Used as a collier and gunpowder carrier.
1903 Sold to British Columbia Salvage Co. Manager: W. Fitzherbert Bullen. **1914** Dismantled.

OTTER (I)

PRINCESS LOUISE (I)

54 OTTER (I)

B 1900 Canadian Pacific Navigation Co's yard, Victoria. **T** 366g, 232n.
D 128/39.01 x 24.4/7.44 x 11/3.35.
E Sgl scr, 2 cyl comp, 24 rhp, 8 kts. By T. Gowen, Victoria, B.C.
H Wood. 2 dks. **P** 44 in 2-berth cabins along the main deck.
1900 Built for CPN. Her engines dated from 1887 and came from a vessel named *Rainbow*.
She was used to connect all the smaller landings serviced by CPN.
1901 May 15: Taken over by CPR. During her subsequent career she had her passenger
accommodation reduced and the lifeboats amended in line with this. **1928** Laid up for sale.
1931 Sold to Gibson Bros., Vancouver Island, who were fish canners.
1937 May 12: Lost by fire.

55 PRINCESS LOUISE (I)

B 1869 J. Inglis, New York. **T** 932g, 544n. **D** 180/54.86 x 30/9.14 x 13/3.96.
E Pad, 1 vertical cyl, overhead beam, direct acting; for manoeuvering each of her massive
paddles could be manually disconnected but the engine had to be stopped for this to be done
(a state of affairs which took a couple of minutes and was generally disliked and seldom used).
75 rhp. 10 kts. By J. Roach & Sons, New York.

H Wood, white oak. 2 dks. Brig rigged. A luxurious passenger ship.

1869 Completed as *Olympia* for Finch & Wright's Oregon Steam Navigation Co. Black hull, white uppers. Black funnel with brass bands. Dec 7: M/v New York-Cape Horn-Olympia. Service Olympia-Seattle-Port Townsend-Victoria, She was the fastest vessel on the route - but did not hold the $36,000 per annum mail contract; this was held by a Mr Nash.

1871 June 27: The famous pre-arranged race between *Olympia* and *North Pacific* (Starr Line) took place on the Tacoma-Port Townsend run. *North Pacific* won but only by minutes. Starr's now paid $7,500 per annum for *Olympia* to be taken off the route. She went to San Francisco where another subsidy was paid to have her withdrawn. Next a coastal service Portland-Humboldt was started but was only viable because of the Starr subsidy.

1878 The Starr annual payment ceased. Oct: Sold to the Hudson's Bay Company.

1879 R/n *Princess Louise* after the Duchess of Argyll, wife of the Governor General of Canada and the fourth daughter of Queen Victoria. Registered at London.

1883 Transferred to CPN. Same name. Victoria-Vancouver service.

1901 May 15: To CPR with the CPN fleet. She introduced the 'Princess' nomenclature system.

1906 Sold to Marpole McDonald, Victoria.

1908 Converted into a barge by the Vancouver Dredging & Salvage Co.

1916 Her owners were the Britannia Mining and Smelter Co. **1919** Sank at Port Alice, B.C.

---

56 QUEEN CITY

B 1894 R. Brown & Co., Vancouver. **T** 391g, 244n.
D 116/35.36 x 27/8.23 x 10/3.05. **H** Wood. 2 dks.
1894 Built as a schooner. **1897** Acquired by CPN.
1898 Fitted by Albion Iron Works Co., Victoria, with a 2 cyl comp eng, 34 rhp.
1901 May 15: Taken over by CPR.
1916 Sept 19: Damaged by fire at Victoria. Sold to the Pacific Line Co. Rebuilt and new engine fitted. Local delivery work. **1918** Sold to Kingsley Nav. Co., Vancouver.
1920 Converted into a petrol barge. Nov: Caught fire and became a total loss.

R.P. RITHET

TRANSFER

57 R.P. RITHET

B 1882 A. Watson & Co., Victoria. **T** 217g. **D** 117/35.66 x 33/10.06 x 8/2.44.
E Stern-wheeler, 2 cyl comp horizontal trunk, direct acting. 8 kts.
H Wood. 1 dk. **P** 200 including 24 berthed.
1882 Apr 20: Launched for Captain Irving's Pioneer Line. With electric light she was the most luxurious yet for her intended service. June 10: New Westminster-Fraser River service. R.P. Rithet, a friend of Irving, owned the flour mills at Enderby, Lake Kamloops. He was a shareholder.
1883 Amalgamated into Canadian Pacific Navigation Co. when it was formed. Placed on a Fraser River-Victoria service.
1885 July 28: Off Victoria, collided with and sank the paddle steamer *Enterprise*. 2 dead. *R.P. Rithet* was held to blame.
1886 June 28: With the introduction of the through service Montreal-Vancouver she was one of the steamers used to connect the CPR Vancouver terminus with Victoria. It cemented even further the CPR/CNR liaison. It was inevitable that CNR would eventually be purchased.
1901 May 15: Taken over by CPR. Their oldest ship.
1909 Apr: Sold to the Terminal S.N. Co. R/n *Baramba*.

1917 Sold to Pacific Lime Co., Vancouver. Reduced to a barge.
1918 Taken over by the Kingsley Nav. Co. Same name. **1927** Circa: Dismantled.

58 TRANSFER

As *R.P. Rithet* except: **B** 1893 at the New Westminster yard. **T** 264g.
D 122/37.18 x 24/7.31 x 5/1.52.
1893 Built for CPN's Fraser River service.
1894 June: The Fraser River reached record flood levels and inundated the valley bottom. *Transfer* was one of three sternwheelers which steamed inland - where none had ever been before - to rescue stranded people and cattle. She even tied up at a barn to pick up cattle and one settler boarded her by a gangway from his upstair's window.
1901 May 15: To CPR with the fleet. Placed on the New Westminster-Lardner-Steveston daily service. Her competitor was the slower *Ramona*.
1909 Sold to Robert Jardine, New Westminster. He converted her into a power plant for his cannery at Redonda Bay. Trace lost.

TEES

WILLAPA

59 TEES

B 1893 Richardson, Duck & Co., Thornaby-on-Tees. **T** 679g, 441n.
D 165/50.29 x 26/7.92 x 10.85/3.28.
E Sgl scr, 3 cyls, tpl exp, 80 rhp, 1 sgl blr, 180 psi. 9 kts. By Blair & Co., Stockton.
H Steel. 1 + shelter dk. **P** 16, aft in poop accommodation.
1893 May: Completed for the Tees Union S.S. Co., Newcastle.
1896 Sold to Hudson's Bay Co. who passed her on to CPN when the two amalgamated their Pacific coast vessels. **1901** May 15: Merged into CPR.
1923 Sold to Pacific Salvage Co. R/n *Salvage Queen*.
1933 Reduced to a timber barge towage. R/n *Island Queen* by Island Tug & Barge Co.
1937 After hull damage, due to colliding with her tow, she was deemed to be beyond economic repair and was scrapped at Vancouver.

60 WILLAPA

B 1882 Ilwaco Nav. Co. Portland, Oregon. **T** 373g, 245n. **D** 136/41.45 x 22/6.7 x 10/3.05.
E Sgl scr, 2 cyl comp, 43 rhp, 10 kts. By Pusey & Jones, Wilmington, Cal. **H** Wood. 2 dks.
1882 Built as the Ilwaco Nav. Co's Columbia River bar tug *General Miles*. Employed to take sailing ships through the deep port entry channels but used also for towing between the Columbia River and Grey's Harbor.
1889 Capsized at Coos Bay on the sand banks while acting as bar tug. Righted and towed to Portland for repairs. Acquired by Captain Beecher she was lengthened by 36ft/10.97, had superstructure added and emerged as the passenger vessel *Willapa*. She operated Puget Sound ports to British Columbia.
1893 Sold to Peabody & Roberts to become the first vessel of the newly formed Alaska Steamship Co. They then formed the Puget Sound Navigation Co. to operate their remaining Puget Sound ships. **1894** Transferred to the new concern.
1896 Feb: Stranded on the inside passage enroute Alaska-Puget Sound. Abandoned to the underwriters. Sold to Captain Irving's Pioneer Line. Refurbished for BC coasting service.
1898 Owned entirely by CPN.
1901 May 15: Transferred to CPR. During the Alaska gold rush she operated to Nome.

1902 Sold to Rex Thompson's Bellingham Bay Transportation Co. R/n *Bellingham*.
1908 Sold back, with Thompson's interests, to the Puget Sound Nav. Co., (the Black Ball Fleet). Based Port Townsend. Later served Seattle-Neah Bay.
1912 Sold to the Inland Navigation Co.
1915 Engines and boiler removed. Used as a US Army barge.
1919 Tied up in sinking condition at San Juan Island dock.
1950 After being taken over and stripped by Otto Shively *Bellingham* was burned as a spectacle at the Seattle Sea Fair.

61 YOSEMITE

B 1862 J.W. North, San Francisco. **T** 1,525g, 1,055n. **D** 282.3/86.03 x 34.9/10.62 x 13.2/4.01.
E Pad, 1 cyl vertical, beam direct acting, 153 rhp, 9 kts. By Allaire Works, New York.
H Wood. 1 dk. **P** 500 (but carried 1,500 on day excursion work).
1862 Built for the Central Pacific Railroad Co.'s California Steam Navigation Co. for the San Francisco-Sacramento service; she operated with *Chrysopolis*. Black hull and funnel.
1865 Oct: Leaving Rio Vista her boiler burst. In the ensuing fire her freight deck collapsed and 55 lives were lost. Rebuilt, a 35ft/10.67m splice being inserted amidships and new boilers fitted. Still with a black hull.
1883 Sold to Capt. Irving's Pioneer Line. Same name. Victoria-New Westminster.
1890 Transferred to CPN. White hull, buff funnel, black top.
1901 May 15: Taken over with the fleet by CPR.
1906 Sold to the Puget Sound Excursion Co., Seattle. T. Grant manager-captain. Overhauled at Eagle Harbor. Used for excursion work.
1907 Aug: While entering her berth at Seattle, from Wilson Park, Captain Grant rang for full astern. However the engineer inadvertently gave full ahead and *Yosemite* rammed her way 30ft/9.14m into Railroad Avenue upsetting a horse and cart. She is thus remembered as the ship that rammed a horse. Also, boxing was illegal in the US Puget Sound counties but there was a patch of water off Whidbey Island which was outside their respective boundaries. On a famed occasion *Yosemite* steamed in circles within these limits while a 20 round fight took place watched by over 300 men.
1909 July 9: Returning from an excursion to Bremerton the ship suddenly veered off course and was wrecked in Port Orchard Narrows, Bremerton.

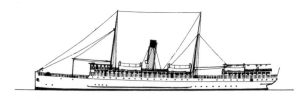

62 PRINCESS MAY

B 1888 Hawthorn, Leslie & Co., Newcastle. **T** 1,394g, 892n.
D 249/75.89 x 33.2/10.11 x 17.7/5.38.
E Tw scr, 2 x tpl exp, 287 nhp. 15 kts. By builder.
H Steel. 2 + part shade dk. **F** 46/14.02. **P** 150.
1888 Feb 29: Launched as *Cass* for the Formosa Trading Co. Taipeh-Shanghai service.

1894 Acquired by the Government of Formosa. Operated by Europeans under license. R/n *Arthur*. Same service. Her name however then reverted temporarily to *Cass*.
1896 Became *Ningchow*, Government of China. Coastal services.
1899 Sold to Marty & D'Abbie, Haiphong. R/n *Hating*.
1901 March: Acquired by CPR. R/n *Princess May*. Vancouver-Southeast Alaskan ports route. It was her renaming which confirmed the use of *Princess* for the CPR coastal vessels.
1910 Aug 5: Went aground on Sentinel Island enroute Skagway-Vancouver. At low tide the vessel was completely high and dry and perched at a steep angle. However she came off safely on the next high tide.
1919 Sold to Princess May S.S. Co., managed by the Standard Fruit Company. Served in the Caribbean. **1930** Towed out from Kingston, Jamaica, and scuttled.

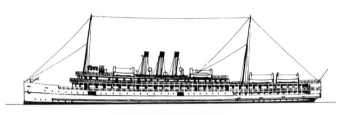

PRINCESS VICTORIA

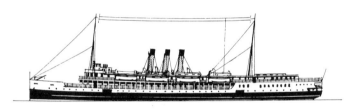

PRINCESS VICTORIA as rebuilt in 1930

63 PRINCESS VICTORIA

B 1903 C.S. Swan & Hunter, Newcastle. **T** 1,943g, 428n. **D** 300/91.44 x 40.5/12.34 x 15.3/4.67.
E Tw scr, 2 x tpl exp, 434nhp. 19½ kts. By Hawthorn, Leslie & Co., Newcastle.
H Steel. 1 + promenade dk. **P** 1,900.
1902 Nov 18: Launched by Mrs Archer Baker.
1903 Jan 26: Trials. Jan 28: Left for Victoria, BC. Mar 28: Arrived, via Cape Horn. For the passage the incomplete superstructure was boxed in and the final decking and fitting out took place at Robertson & Hackett's Vancouver yard with furnishing etc installed by CPR at Victoria, BC. Aug 17: When she entered service *Princess Victoria* became the fastest vessel on the triangular route Vancouver-Victoria-Seattle. Affectionately known as the *Princess Vic* she carried a broom at her foremast top to signify her all conquering speed.
1906 July 21: Collided with the stern wheeler *Chehalis* (owned by her master Captain Hyde) in Burrard Inlet. Neither vessel sank but the wooden *Chehalis* had to be beached and never sailed again.
1914 Aug 26: Collided in fog with the Pacific Alaska SS Co's *Admiral Sampson* which sank with the loss of 12 lives.
1930 Converted into a car ferry carrying 50 vehicles (as drawn).
1950 Aug 28: Final sailing Vancouver-Nanaimo. Sept 5: Laid up at Victoria.
1952 Feb: Sold to Tahsis & Co., Vancouver. R/n *Tahsis No. 3* as a fuel delivery barge.
1953 Mar 10: While in tow of the tug *Sea Giant* struck a rock in Welcome Passage and sank.

ELDER DEMPSTER NORTH ATLANTIC INTERESTS PURCHASED TOGETHER WITH THREE MERSEY TUGS AND FIFTEEN OTHER VESSELS

MERSEY TOWING COMPANY

BEAVER	*PANTHER*	*AFRICAN / OTTER (II)*

64 BEAVER (II)

B 1898 Elliot & Jeffery, Cardiff. **T** 154g, 13n. **D** 106.3/32.41 x 20/6.1 x 11.2/3.4.
E Sgl scr, 2 cyl comp, 75 rhp, 1 sgl blr, 100 psi. 8 kts. By builder.
H Steel, iron frames. 1 dk.
1898 Tug. Built as *Powerful* for J. Elliot, Cardiff. **1899** R/n *Lady Lewis*; same owners.
1901 Acquired by Elder, Dempster & Co. to form part of the fleet of Mersey Towing Co., Liverpool. R/n *Beaver*.
1903 Apr 6: Acquired by CPR. **1922** Sold to J. Davies & Co., Cardiff.
1938 Broken up by Reese & Co., Llanelly.

65 PANTHER

B 1884 Elliot & Jeffery, Cardiff. **T** 150g, 19n. **D** 105.2/32.05 x 19.8/6.02 x 10.7/3.25.
E Sgl scr, 2 cyl comp, 70 rhp. 8 kts. By builder. **H** Iron. 1dk.
1884 Built as the tug *Elliot & Jeffery* for J. Elliot, Cardiff.
1901 Acquired for the Mersey Towing Co., Liverpool. R/n *Panther*.
1903 Apr 6: Taken over by CPR. **1921** Sold to Coulson Tug Co., Newcastle.
1925 Bought by France Fenwick Tyne & Wear Co. when they took over the Coulson fleet.
1926 Broken up.

66 AFRICAN / OTTER (II)

B 1887 Elliot & Jeffery, Cardiff. **T** 159g, 13n. **D** 105.5/32.13 x 19.8/6.02 x 10.5/3.2.
E sgl scr, 2 cyl comp, 80 rhp. 8 kys. By builder. **H** Iron. 1 dk.
1887 Completed as the two funnelled tug *Sir W.T. Lewis* for J. Elliot & Co.
1901 Acquired by Mersey Towing. R/n *African*.
1903 Apr 6: Taken over by CPR. Tender duties.
1906 Oct: Rebuilt with one funnel. R/n *Otter*. Used only as a tug. *Bison* (88) replaced her.
1922 Sold to the Liverpool Screw Towing & Lighterage Co. R/n *Marsh Cock*.
1946 May 27: Sold for scrap to Rootledge & Co. Broken up at Bromborough, Cheshire.

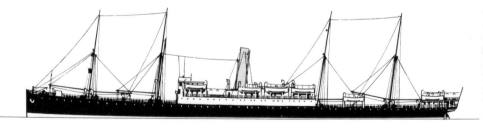

LAKE ERIE, LAKE CHAMPLAIN

67 LAKE ERIE / TYROLIA

B 1900 Barclay, Curle & Co., Glasgow. **T** 7,550g, 4,814n.
D 446/135.94 x 52/15.85 x 35.5/10.82.
E Tw scr, 2 x tpl exp, 660 nhp, 3 dbl blrs, 18 furn, 180 psi. 14 kts. By builder.

H Steel. 2 + shelter dk. **P** 100 1st, 80 2nd, 500 3rd. Crew 90.
1899 Nov 21: Launched. Beaver funnel but Elder, Dempster owned.
1900 Jan 30: M/v Liverpool-Cape Town as a Boer War transport.
1901 In all, made eight voyages before being released onto the Liverpool-Quebec-Montreal service. Transferred to British & African S.N. Co. ownership but retained her Atlantic Beaver funnel.
1903 Mar 3: Final Beaver sailing. Apr 6: One of the fifteen ocean-going vessels acquired by CPR. Handed over at Liverpool. Her accommodation was then changed to 150 2nd, 1,050 Steerage, as drawn. Apr 26: Arrived at Halifax on her first sailing having been re-directed from Quebec due to later than usual St Lawrence ice. **1906** Yellow funnel, black top.
1910 May: Chartered to the Allan Line when they strengthened their London sailings (from monthly to weekly) and with whom CPR were in close collaboration; in fact they secretly owned the company.
1913 Mar 29: R/n *Tyrolia* and placed on the new Trieste-Canada service.
1914 Oct 28: Employed as a troopship UK-France. Nov: Converted into the dummy battleship HMS *Centurion*. Based Scapa Flow with the Special Services Squadron.
1915 The squadron was disbanded. Used as a store ship.
1916 June 27: Bought by the Admiralty. Converted into a 5,000 ton capacity circular-tank oiler. R/n *Saxol*. Oct 7: Lane & MacAndrew became the managers. R/n *Aspenleaf*. Dec 30: Hit a mine in the English Channel laid by *UC-16*. Towed into port.
1917 Nov 7: Taken over by the Shipping Controller,
1919 Sept 12: Bought by Anglo-Saxon Petroleum Co. Same name. **1921** Jan 11: R/n *Prygona*.
1925 Feb 6: Sold for breaking up by Petersen & Albeck, Copenhagen.

68 LAKE CHAMPLAIN / RUTHENIA

As *Lake Erie* except: **T** 7,392g, 4,685n.
1900 Mar 31: Launched for British & African S.N. Co. but intended for the Beaver Line service in their livery. May 15: M/v Liverpool-Quebec-Montreal. An attempt to use her for Boer War work was frustrated by representations from the Canadian Government. They wanted the service to continue.
1901 May 25: Became the first British merchantship to be fitted with wireless telegraphy
1903 Apr 6: Taken over by CPR. Yellow funnel. Apr 14: Made CPR's first Atlantic sailing to Saint John, NB., via Halifax. **1906** Black topped funnel.
1911 Apr: Hit an iceberg off Newfoundland, fortunately with little damage. Put into St Johns, Newfoundland.
1913 R/n *Ruthenia* and placed, with her sister, on the Trieste route.
1914 Aug: Taken over by the Admiralty; initially as a cross channel troopship then converted into the dummy battleship HMS *King George V*. Joined the others at Scapa Flow.
1915 Dummy outline removed and used as a store ship. Reverted to *Ruthenia*.
1916 Jan 29: Purchased by the Admiralty. Converted into an oil tanker, similar to her sister. Based Hong Kong with the China Fleet. The ship was never renamed *Regina* as stated in many records. **1929** Served as a naval oil hulk at Singapore.
1942 Feb 16: Scuttled when the Japanese took the city. Raised and put back into merchant service as *Choran Maru*, a troop carrier - mainly Singapore-Indonesia.
1945 Retaken at Singapore by the British. Used to move Japanese p.o.w's.
1949 Apr 3: Left Singapore in tow of the tug *Englishman* (United Towing) for the Clyde. June 18: Arrived and then broken up by BISCO at W. Arnott Young & Co., Dalmuir and Troon.

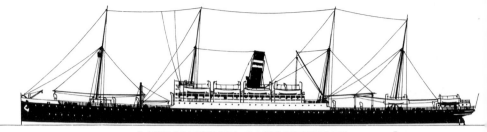

LAKE MANITOBA, LAKE MICHIGAN

69 LAKE MANITOBA

B 1901 C.S. Swan & Hunter, Newcastle. **T** 8,852g, 6,276n.
D 469.5/143.1 x 56.2/17.12 x 31.9/9.7.
E Tw scr, 2 x tpl exp, 832 nhp, 5 sgl blrs, 15 furn, 180 psi. 14 kts. By Richardsons, Westgarth & Co., Hartlepool.
H Steel. 2 dks. **P** 122 1st, 130 2nd, 500 3rd. Crew 110.
1901 June 6: Launched for the Beaver Line. She had special arrangements for the carriage of troops and their horses. Sept 24: M/v Liverpool-Quebec-Montreal. As drawn.
1902 Boer War transport HMT *No 23*. She was given an extra pair of lifeboats abreast the mizzen mast. Wash rooms were placed midway betweem the fore mast and the derrick posts and repeated between the mizzen and jigger masts. Sept 1: Liverpool-Cape Town. Sept 24: Cape Town-Bombay repatriating Indian troops. Made two such voyages to Bombay then reverted to Liverpool-Saint John (NB).
1903 Apr 6: Transferred to CPR. Yellow funnel. May 5: Took CPR's very first Liverpool-Quebec, then, on to Montreal sailing. **1906** Black topped funnel.
1914 Oct 29: Used as a p.o.w prison. **1915** Apr 17: Employed as a troop ship.
1916 Aug: Taken over by the Ministry of Shipping under the Liner Requisition Scheme and put back on the Canadian route.
1918 Aug 26: Scuttled at Montreal to extinguish a fire which gutted the ship. Oct 8: Sold by the underwriters to Bishop Navigation Co., Montreal. R/n *Iver Heath* and converted at Halifax into a cargo vessel.
1921 Sept 28: Sold to the Canada Steamship Line. Same name.
1923 July 25: Acquired by Stelp & Leighton's Crete Shipping Co. **1924** Scrapped.

70 LAKE MICHIGAN

Sister to *Lake Manitoba* except: **B** 1902. **T** 8,200g, 5,340n.
1901 Sept 28: Launched for the Beaver Line.
1902 Mar 21: M/v Liverpool-Saint John, NB-Cape Town (Boer War transport)-Liverpool.
1903 Apr 6: To CPR. Yellow funnel. May 26: Her first sailing Liverpool-Quebec-Montreal.
1904 Feb 21: During a gale in the English Channel she collided with the sailing ship *Matterhorn* (J.R. de Wolf, Liverpool). Had to be beached on Dungeness. Feb 25: Towed into Gravesend for repairs. Aug: Placed on the London-Antwerp-Quebec-Montreal service. **P** 3rd increased to 2,150. **1906** Yellow funnel black top.
1914 Aug 4: Requisitioned on the first day of the war; carried troops Liverpool-France.
1915 Oct: Loaned to the French for trooping to the Salonika campaign. She then reverted to British Expeditionary Force control.
1916 Nov 15: Enroute Montreal-Brest-London with a general cargo and horses (for Brest), hit a mine, laid by *UC-18* on Nov 10, nine miles off Brest and towed in.
1918 Apr 16: Torpedoed by *U-100* 93 miles north west of Eagle Island, Ireland enroute Clyde-Saint John with a general cargo. Only her captain was lost.

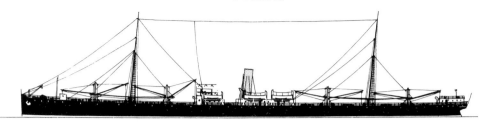

71 MILWAUKEE

B 1897 C.S. Swan & Hunter, Newcastle. **T** 7,323g, 4,784n, 12,272dwt.
D 470/143.26 x 56.1/17.09 x 31.95/9.73.
E Sgl scr, tpl exp, 502 nhp, 180 psi, 3 sgl blrs, 9 furn. 12 kts. By North East Marine Eng'g Co.,
Newcastle. **H** Steel. 2 + shelter dk.
1896 Nov 7: Launched for Alfred Jones ownership with Elder, Dempster & Co. as managers.
Their largest ship to date.
1897 Jan 16: M/v Tyne-New Orleans. nearing her destination she suffered engine failure.
Towed by Heyn's *Bengore Head* into Port Eads at the mouth of the New Orleans Channel.
1898 Transferred to Elder, Dempster & Co. ownership. May 1: Placed on the Montreal service.
Sept 16: Went hard aground on rocks near Peterhead, Scotland. Explosives were used to break
her in two at the bridge front. Oct 21: Refloated minus 180ft/54.86m of her bow.
1899 Apr 12: A new fore part was launched by her builders. June 24: Resumed Tyne-Montreal.
1900 Feb 21: Halifax-Cape Town as a Boer War transport for cavalry troops without their
horses. Next to New Orleans for the horses; for this a continuous deck stall was added aft from
the superstructure to the stern lifeboat. An extra pair of boats was added in front of the bridge.
She next carried Boer prisoners of war to internment at St Helena.
1902 Repatriated Boer prisoners St Helena-Cape Town.
1903 Apr 6: Transferred to CPR. Her sister *Monarch* remained with Elder, Dempster.
1906 Black topped funnel. **1914-18** Remained on company service.
1918 Mar 31: Missed by a torpedo in the Irish Channel. Aug 31: Torpedoed by *U-105* 260 miles
southwest of Fastnet. One lost.

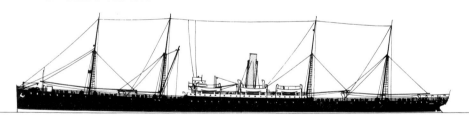

MONTCALM (I), MONTROSE (I), MONTEREY

72 MONTCALM (I)

B 1897 Palmers' Co., Jarrow. **T** 5,478g, 3,732n. **D** 445/135.64 x 52.5/16 x 27.6/8.41.
E Sgl scr, tpl exp, 664 nhp, 3 dbl blrs, 18 furn, 180 psi. 13 kts. By builder.
H Steel. 2 + a 126/38.4 shade dk which was fitted to carry emigrants outbound and live cattle
inbound. This practice became increasingly unpopular with the Press.
1897 May 17: Launched for the African S.S. Co., Elder, Dempster & Co. managers.
Sept 3: M/v Avonmouth-Montreal. As drawn.
1898 Chartered to the Atlantic Transport Line. Nov 13: First sailing to New York for them.
1898 The shade deck was enclosed. **T** 6,981g, 5,284n.
1900-02 Boer War transport; mainly New Orleans-Cape Town with mules.
1903 Apr 6: Taken over by CPR. Passenger accommodation added. 70 2nd, amidships, 1,800
3rd, shade deck. **1906** Black topped funnel.

1914 Oct: Taken over as a commissioned merchant ship for navy use.

1915 Aug: Acquired by the Admiralty and initially intended to be sunk as a block ship at Scapa Flow. Correctly the idea was vetoed. Trooped to France for the British Expeditionary Force. Oct: Converted to resemble the battleship HMS *Audacious*. Based Scapa Flow. Note: the real *Audacious* had already been sunk by mines off Ireland in Oct 1914 but the fact had been kept secret.

1915 Sept: When the Special Services Fleet was disbanded she served as a store ship.

1916 Feb 18: Transferred by the Admiralty to Frederick Leyland & Co. management.

Oct 26: Sold to Anglo-Saxon Petroleum Co. Nov 18: R/n *Crenella* and used as an oil tanker.

1917 Oct 11: Taken over by the Shipping Controller as *Oiler No 143*.

Nov 26: Torpedoed off the south coast of Ireland by *U-101*. Reached port.

1919 Nov 26: Reverted to Anglo-Saxon ownership. Laid up in the Gare Loch awaiting her turn for refurbishing.

1920 Oct 10: Sold to Walter Runciman's Velefa Shipping Co., same name with Runciman (London) Ltd. as managers. Spent most of the time laid up in the Tyne.

1923 June 20: Sold to Christian Nielsen & Co's A/S Larvik Hvalfangerselkskib. Used as a whaling fleet oil and store depot ship. Oct: R/n *Rey Alfonso*.

1925 Owned by H.M. Wrangell & Co., Haugesund. Same name.

1927 Sold to Anglo-Norse Co., Tonsberg. Hans Borge manager. R/n *Anglo-Norse*. Based South Shetland Islands. Fitted with 4 x 50 ton derricks for lifting whales aboard for flensing (by now newly built whale factory ships had stern ramps).

1929 R/n *Polar Chief*, Falkland Whaling Co., Jersey.

1930 Spent this season laid up at Tonsberg.

1941 July 2: Taken over by the Ministry of War Transport. Nov 17: R/n *Empire Chief* with Christian Salvesen & Co. as managers.

1946 Aug 3: Acquired by Salvesen. R/n *Polar Chief*. Owned by South Georgia Co. Ltd., Leith.

1952 Apr 29: Arrived at Dalmuir for scrapping by W.H. Arnott Young & Co.

73 MONTROSE (I)

Details as *Montcalm* except: **B** Sir Raylton Dixon & Co., Middlesbrough. T 5,440g, 3,453n.

E By T. Richardson & Sons, Hartlepool. At the behest of the Ministry of Food she was fitted with Linde Refrigeration for the carriage of dairy produce from Canada.

1897 June 17: Launched for Elder, Dempster & Co. Sept 12: M/v Middlesbrough-Quebec-Montreal.

1900 March: Boer War transport duties as HMT *No. 93*. Carried 30 Officers and 1,250 men.

1903 Jan: Released from trooping. **P** Now 70 2nd, 1,800 3rd. Laid up.

Apr 6: Transferred to CPR. Apr 20: First CPR sailing. **1906** Black topped funnel.

1910 July 20: Left Antwerp for Quebec with the wife murderer Dr Hawley Crippen and his lover Ethel Le Néve (disguised as a man) aboard under the names of Mr and Master Robinson. July 22: They were detected (too furtively amorous to be males) and the details were wirelessed. The two Scotland Yard detectives took White Star's *Laurentic*, a faster vessel, and arrested the pair on *Montrose*'s arrival off Quebec and before they set foot on Canadian soil. This was important because Dr Crippen was an American by birth. The occasion was the first time that radio had been used in the pursuit of crime. Nov 23: Crippen was hanged at Pentonville prison.

1914 Aug 8: When the war started (Aug 4) CPR's *Montreal* (78) was undergoing engine overhaul at Antwerp. Faced with the rapidly advancing German Army *Montrose* towed the powerless *Montreal*, crammed with refugees, back to London. Oct 28: Acquired by the Admiralty for use as a blockship and extra wharf at Dover. For this she was filled with concrete and was fitted with bridging, decking and several gantries. Dec 28: While moored in the outer harbour awaiting positioning she broke loose from her moorings in a fierce 86 mph northerly gale and drifted out of the Eastern Entrance. A tug of the Downs Boarding Flotilla tried to save her and came alongside where four volunteers jumped aboard in an effort to fix a tow but they had to jump back as the ship grounded on the East Goodwin sands where she broke in two and was lost.

74 **MONTEREY**

As *Montcalm* except **B** 1898. **T** 5,445g, 3,489n.
1897 Nov 25: Launched for Elder, Dempster & Co.
1898 May 25: M/v Tyne-Montreal-Avonmouth.
1899 July: Took the first sailing of Beaver's Avonmouth-Queenstown-Rimouski mail contract.
1900 Mar 16: Taken up for Boer War transport duties. Halifax-Cape Town and then 7 voyages New Orleans-Cape Town with horses.
1903 Apr 6: Transferred to CPR. July 14: Wrecked on Platt Point, Miquelon Island enroute Montreal-Bristol with general cargo and cattle.

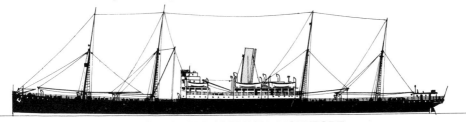

MONTEAGLE / BELTON, MONTFORT

75 **MONTEAGLE / BELTON**

As *Montclam* except: **B** 1899. **T** 5,468g, 3,485n.
1898 Dec 13: Launched for Elder, Dempster & Co.
1899 Mar 3: M/v Tyne-New Orleans then Liverpool-Saint John, NB until the thaw when Montreal became the Canadian terminus. May 13: Avonmouth-Montreal for 11 voyages.
1900 Feb: Became Boer War transport HMT *No 87.*
1902 May 24: Resumed her Avonmouth-Canada service.
1903 Apr 6: Transferred to CPR. Made their first sailing on the Avonmouth-Canada regular mail route.
1906 March: Transferred, via Tenerife, Durban to Hong Kong, to strengthen the trans-Pacific service. **P** 97 cabin, 1,200 3rd. Retained a buff funnel. Her lifeboats were now raised as drawn. Some of her sisters were similarly modified during their career. May 2: First sailing from Hong Kong. Sept 18: Driven ashore at Hong Kong by a typhoon, breaking her stern post. Salvage and repairs took six months.
1914 Sept: Requisitioned at Vancouver; sent to Bombay to act as an Indian cavalry troopship to Marseilles.
1915 Feb: Reverted to a skeleton Hong Kong-Vancouver service with *Empress of Japan* (10).
1918 Feb: Made three voyages to Vladivostok to repatriate Serbian p.o.w's and including Polish troops all of whom had walked right across Russia.
1919 Jan: Made a further visit to Vladivostok, this time to collect Austrian and Czecho-Slovak p.o.w's following their march across Russia. May: After overhaul, at Hong Kong where she was fire damaged in dry dock, resumed her trans-Pacific run. Buff funnel, black hull with white band.
1921 Apr: Rescued the crew of the French steamer *Hsin Tien* off the Amoy coast. Her captain received the French Medaille d' Honneur.
1922 Sept 22: Transferred to the Atlantic. Left Vancouver for Montreal, loaded with lumber. Nov 17: Reverted to the Montreal-Avonmouth route.
1923 Jan 29: When all the cargo ships were given 'B' names r/n *Belton* by CP Ocean Services. Spent most of her time laid up in the East India Dock.
1924 Laid up at Southend.
1926 Sold for £10,750. Apr 27: At Blyth and scrapped by Hughes, Bolckow.

76 **MONTFORT**

As *Montcalm* except: **B** 1899. **T** 5,481g, 3,490n. **P** 15 1st.
1899 Feb 13: Launched for Elder, Dempster & Co. Apr 26: M/v Tyne-Quebec-Montreal.

Nov 11: Boer War transport. Liverpool-Cape Town for three voyages.
1900 Passenger accommodation added: 30 2nd, 1,200 3rd. Owned by Elder Line Ltd.
July 17: Resumed service.
1901 July: Went aground on the Isle of Wight leaving Southampton with troops for Durban.
1903 Apr 6: Transferred to CPR. Liverpool-Canada service.
1918 Oct 1: Torpedoed by *U-55* 170 miles south-west of Bishops Rock. Five lives lost.

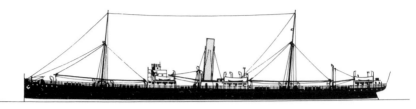

77 MONMOUTH

B 1900 Sir Raylton Dixon & Co., Middlesbrough. **T** 4,078g, 2,569n.
D 375.1/114.33 x 48.1/14.66 x 25.6/7.8.
E Sgl scr, tpl exp, 363 nhp, 3 sgl blrs, 12 furn, 180 psi. 10 kts. By Furness, Westgarth & Co., Middlesbrough. **H** Steel. 2 dks.
1900 May 1: Launched for Elder, Dempster & Co. Sept: Delivered to British & African S.N. Co. Placed on the Atlantic service. She was the third ship of this name for them.
1903 Apr 6: Transferred to CPR. **1906** Black topped funnel.
1914 Became a Canadian Expeditionary Force troopship.
1916 Loaned to the French. Trooped North Africa-Cherbourg. Nov 17: Mined off Cherbourg. Laid on Nov 16 by *UC-26*. Two French tugs took her into Cherbourg - her destination from Newport News. Repaired at Portsmouth.
1917 Oct: Used to carry ammunition to Murmansk and later (1918) to the Mediterranean.
1918 Sept 7: Attacked by submarine gunfire but escaped under smoke and return of fire.
1919 Dec 31: Sold to the Imperial Oil Co., Sarnia with C.O. Stillman & Co. as managers. Converted into an oil carrier. Same name. **1922** Transferred to C.O. Stillman & Co.
1923 Sold to Kishimoto Shokai K.K., Dairen. R/n *Shinzan Maru*.
1929 Sold to Dalgosrybtrest, Vladivostok. R/n *Treti Krabolov*.
1960 Deleted from Lloyd's Register. Probably broken up before this date.

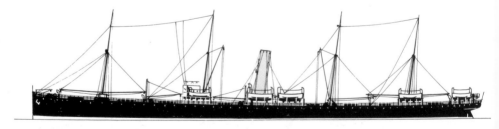

78 MONTREAL (I)

B 1900 C.S. Swan & Hunter, Newcastle. **T** 8,644g, 6,443n.
D 469.5/143.1 x 56.2/17.12 x 31.95/9.73.
E Tw scr, 2 x tpl exp, 702 nhp, 4 sgl blrs, 12 furn, 180 psi. 12 kts. By Wallsend Slipway & Eng'g Co., Newcastle. **H** Steel. 2 dks. **P** 12.
1899 Apr 28: Launched for the British & African S.N. Co. with Elder, Dempster as managers.
1900 July: Completed with the yellow funnel of the Atlantic fleet. Oct: Boer War transport carrying horses and mules New Orleans-Cape Town. **1902** May: Resumed normal service.

1903 Apr 6: Transferred to CPR. **1906** Black topped funnel.
1914 Aug 4: *Montreal* was in Antwerp with dismantled engines when the German advance into Belgium commenced. Her coal was transferred to CPR's *Montrose* (73) and this ship then towed *Montreal* to England. Both ships were crowded with refugees.
1915 Apr 1: Taken over as a troop ship.
1918 Jan 29: Bound for Saint John, NB, in convoy HG 47, she was rammed by White Star's *Cedric* off Morcambe Bay. Taken in tow she sank next day only 14 miles short of the River Mersey. 2 dead. The wreck was a danger to navigation and was marked with special buoys.

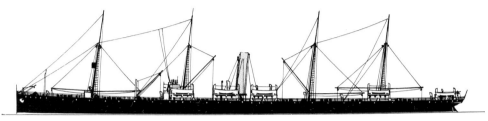

79 MOUNT ROYAL

B 1898 C.S. Swan & Hunter, Newcastle. **T** 7,054g, 4,599n, 12,200dwt.
D 470/143.26 x 56.1/17.09 x 31.95/9.73.
E Sgl scr, tpl exp, 500 nhp, 180 psi, 3 sgl blrs, 9 furn. 12 kts. By Central Marine Eng'g Works, West Hartlepool. **H** Steel. 2 + shelter dk.
1898 Aug 17: Launched for Elder, Dempster & Co. Nov 30: M/v Tyne-New Orleans.
1899 Nov 5: Boer War transport. Naples-Cape Town with mules and New Orleans for horses.
1900 Owned by Elder Line Ltd. Cargo and cattle carrier; Canada trade.
1903 Apr 6: Transferred to CPR. **1906** Black topped funnel.
1914 Oct: Rebuilt as the decoy battleship HMS *Marlborough*, Special Services Squadron.
1915 Converted into an oiler with circular tanks. R/n *Rangol* by the Admiralty.
1916 Placed under the management of Lane & MacAndrews. R/n *Mapleleaf*.
1917 Nov 11: Acquired by the Shipping Controller. Same name and management.
1919 Oct 4: Purchased by British Petroleum. **1920** Oct 19: R/n *British Maple* (I).
1922 June 6: Became a bunker depot ship at Southampton. Anchored off Hamble.
1932 Dec 10: Sold for scrap for £4,000 and broken up at Rosyth by Metal Industries Ltd. (Arrived Jan 25, 1933).

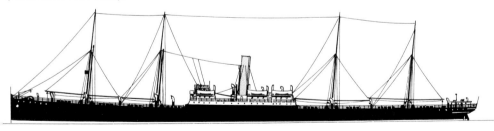

MONTEZUMA, MOUNT TEMPLE

80 MONTEZUMA (I)

B 1899 Alex. Stephen & Sons, Linthouse. **T** 7,345g, 5,358n.
D 485/147.83 x 59/17.98 x 30.5/9.3.
E Tw scr, 2 x tpl exp, 660 nhp, 3 sgl blrs, 12 furn, 180 psi. 14 kts. By builder.
H Steel. 2 dks. **B** 107/32.61.
1899 July 11: Launched for Elder, Dempster & Co. Sept: M/v Liverpool-New Orleans. Then used for Boer War duties New Orleans-Cape Town.

1901 Transferred to British & African S.N. Co. Yellow funnel, not their usual black.

1903 Apr 6: Taken over by CPR. Given extra lifeboats; a housed pair midway between mizzen and jigger masts and four abreast on the after deckhouse. **P** 500 3rd, emigrants.

1914 Oct: Converted to resemble the battleship HMS *Iron Duke*. Based at Scapa Flow where her name was HMS *Iron Duke A* - referred to only as 'A'.

1915 July 7: Acquired by the Admiralty, when the Special Services Squadron was disbanded, converted into an oiler. R/n *Abadol*.

1917 Feb 7: Transferred to Lane & MacAndrew Ltd. R/n *Oakleaf*.

July 25: Torpedoed by *UC-41* sixty four miles northwest of the Butt of Lewis.

81 MOUNT TEMPLE

As *Montezuma* except **B & E** 1901 Armstrong, Whitworth & Co., Newcastle. **T** 8,790g, 6,661n.

1901 June 18: Launched for Elder, Dempster & Co. North Atlantic service.

1903 Apr 6: Transferred to CPR. Modified like her sister. **P** 500 emigrants.

1906 Black topped funnel.

1907 Dec 1: Went aground on West Ironbound Island, Lahave, Nova Scotia. A 200ft/60.96 breeches buoy was erected and 600 people were safely put ashore. Next day the Canadian Government's *Laurier* took the survivors to Halifax, NS.

1908 Apr 16: The ship was refloated and taken to Halifax for repairs.

1914 Sept: Taken up for trooping.

1915 Late: Returned to commercial service to bring food from Canada.

1916 Dec 6: Enroute Montreal-Brest with a general cargo and 710 horses, captured and then sunk on the second cruise (ended March 21, 1917) of the German commerce raider *Möwe* (ex-*Vineta*, ex-*Pungo*, Laeisz) 620 miles off Fastnet. 3 dead, and 108 taken prisoner. They were later transferred to the captured *Yarrowdale* (Mackill S.S. Co) and, with the added crews of *Voltaire* (Lamport & Holt) and *King George* (Freshfield SS Co.) arrived at Swinemunde on Dec 31 for internment.

PRINCESS BEATRICE

CITY OF NANAIMO, JOAN

82 PRINCESS BEATRICE

B 1903 British Columbia Marine Rly Co., Victoria. **T** 1,290g, 635n.

D 193.3/58.93 x 37.3/11.38 x 15.2/4.62.

E Sgl scr, tpl exp, 150 nhp. 13 kts. By Bow, McLachlan & Co., Paisley.

H Wood. 1 + awning dk. **P** 350 but cabins for approximately 50.

1903 The ship was being built for her builder's service when she was taken over by CPR.

1904 Inaugurated the Victoria-Seattle, USA, route.

1920 Acted as an extra and summer excursion vessel

1928 Sold to B.L. Johnson for breaking up.

THREE SHIPS (83-85) TAKEN OVER WITH THE 1905 PURCHASE OF THE ESQUIMALT AND NANAIMO RAILWAY CO., VICTORIA

83 CITY OF NANAIMO

B 1891 McAlpine & Allen, Vancouver. **T** 761g, 518n. **D** 159/48.46 x 32/9.75 x 9.45/2.76.

E Tw scr, 2 x 2 cyl comp, 58 rhp. 11 kts. By J. Doty Engine Co., Toronto. **H** Wood. 1 dk.

1891 Entered service. **1897** Acquired by the Esquimalt & Nanaimo Rly Co.

1905 Taken over by CPR. Vancouver-Nanaimo service.

1912 Sold to the Terminal S.N. Co., Vancouver. R/n *Bowena*.
1922 When Terminal's fleet was taken over she became *Cheam* of the Union SS Co., Vancouver. Used for day excursion work out of Vancouver. **1926** Broken up.

84 JOAN
B 1892 Albion Iron Works, Victoria. **T** 821g, 544n. **D** 176.85/53.87 x 30/9.15 x 11/3.35.
E Tw scr, 2 x 2 cyl comp, 85 rhp. 13 kts. By builder. **H** Wood. 1 dk.
1892 Built for the Esquimalt & Nanaimo Rly Co. A look-alike sister to *City of Nanaimo* but with two masts.
1905 Taken over by CPR. Vancouver-Nanaimo service.
1914 Sold to Terminal S.N.Co. R/n *Ballena*.
1920 Nov 13: Burnt out at Vancouver and broken up by Vancouver Dredging & Salvage Co.

85 CZAR
B 1897 T.H. Trakey, Victoria. **T** 152g, 93n. **D** 101/30.78 x 21.5/6.55 x 11/3.35.
E Sgl scr, quad exp, 4 cyl, 56 rhp. 10 kts. By Hinckly, Spear & Hayes, San Francisco.
H Wood. 1 dk.
1897 Operated by J. Dunsmuir as a tug at Victoria. The first quadruple engine in BC waters.
1902 Acquired by Esquimalt & Nanaimo Rly Co. Barge towing.
1905 Taken over by CPR. Remained at Victoria. **1914** Sold to G.F. Payne.
1918 Sold to the Imperial Munitions Board, Vancouver. Towed explosive laden barges.
1930 Broken up by the Pacific Construction Co., having been out of service for some time.

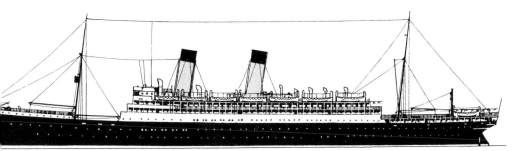

EMPRESS OF BRITAIN (I) / MONTROYAL. EMPRESS OF IRELAND

86A MONTROYAL

86 EMPRESS OF BRITAIN (I) / MONTROYAL
B 1906 Fairfield SB & E Co., Glasgow. **T** 14,189g, 8,024n.
D 548.8/167.26 x 65.6/19.99 x 36.6/11.15.
E Tw scr, 2 x 4 cyl quad exp, 3,168 nhp, 6 dbl + 3 sgl blrs, 60 furn, 220 psi. 18 kts. By builder.
H Steel. 4 dks. **F** 95/28.96. Prom 405/123.44. **P** 310 1st, 350 2nd, 800 3rd. Crew 250.

1905 These two ships were originally announced as *Empress of Austria* and *Empress of Germany*. They were designed with the mail contract in mind and had to maintain 17 knots in all weathers. They thus had a higher freeboard than many larger contemporaries. Nov 11: Launched by Mrs Arthur Piers.

1906 May 5: M/v Liverpool-Quebec. On her second voyage took the record Father Point-Liverpool with a time of 5 days, 12 hours, 15 minutes.

1907 Jan: Reduced the Liverpool-Halifax record to 5 days, 8 hours, 18 minutes. She continued to reduce her times over the ensuing year or two.

1912 July 27: Collided with and sank the steamer *Helvetia* (W. Lowden & Sons) off Cape Madelaine.

1914 Aug 16: Requisitioned for use as an Armed Merchant Cruiser. Southern Atlantic. Initially she was posted to Admiral Stoddart's South Atlantic Squadron in order to protect the River Plate food ships. She was too ponderous for the task of facing any real German warship and was moved onto the Cape Verde-Finisterre patrol.

1915 Converted for trooping duties. May 12: Commenced trooping to the Dardanelles. Her number was No 628. Oct: Damaged by fire while at anchor in the Mersey.

1916 Allocated, for the duration, to the Canadian Expeditionary Force.

1919 Mar 23: Resumed Canadian service Liverpool-Saint John. NB. Aug: Reconditioned by her builder and converted to burn oil fuel. Bunkers 3,500 tons; sufficient for a round voyage. Emerged with the plain buff funnels which now became standard for Canadian Pacific Ocean Services on both the Atlantic and Pacific vessels (but not those in coastal water).

1921 Logged the then fastest CP round voyage Liverpool-Quebec-Liverpool in 15 days, 9 hours, 30 minutes. **1922** Placed on the Southampton-Quebec service.

1924 Converted to cabin class. **P** 600 Cabin, 800 3rd. Since all the Cabin class ships were being given 'M' names she was renamed *Montroyal*. Apr 16: Resumed Liverpool-Quebec.

1927 Placed on the Antwerp-Southampton-Cherbourg-Quebec route.

1929 Sept 7: Final voyage.

1930 June 17: Sold to Stavanger Shipbreaking Co., Stavanger. Her smoke room was dismantled and rebuilt on the Sola Strand Hotel as the Montroyal Ballroom.

87 EMPRESS OF IRELAND

Details as *Empress of Britain* except: **B** 1906 **T** 14,191g, 8,028n.

1906 Jan 27: Launched by Mrs Alexander Gracie. June 29: M/v Liverpool-Quebec.

1913 July 11: Took part in the Mersey Royal Review of merchant and naval vessels by King George V and Queen Mary.

1914 May 29: Left Quebec at 16.30 hrs, carrying in all 1,477 passengers and crew. Her commander was Captain Kendall. That evening she encountered patchy fog. May 30: Below Rimouski the look out reported an incoming vessel well to starboard, which by the rule of the road would maintain her course and thereby pass *Empress of Ireland* on her starboard side. But ships directly approaching each other head-on must 'keep to the right' and pass port to port. Swirling fog came down and masked the two ships. Captain Kendall stopped, put his ship astern and blew three blasts on the siren to indicate that he had done so. The fog had become very dense when suddenly the other ship appeared and struck the *Empress of Ireland* midway between her funnels. She had been rammed by the Norwegian collier *Storstad* (A.F. Klaveness) five miles east of Father Point in the St Lawrence River. *Empress of Ireland* was mortally holed above and below the waterline, her engine room flooded so that the watertight doors could not be operated. Nor was there steam left to attempt to beach the ship. An SOS was immediately sent out. Captain Kendall told *Storstad* to keep her engines running and to push her bow hard into the gash but she was so damaged that she drifted away and *Empress of Ireland* heeled to starboard and sank within 15 minutes in 15 fathoms (45 feet). The time was 01.55 hrs and few of the sleeping passengers and crew managed to reach the open deck and were drowned in their cabins. Only four lifeboats got away and 1,024 persons perished, of these 840 were passengers of whom 150 (out of the 200 aboard) were senior members of the Salvation Army. (By comparison *Titanic* lost only 807 passengers). Two Canadian Government steamers,

Eureka and *Lady Evelyn* were at Father Point and Rimouski, respectively, both with steam up, and they put out and assisted in picking up many of the 463 who were saved from the near freezing water. The spot where she sank is still marked by a red 'wreck' buoy.

1914 June: The Court of Enquiry, headed by Lord Mersey and which called sixty-one witnesses, placed the main blame on the Norwegian vessel for changing course to pass 'port to port'. The Norwegians claimed that, by going astern, Captain Kendall had changed course and had placed his ship across the path of *Storstad* which would have otherwise, as she had intended, passed safely astern and 'port to port'. The Court pointed out that *Storstad* had hazardously and erroneously changed course towards *Empress of Ireland* in conditions of bad visiblity. This invited a collision and it was not, therefore, surprising that it occurred. Norway disagreed with the verdict. Unable to meet their liabilities the owners sold their ship. The value of *Storstad* was only $175,000 which was insufficient to meet Canadian Pacific's damage claims.

88 BISON

B 1906 Garston Graving Dock & SB Co., Liverpool. **T** 274g, 37n.
D 125/38.1 x 24.1/7.34 x 11.5/3.48.
E Sgl scr, tpl exp, 90 rhp,1 sgl blr, 100 psi. By Crabtree & Co., Great Yarmouth.
H Steel. 1 dk. Shade dk 77/23.47. **P** 316. Crew 11.
1906 Passenger tender which replaced *Otter* (65), Owned by the Mersey Towing Co. CPR managers. Based Liverpool.
1936 Her passenger licence was increased to 537.
1941 May 4: During the 'May Blitz' she was sunk by a bomb but raised and repaired.
1946 Nov 9: Sold to John Latsis, Piraeus. R/n *Niki*. Tender duties.
1954 Purchased by N. Lambiris. Re-engined and r/n *Hydra*. Used for day excursion work to Hydra Island. (The ship was also once shown as owned by Valarisias Kattoulas).
1957 R/n *Nicolas L*. Same owner.
1964 Became *Aghios Georgios* of A. Alexiadis & P Iliadis, Piraeus. Harbour work.
1966 Broken up at Skaramanga.

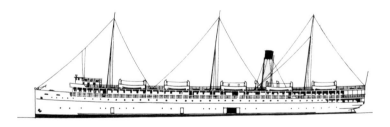

ASSINIBOIA, KEEWATIN

89 ASSINIBOIA

B 1907 Fairfield SB & E Co., Govan, Glasgow. **T** 3,880g, 2,486n.
D 336.5/102.56 x 43.85/13.33 x 14.3/4.67.
E Sgl scr, 4 cyl quad exp, 524 nhp, 4 shl blrs, 12 furn, 220 psi. 14 kts. By builder.
H Steel. 1 dk. F & B 295/89.92. **P** 400 (but only 280 berthed). Crew 80.
1907 June 25: Launched for the Port McNicoll-Fort William route (542 miles; journey time 38 hours). As with the earlier ships she was built so that she could be divided into two halves for the transit up to the Great Lakes. When completed she had a black hull and three masts. Her cargo was loaded through side doors in the hull, much of it was an early form of palletisation. Sept: Divided by Davie Shipyard, Levis, Lauzon. Nov: Arrived at Owen Sound for re-joining.

1908 July 4: Entered service, summer only with winter lay up.

1909 June 9: In Soo Lock, waiting to be dropped 22ft/6.71m to Lake Huron, she was being joined by *Crescent City* (Pittsburgh SS Co.) and the upper lock gates were not yet closed. Downstream of the lock *Perry G. Walker* (J.C. Gilchrist), coming up river, failed to stop and rammed the lower gates releasing the water therein plus *Assiniboia* and *Crescent City* both of which shot out on a torrent of water which was reinforced by the might of Lake Superior. The two ships hit *Perry G. Walker*, which was now also being washed down stream, *Crescent City* smashed into one of the lock gates as she passed. Fortunately the upper Soo Lock gates now closed (they were designed, in an emergency, to close by the pressure of upstream water). Amazingly none of the three ships was lost and, after being halted by tugs, they each docked under their own power with varying degrees of hull damage.

1953 Converted to oil burning. White hull (as drawn). **1955** Reboilered. Main mast removed.

1965 Oct: At the end of the summer season she ceased to carry passengers and was reduced to cargo only - but her profile remained the same.

1967 Nov 26: Arrived at Port McNicholl and laid up for the winter.

1968 May 19: Sold to JAL Steamship Line for further service. Nothing came of this and in August she was towed to West Deptford, New Jersey, for use as a restaurant. Nov: The ship was destroyed by fire and her hull scrapped.

90 KEEWATIN

Sister to *Assiniboia*. T 3,856g, 2,470n.

1907 July 6: Launched. Sept 14: Left the Clyde. Oct 5: At the Davie yard for dividing. Oct 10: Left in tow for Buffalo.

1908 July 10: Entered service. **1953** Converted to oil fuel. White hull.

1955 Given the same two masted livery as her sister.

1965 Oct: Withdrawn from passenger service but continued to carry cargo only.

1966 Nov 8: Sold to the Marine Salvage Co., Port Colbourne.

1967 Resold to River Queen Boat Works, Gary, Indiana to became a museum at Saugatuck, Kalamazoo River.

CRUIZER

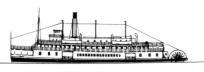

KUSKANOOK

91 CRUIZER

B 1895 Wm. Hamilton & Co., Glasgow. **T** 380g, 24n. **D** 150/45.72 x 24.5/7.47 x 13/3.96.

E Sgl scr, tpl exp, 127 nhp, 180 psi. 9 kts. By Rankin & Blackmore, Greenock.

H Iron. 1 dk.

1895 Completed as the *Flying Buzzard*, Clyde SS Co., Glasgow. Clyde tender duties mainly with Allan, Anchor and Donaldson ships which gave her a daily roster.

1900 Purchased by the Liverpool Steam Tug Co., r/n *Cruizer*.

1907 Acquired by CPR for the Mersey Towing Co. - but not owned by them. CPR owned.

1913 Sold to C. Bristler & Co., Halifax.

1925 Sold to Cruizer Shipping Co., Halifax. Owned by the Dominion Coal Co.

1952 Scrapped by Dominion Steel Co., Halifax.

92 KUSKANOOK

B 1906 J.M. Bulger, CPR, Nelson. **T** 1,008g. **D** 194/59.13 x 31/9.45 x 7/2.13.

E Stern wheeler, 1 cyl, horizontal trunk, 32 rhp. By Polson Iron Works, Toronto.

H Wood. 1 dk. **P** 400.

1906 Constructed for the Kootenay Lake and Nelson, Columbia River service, Kootenay

Landing being a small township at the southern end of the lake. May 5: Launched. Cost $150,000. July 8: Delivered. her maiden voyage was an excursion with 300 passengers. A fast ship capable of '20 miles per hour'. **1931** Ended her service and laid up. **1934** Became an hotel at Nelson. **1949** Beached and abandoned.

OKANAGAN

PRINCESS ENA

93 OKANAGAN (I)

Details as *Kuskanook* except: **B** 1907 J.M. Bulger, CPR, Okanagan Landing.
1907 Apr: launched for the Okanagan Lake services. She illustrates how the profiles of two vessels built to the same hull plan can differ. June 6: Entered service; six times a week Okanagan Landing-Summerland-Peachland-Kelowna-Penticton. P 250. Photographs of her have a black funnel.
1916 Laid up when the Kettle Valley railway was completed. Used intermittently.
1928 Cargo only. **1934** Laid up at Okanagan Landing.
1938 Hulked. Her machinery was removed and some of it re-used locally.

94 PRINCESS ENA

B 1907 Garston Graving Dock & SB Co., Liverpool. **T** 1,368g, 827n.
D 195.1/59.46 x 38.2/11.63 x 14.8/4.5.
E Sgl scr, 2 cyl comp, 75 rhp, 2 sgl blrs, 130 psi. 10½ kts. By Crabtree & Co., Great Yarmouth.
H Steel. 1 + spar dk. B 61/18.59. **P** 5. **C**: 1,300 tons + 800 head of cattle.
1907 Her builders were owned by H & C Grayson and reverted to that name in 1912. Oct 31: Left Liverpool via Montevideo for Vancouver.
1908 Jan 22: Arrived and entered service as a cargo vessel.
1916 Served Vancouver-Vladivostok with munitions.
1926 Fitted with steel tanks for 75,000 gallons/283,905 litres of fish oil.
1931 Sold to F. Millard & Co., same name. **1938** Broken up by the Dulien Steel Works, Seattle.

PRINCESS ROYAL

NANOOSE

95 PRINCESS ROYAL

B 1907 British Columbia Marine Rly Co., Victoria. **T** 1,997g, 981n.
D 228/69.49 x 40/12.19 x 16.5/5.03.
E Sgl scr, tpl exp, 302 nhp, 3 sgl blrs, 180 psi. 15 kts. By Bow, McLachlan & Co., Paisley.
H Wood. 1 + awning dk. **P** 700.
1907 Built for the Vancouver-British Columbia coastal ports-Alaska service.
1931 Stripped down to a hull and used as a sawdust carrier.
1933 Broken up by H.B. Elworthy & Co.

96 NANOOSE

B 1908 British Columbia Marine Rly Co., Victoria. **T** 305g, 165n.

D 116/35.36 x 24.6/7.49 x 14/4.27. **E** Sgl scr, 2 cyl, comp, 63 rhp, 1 sgl blr, 3 furn, 130 psi. 9 kts. By builder. **H** Steel. 1 dk.
1908 Employed as a CPR tug at Victoria. Tall funnel (as drawn), much later replaced by a thicker and shorter version. **1940** Withdrawn from service and laid up.
1946 Sold to Comox Logging & Rly Co. and sunk as a breakwater.

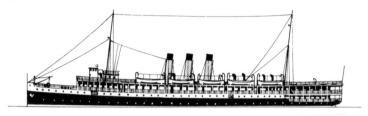

97 PRINCESS CHARLOTTE

B 1908 Fairfield SB & E Co., Glasgow. **T** 3,844g, 1,999n.
D 330/100.58 x 46.6/14.2 x 23.7/7.21.
E Tw scr, 2 x tpl exp, 795 nhp, 6 sgl blrs, 18 furn, 180 psi. 19½ kts. By builder.
H Steel. 2 + shelter and promenade dk. **P** 1,500. Later: 15 motor cars.
1908 June 26: Launched. Used on the Channel and Puget Sound plus coastal ports between Seattle and Skagway. **1909** Jan 11: First coastal sailing.
1949 June 14: Withdrawn from service. Dec: Sold to Typaldos Bros, Piraeus. R/n *Mediterranean*. Converted into a cruise liner with a single oval conical funnel which covered the two funnel uptakes of the original after pair of stacks. Venice-Piraeus-Istanbul route.
1965 Mar: Broken up by Sidiremboriki Soc. Anon., Perama, Greece.

Appearance as Valhalla (46)
98 HOSMER

B 1909 J.M. Bulger, CPR, Nelson. **T** 154g.
D 110/33.53 x 21/6.4 x 8/2.44.
E Sgl scr, 2 cyl comp, 37 rhp. **H** Wood. 1 dk.
1909 River towage tug based at Vancouver. Named after Hosmer the main township on the Crow's Nest railway line into Montana.
1931 Withdrawn from service and laid up. **1934** Broken up.

Appearance as Valhalla (46)
99 WHATSHAN

B 1909 J.M. Bulger, CPR, Nelson. **T** 106g. **D** 89.7/27.33 x 19/5.79 x 8/2.44.
E Sgl scr, 2 cyl comp, 30 rhp. By Polson Iron Works, Owen Sound. **H** Wood. 1 dk.
1909 Built as a barge towing tug for Lake Kootenay. Named after Whatshan Lake. Ident: No davited lifeboat, carried one on chocks on deck.
1920 Sept: Dismantled. Her engine was then installed in *Kelowna* (168).

KALEDEN

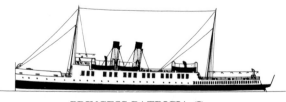

PRINCESS PATRICIA (I)

100 KALEDEN

B 1910 J.M. Bulger, CPR, Okanagan. **T** 180g. **D** 94/28.65 x 18/5.49 x 4/1.22.
E Stern-wheeler, 2 cyl comp, direct acting. By builder. **H** Wood. 1 dk.
1910 Cargo carrier. Built for a new service on Skaha Lake between Penticton-Kaleden-Okanagan Falls. But first a new route was tried. For this she is notorious. On her maiden voyage of 12 miles between Okanagan Lake and Dog Lake the river was so shallow that it took 3 days to go down and 7 days to return up stream. The captain lost count of how many times she grounded - 'more than the days of the year'. He also said 'I can sail this darned ship in 6 inches of water but not two.' She was immediately transferred onto Okanagan Lake and then became the work-boat for the construction of the Kettle Valley Rly.
1916 Laid up when the railway was completed. **1920** Dismantled.

101 PRINCESS PATRICIA (I)

B 1902 Denny Bros, Dumbarton. **T** 665g, 558n. **D** 270/82.3 x 32.1/9.78 x 11/3.25.
E Five screws on 3 shafts (2 propellers on the outer shafts), 3 turbines, one per shaft, 1 dbl blr, 450 rhp, 150 psi. 18 kts. By Parson's Steam Turbine Co., Newcastle.
H Steel. 1 dk. **P** 900 deck (1st aft, 2nd amidships).
1902 Apr 2: Launched. May 19: Trials. On the measured mile she achieved 21.95 knots with 2,240 shp on the centre shaft and 1,109 shp on the outer shafts, at 756 rpm. May 28: Delivered as *Queen Alexandra* for J. Williamson's 'Turbine Steamers Ltd'. Cost £38,688. She was only the second commercial turbine vessel to be constructed (*King Edward* being the first). Her shareholders were Denny Bros, Parsons and J. Williamson (Known as the Turbine Steamer Syndicate). After one experimental run from Fairlie to Oban where she remained for about a week for fine tuning, she was placed, at the beginning of the season, on the year round Ardrossan-Campbeltown service.
1910 Sept: Gutted by fire at Greenock and abandoned to the underwriters.
1911 Acquired by CPR and reconditioned by her builder. Screws reduced to one per shaft. R/n *Princess Patricia* after the Duke of Connaught's daughter. **T** 1,158g.
1912 Jan 12: Left the Clyde via Cape Horn for Victoria. The voyage took 43 days, 21 hours. May 11: First sailing Vancouver-Nanaimo. Her consort was *Motor Princess* (178)
1928 May 5: Final Nanaimo sailing. Replaced by *Princess Elizabeth* (198). Relegated to summer excursion work. **1932** Laid up at Esquimalt.
1937 May: Sold to Capital Iron & Metals Co. for scrap. The hull was burnt to remove all but the metalwork.

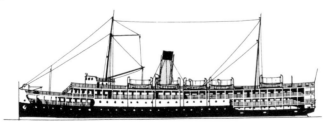

102 PRINCESS ADELAIDE

B 1910 Fairfield SB & E Co., Glasgow. **T** 3,016g, 1,910n.
D 290.5/88.54 x 46.1/14.05 x 15/4.57.
E Sgl scr, tpl exp, 4 cyl (2 x LP), 616 nhp, 4 sgl blrs, 12 furn, 180 psi. 18 Kts. By builder.
H Steel 1 + promenade dk. **P** 1,200. 6 motor cars.
1910 July 10: Launched. Oct 4: Left Glasgow for Vancouver via the Straits of Magellan.
1911 Jan 24: First coastal voyage.
1920 The post war price of oil and the irregularity of supply led CPR to convert their coastal vessels back to coal. *Princess Adelaide* was the first to be done.

1948 Oct 14: Withdrawn from service.
1949 July: Sold to Typaldos Bros, Piraeus. R/n *Angelika.* Venice-Piraeus route.
1967 Laid up as the company ran into financial trouble and then broken up.

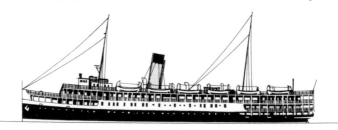

103 PRINCESS ALICE

As *Princess Adelaide* except: **B** 1911 Swan, Hunter & Wigham Richardson, Newcastle.
T 3,099g, 1,904n. **E** By Wallsend Slipway & Eng'g Co., Wallsend.
1911 May 29: Launched. Her profile differed as drawn due to the engine room layout differing
from her sister.
1919 Carried the Prince of Wales (Edward VIII) Victoria-Vancouver during his 'Ambassador
of the Empire' tour.
1949 June: Sold to Typaldos Bros. R/n *Aegaeon.*
1966 Dec: Left Piraeus in tow of the tug *Eyforia* (Typaldos Bros.) for breaking up at La Spezia.
In a storm she broke adrift and was wrecked at Civitavecchia.

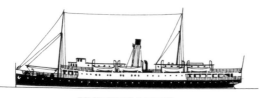

PRINCESS MARY

MUSQUASH, GOPHER

104 PRINCESS MARY

B 1910 Bow, McLachlan & Co., Paisley. **T** 1,697g, 1,011n. **D** 210/64 x 40.1/12.22 x 14/4.27.
E Tw scr, 2 x tpl exp, 388 nhp, 2 sgl blrs, 8 furn, 180 psi. 15 kts. By builder.
H Steel. 1 + promenade dk. **P** 700.
1910 Sept 21: Launched. Nov 22: Left for Victoria via the Straits of Magellan. Placed on the
Comox-Union Bay-Powell River service.
1914 Lengthened to 248ft/75.59 by Yarrow's Esquimalt yard.
1926 Operated cruises out of Vancouver.
1952 Sold to the Island Tug & Barge Co. Her coffee shop and dining room were removed to
become a restaurant at Victoria.
1953 Sold to the Union SS Co. R/n *Bulk Carrier No. 2.*
1954 Apr 15: In a gale the tow line to her tug *Chelan* (Union SS Co.) broke and she commenced
to drift ashore. The tug stood by and attempted to put a line aboard. Next she tried to take
off the crew. Apr 19: Both she and *Chelan* were wrecked on Cape Decision with the loss of
all aboard both.

105 MUSQUASH

B 1910 Garston Graving D & SB Co., owned H & C Grayson & Co., Garston, Liverpool.
T 198g. **D** 100.2/30.53 x 23.1/7.04 x 12/3.66.

E Sgl scr, tpl exp, 90 rhp, 1 blr, 180 psi. By Crabtree & Co, Gt Yarmouth. **H** Steel. 1 dk.
1910 Sept 20: Launched for the Mersey Towing Co. CPR as managers.
1914 Requisitioned by the Admiralty but not retained. June 3: Left Liverpool, in company of
Gopher, for Quebec via Moville, Ireland, and St Johns, Newfoundland. June 20: Arrived.
Transferred to the ownership of the Quebec Salvage & Wrecking Co., CPR owned.
1920 Sold to the Atlantic Salvage Co., Halifax.
1921 Aug 4: Sunk by collision off Anticosti Island.

106 GOPHER

Sister to *Musquash*.
1910 Nov: Launched for the Mersey Towing Co.
1914 Also taken over by the Admiralty but not retained. Went to Quebec with her sister.
Transferred to Quebec Salvage & Wrecking Co. ownership.
1923 Sold to the St John Dry Dock Co. R/n *Ocean King*.
1926 Bought by Davie SB & Repair Co., Lauzon. R/n *Chateau* (II).
1961 Oct 30: Sold for scrapping.

107 WILL W. CASE

B 1878 S Starrat, Rockland, Maine. **T** 538g. **D** 143/43.58 x 31/9.45 x 17/5.18.
H Wood. 1 dk. sailing vessel, 3 masted barque rig.
1878 Built for the Atlantic coastal trade out of Rockport.
1910 Acquired by CPR. Reduced to a 3-masted barge and used as a towed collier to service
the lesser BC ports. These had earlier been wood-burning depots but with the advent of coal
fired ships the new supply service was necessary.
1924 Sold to the Canadian Government and sunk, loaded with stone, as a breakwater at
Sydney, BC.

108 MELANOPE

B 1876 W.H.Potter & Co., Liverpool. **T** 1,624g.
D 258/78.64 x 40/12.19 x 24/7.31. **H** Iron. 1 dk. 3 masted barque rig.
1876 Built as a fast barque for the Heap's celebrated Australian Shipping Co.
1882 William Gracie and Edwin Beazley formed Gracie, Beazley & Co. to take over the Heap
vessels. Nov 8: Transferred; same name. Placed on the Melbourne route. Her first passage for
the new owners was 82 days. Then she operated to Calcutta, Australia and the USA.
1891 Feb 10: Made her first voyage as a petrol carrier when she left New York with 57,750
cases; her largest load to date.
1898 Dec: Sold at Antwerp to a Captain-owner who brought his wife aboard. She died at
Panama and a few days later the Captain jumped overboard. The mate continued the voyage
to San Francisco where, to pay off the crew, the ownerless ship was sold to J.J. Moore, San
Francisco. The crew blamed the vessel's many mishaps to a curse bestowed on the ship by an
old woman apple-vendor who had been forcibly removed. Her new captain was N.K. Wills.
1906 Dec: Abandoned, beam ended, after being hit by a squall. The barque drifted into the
calm water of the Columbia River where the captain and crew were able to reboard her.
1907 Converted into a coal barge. Steam cranes replaced her masts.
1911 Acquired by CPR for use as a coal hulk. She was the store to supply *Will W. Case* but
also coaled the 'Empresses'.
1946 Sold to the Comox Logging & Rly Co. and sunk as a breakwater at Royston, BC.

QUALICUM   **PRINCESS SOPHIA**

109 QUALICUM
B 1904 Heafie & Levy, Philadelphia. **T** 200g, 98n. **D** 96/29.26 x 22/6.7 x 12/3.66.
E Sgl scr, 2 cyl comp, 43 rhp. By builder. **H** Steel. 1 dk.
1904 Built as the tug *Colima* (US Army Construction Corps), as drawn.
1907 Engaged in the construction of the Panama Canal.
1911 Acquired by CPR. R/n *Qualicum* after Qualicum Beach. Used to tow *Will W. Case*.
1946 Sold and her steel hull was used as a breakwater.

110 PRINCESS SOPHIA
B 1911 Bow, McLachlan & Co., Paisley. **T** 2,320g, 1,466n.
D 245.2/74.73 x 44.1/13.44 x 24/7.31.
E Sgl scr, tpl exp, 366 nhp. 3 sgl blrs, 9 furn, 180 psi. 14½ kts. By builder.
H Steel. 1 + awning dk. **P** 350.
1911 Nov 8: Launched.
1912 March: Placed on the Vancouver-Victoria night service. Summer: Alaska route.
1918 Oct 25: Left Skagway for Vancouver; the last southbound sailing of the season and therefore filled with passengers which included the whole crew of the sternwheeler *Casca* (White Pass & Yukon Co.). Among them was chief engineer Richard Calvert Haws, my great uncle, formerly chief engineer aboard *Okanagan* (94). Oct 26: Four hours out she ran into a snow storm and slewed off course so that, at 02.00, she grounded on Vanderbilt Reef in the Lynn Channel. Although two-thirds of the ship was high and dry she appeared to be safe and the passengers and crew remained on board for forty hours waiting for the snow to abate. Two anchors were fixed to the shore to hold her where she lay and ships from Juneau stood by. But with the next rising tide a vicious blizzard off-shore gale sprang up which drove the attending ships to shelter. Suddenly *Princess Sophia* was washed off the rocks into deeper water where, against the rocks, she broke up in the heavy seas with the loss of all 343 persons aboard. The last message from the ship, timed at 06.30, was 'Good-bye, we're going'. Next day all that remained to be seen was her fore mast. The bodies of several women and children were found frozen to life rafts. The pocket watch of R.C. Haws had stopped at 06.50. This was the worst North Pacific coastal service disaster (*Pacific*, in 1875, lost 275 on Cape Flattery).
1919 A joint Seattle-Vancouver syndicate attempted salvage. All that was recovered was the purser's safe which contained $12,000.
Ironically *Casca* is still preserved at Whitehorse.

SIX DOMINION ATLANTIC RAILWAY COMPANY SHIPS
(111 - 116)

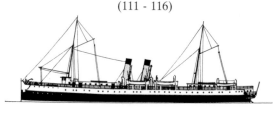

BOSTON

111 BOSTON

B 1890 Alex. Stephen & Sons, Linthouse. **T** 1,694g, 734n. **D** 245/74.68 x 36.1/11 x 20/6.1.
E Sgl scr, tpl exp, 568 nhp, 4,763 ihp, 15 kts. By builder.
H Steel. 2 dks. **P** 1,200 unberthed, 300 berths.
1890 Oct: Built for the Yarmouth SS Co. On trials she achieved 18 1/4 knots to become the
fastest sea-going single screw ship of her size. Yarmouth, NS - Boston, Mass. service.
1901 June: The Yarmouth SS Co. and its ships were taken over by the Dominion Atlantic Rly
Co. Same service.
1912 Jan 1: The Dominion Atlantic Rly Co. and its six ships was leased to CPR but the Canada-
USA route was not included in CPR's terms of Government lease. Only the Bay of Fundy
service was to continue. *Boston* was put up for sale.
1912 Aug 20: Sold to the Eastern Steamship Co. who took over the service. Same name.
1917 Laid up at Boston, Mass. **1920** Scrapped.

PRINCE GEORGE, PRINCE ARTHUR

112 PRINCE GEORGE

B 1898 Earle's Co., Hull. **T** 2,194g, 863n. **D** 290.5/88.54 x 38/11.58 x 16.5/5.03.
E Tw scr, 2 x tpl exp, 718 nhp, 4 sgl blrs, 180 psi. 16 kts. By builder.
H Steel. 2 dks. **P** 200 overnight berths, 700 deck. Crew 65.
1898 Built for the Dominion Atlantic Rly Co's Yarmouth, Nova Scotia-Boston service.
R.L. Campbell manager. As drawn.
1912 Jan 1: Taken over with the company by CPR. Same name and service. Aug 20: Sold to
the Eastern SS Corp., Boston, Mass. Registered as owned by the Boston, Yarmouth SS Co.
1917 May: Following the April entry of the USA into World War I the ship returned to the
UK and was used as a cross channel hospital ship. The lifeboats of both sisters was increased
to seven each side.
1919 Released back to her owners. **1929** Sold to the Boston Iron & Metal Co. for scrap.

113 PRINCE ARTHUR

As *Prince George* except: **B** 1899. **T** 2,041g, 923n.
1899 Completed for the Dominion Atlantic Rly Co. Same service as her sister. These two
vessels had exactly parallel careers.
1912 Jan 1: Taken over by CPR. Aug 20: Sold with her sister to Eastern. Owned by the Boston,
Yarmouth SS Co.
1917 May: Went with her sister for cross channel hospital ship work.
1919 Reverted to her owners.
1929 Sold with her sister to Boston Iron & Metals for demolition.

114 PRINCE ALBERT

B 1902 J. McGill, Shelburne, Nova Scotia. **T** 112g. **D** 97/29.57 x 20/6.1 x 8/2.44.
E Sgl scr, 2 cyl comp, 24 rhp. 9 kts. By W & A Moir, Yarmouth. **H** Wood. 1 dk. **P** 180 deck.
1902 Built as *Messenger* for S.E. Messenger of Yarmouth. Used on coastal passenger services.
1904 Acquired by the Dominion Atlantic Rly Co. to replace *Evangeline* on the Kingsport-
Parrsboro service across Minas Basin, Bay of Fundy. R/n *Prince Albert*.
1912 Jan 1: Taken over by CPR. Aug 20: Sold to Eastern SS Corp. Owned by the Boston,
Yarmouth SS Co. Same name and service.

1927 Sold to Albert SS Co. Same name. Based Yarmouth.
1929 Mar 5: Lost in pack ice at Mulgrave, Nova Scotia.

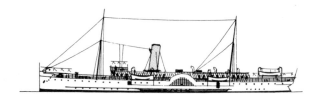

115 **PRINCE RUPERT**

B 1894 Wm Denny & Bros., Dumbarton. **T** 1,158g, 620n. **D** 260/79.25 x 32.2/9.8 x 11.5/3.51.
E Pad, 3 cyl tpl exp, diagonal, 392 nhp, 2 sgl blrs, 160 psi. 18 kts. By builder.
H Steel. 3 dks. **P** 103 1st in 59 cabins aft, 900 unberthed. Crew 40.
1894 May 23: Launched for the Dominion Atlantic Rly Co., Digby, manager R.L. Campbell
Cost £38,868. Intended for the Bay of Fundy service of the Dominion Atlantic Rly Co. of which
John and Archibald Denny were also directors. Aug 15: Trials. 18.69 knots at 54.1 rpm.
Sept 4: Delivered to Southampton. Her livery was, at this time, white with a pale yellow funnel.
The first and only paddler on the route, her paddles were regarded as vulnerable to driftwood
logs and ice and her entry was viewed with some (unjustified) apprehension.
1895 June: Due to a lack of bunker space the vessel had to be towed across the Atlantic to
Halifax. Then served on the Digby-Saint John, NB route.
1912 Jan 1: The Dominion Atlantic Rly Co. became a part of CPR, leased for 999 years. Sir
Willim Van Horne was her registered owner with G.H. Wigham of CPR as manager. The idea
of taking her to Vancouver was abandoned because of her designed bunker space which limited
her to Digby-Saint John.
1914 It was intended to replace her with *St George* (124) but the war intervened before the
end of season action took place.
1917 When *St George* returned to England she maintained the service alone.
1919 Sold to the US flag but no owners recorded. **1924** Broken up in the USA.

116 **YARMOUTH**

B 1887 A. McMillan & Sons, Dumbarton. **T** 1,452g, 725n.
D 220.3/67.13 x 35.2/10.72 x 12.7/3.86.
E Sgl scr, tpl exp, 298 nhp, 1 sgl blr, 180 psi. 12 kts. By W.V.Lidgerwick, Glasgow.
H Steel. 2 + shade dk. **P** Approx 300, half with berths.
1887 Built for the Yarmouth SS Co. Red funnel black top. Black hull, white band at deck
level, brown uppers.
1901 Taken over by the Dominion Atlantic Rly Co. **1912** Jan 1: Taken over by CPR.
1918 Sold to the North American SS Corp, Yarmouth, Nova Scotia. Yarmouth-Boston route.
Nov: Chartered to the Black Star Line. This company was entirely staffed and operated by
black people. She was then hired to carry a cargo of pre-prohibition liquor New York-Havana
but the ship broke down and was towed into a US port only one day after Prohibition

(1918-1933) became law. The cargo was therefore confiscated and the Black Star Line went out of business. **1924** Broken up by Pottstown Steel Corp., USA.

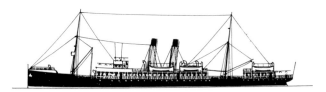

116A PRINCE EDWARD

This vessel was sold before Dominion Atlantic became a part of CPR but is included in order historically to complete the Dominion Atlantic fleet list.

B 1899 Earle's Co., Hull. **T** 1,414g, 700n. **D** 290.5/88.54 x 38/11.58 x 16.5/5.03.
E Tw scr, 2 x tpl exp, 377 nhp, 175 psi, 2 dbl blrs, 15 kts. By builder.
H Steel. 2 + shade dk. **P** Carried berthed and deck passengers.
1899 Aug: Delivered to Dominion Atlantic Rly Co., London. R.L. Campbell manager. Yarmouth-Boston route.
1906 Sold to Rederi Akt. Sverige-Tyskland (= Germany in Swedish), Malmo, for their service Trolleborg-Sassnitz. S. Hedberg manager.
1912 R/n Vasilij Velikij by Ivan I. Burkoff, Archangel-Varanger-Vardo service.
1916 Mar 3: Wrecked enroute to Vardar, Russia.

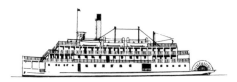

117 BONNINGTON

B 1911 J.M. Bulger, CPR, Nakusp. **T** 1,700g. **D** 202/61.57 x 39/11.89 x 7/2.13.
E Stern wheeler, 2 cyl horizontal, direct acting. **H** Steel. 1 dk. **P** 400.
1911 Apr 24: Launched. Cost $160,000. Built for the intended Arrow Lake run south of Robson but the railway link to Trail was completed. Used out of Nakusp, Upper Arrow Lake.
1931 Laid up, then sold to a Mr Sutherland. Operated, cargo only, according to demand.
1942 Sold to the Government of British Columbia. Her boiler was removed and fitted into *Nasookin* (125). Trace lost.

---

118 CASTLEGAR

B 1911 J.M. Bulger, CPR, Okanagan Landing. **T** 104g
D 94.3/28.75 x 19.3/5.89 x 8.2/2.44.
E Sgl scr, 2 cyl comp, 27 rhp. By Collingwood SB Co., Vancouver. **H** Wood. 1 dk.
1911 Tug. Employed on Okanagan Lake. **1925** Scrapped.

Drawing on page 69

119 EMPRESS OF RUSSIA

B 1912 Fairfield SB & E. Co., Glasgow. **T** 16,810g, 8,789n.
D 570.2/173.79 x 68.2/20.78 x 42/12.8. Dft 29/8.84.
E Quad scr, 4 x stm turb, 6 dbl + 6 sgl blrs, 64 furn, 3,750 nhp, 190 psi. 19 kts. By builder.
H Steel. 4 dks. F & B 394/120.09. Fuel 4,625 tons coal. **C** 338,000/9,571 cu g + 14,300/405 cu refrig in 5 chambers. **P** 1,180.

1912 Aug 28: Launched by Mrs W. Beauclerk, daughter of CPR Chairman Sir T. Shaughnessy. These two ships were built to counter the competition of the Japanese Toyo Kisen Kaisha vessels, *Tenyo Maru* and *Chiyo Maru*, built 1908/9.

1913 Apr 1: M/v Liverpool-Suez Canal-Hong Kong. May 21: First transpacific voyage. She crossed Hong Kong-Nagasaki-Vancouver in 8 days 18 hrs, 31 mins; a record which stood for nine years.

1914 Aug 23: Requisitioned at Vancouver. Sent to Hong Kong for conversion and arming. Given 4 x 4.7 old guns (all there were available) and used for Indian Ocean Armed Merchant Cruiser duties. Nov 9: After HMAS *Sydney* sank the German light cruiser *Emden*, *Empress of Russia* met with *Sydney* and took off 37 survivors from the scuttled *Buresk* (Burdick & Cook) which had *Emden*'s British prisoners aboard (plus a German prize crew of 16). She took these plus the *Emden*'s survivors to Colombo.

1915 Used as guard ship at the entrance of the Red Sea, based at Aden. Her companion was *Empress of Asia*. **1916** Feb 12: Returned to CPR service.

1918 May 6: Taken over for North Atlantic trooping.

1919 Jan 12: Left for Hong Kong where she was refitted. Mar 8: Handed back to CPR. Resumed her trans-Pacific service. In all she made 310 voyages. Black hull, white band.

1927 The Empresses were given white hulls with a yellow band.

1940 Nov 28: Requisitioned for trooping duties. Stripped and equipped at Vancouver.

1941 Feb 6: Left Vancouver for Glasgow as a troopship.

1943 Oct: Repatriated British p.o.w.'s from Stockholm.

1945 Sept 8: Destroyed by fire at Barrow during a refit. Broken up there by Thos.W.Ward.

120 EMPRESS OF ASIA

Sister to *Empress of Russia*. **T** 16,909g, 8,883n.

1912 Nov 23: Launched. **1913** June 14: M/v Liverpool-Cape Town-Hong Kong.

1914 Aug 2: Requisitioned as an Armed Merchant Cruiser.

1915 Served in the Red Sea with her sister.

1916 Mar 20: Returned to CPR's transpacific service

1918 May 3: Taken up for trooping and left Vancouver for New York. Made six transatlantic trooping voyages.

1919 Jan 2: Left Liverpool for Hong Kong to return to CPR service. Black hull white band.

1926 Jan 11: Collided with and sank the steamer *Tung Shing* (Indo China S.N. Co.) at Shanghai. **1927** White hulled.

1941 Jan 1: At the end of her 307th transpacific voyage she was requisitioned at Vancouver for trooping duties.

1942 Feb 5: Sunk by Japanese aircraft off Singapore. A number of the lifeboats escaped to Java where, later, most of the survivors were captured.

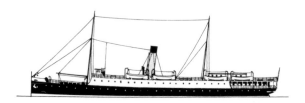

121 PRINCESS MAQUINNA

B 1912 British Columbia Marine Rly Co., Esquimalt. **T** 1,777g, 979n.
D 232.7/70.71 x 38/11.58 x 14.5/4.42.
E Sgl scr, tpl exp, 238 nhp, 13 kts. By Bow, McLachlan & Co., Paisley.
H Steel. 1 dk + awning dk. **B** 142/43.28. **P** 440.

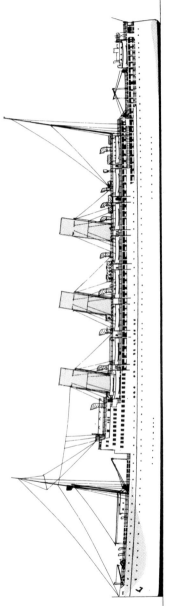

EMPRESS OF RUSSIA, EMPRESS OF ASIA

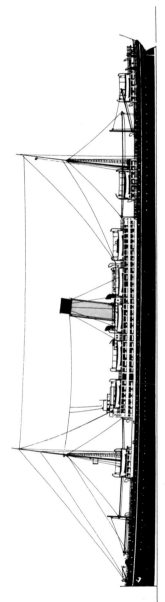

147 SCANDINAVIAN

1912 Dec 24: Launched. Named after the daughter of Chief Maquinna. Designed by Capt Troop.
1913 July: Entered service to over 40 ports on Vancouver Island and the west coast of British Columbia, such places as Col-oose, Kyuquot Whaling Station, Quatsino Cannery, Quiet Cove and Uchuckleseit. **1952** Laid up at Vancouver.
1953 Sold to the Union SS Co., Vancouver. Converted into an ore carrying barge. R/n *Taku*. Used on the Alaska-Trail Smelter Plant service.
1962 July: Scrapped by General Shipbreaking Co., False Creek, Vancouver.

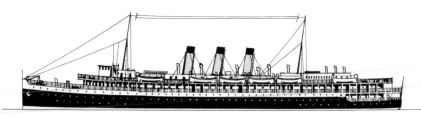

PRINCESS IRENE, PRINCESS MARGARET

122 **PRINCESS IRENE**
B 1913 Wm Denny & Bros, Dumbarton. **T** 5,934g, 2,234n. **D** 395.5/120.55 x 54/16.46 x 28/8.53.
E Tw scr, 2 stm turbines, 15,000 shp, 22½ kts. By builder.
H Steel. 2 dks. Fuel 585 tons oil. **P** Designed for 1,500.
1913 May 25: Ordered. The pair were to be the finest coastal liners in service and were to release some of the smaller ships which were to be replaced by the then existing Vancouver-Victoria vessels.
1914 Oct 20: Launched. Little work was then done. The ship did not enter CPR service.
1915 Jan 20: Taken over by the Admiralty with her sister *Princess Margaret* (123) and converted into a minelayer for 400 mines. 2 x 4.7in guns plus 2 x 3in highangle AA guns. Crew 215.
May 27: While ready for sea but undergoing final commissioning work at Sheerness Dockyard she was destroyed by an explosion. Two columns of flame, estimated at 300 ft/91.44m high shot up in quick succession to be followed, as the mines went up, by a massive roar which totally destroyed the ship. In addition to the naval duty crew 78 workmen were onboard of which only one survived. A memorial exists outside Sheerness Railway Station to the 53 crew and 77 workmen killed. Had the accident occurred 24 hours later over 400 would have been killed.

123 **PRINCESS MARGARET**
Sister of *Princess Irene*.
1913 May 25: Ordered. **1914** June 24: Launched by Mrs R. Redmond, daughter of CPR's Chairman Sir T. Shaughnessy. Oct 23: Trials in CPR livery but with Denny's houseflag (she had not been handed over). Dec 26: Taken over by the Admiralty and converted into a minelayer like her sister. Served off the Belgian coast and the Heligoland Bight.
1918 Acted as a hospital transport vessel for soldiers and later sick refugees.
1919 Purchased by the Admiralty. Served in the Baltic.
1921 Fitted out as an Admiralty yacht for the North Atlantic also with hospital ship capability. Her minelaying equipment was retained and she was thus justified under the various naval estimates of the period. The ship was under-utilised, spending much of her time in port.
1927 With the advent of the fast minelaying cruiser HMS *Adventure* she was laid up.
1929 July 2: Arrived at Blyth and broken up by Hughes, Bolckow & Co. Thus she, too, never served with CPR.

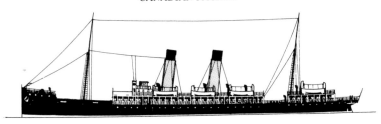

124 ST GEORGE
B 1906 Cammell, Laird & Co., Birkenhead. **T** 2,456g, 1,012n.
D 352/107.29 x 41.1/12.52 x 16.2/4.93.
E Tpl scr, 3 direct drive stm turbs, 8 sgl blrs, 24 furnaces, 185 psi. 20 kts. By builder.
H Steel. 2 + shelter dk. **F** 45/13.71. **P** 1,200.
1906 Sept: Completed for the Great Western Railway Co. and owned by the Fishguard &
Rosslare Railway & Harbour Co. for the Fishguard-Rosslare route. Her sisters were *St David*
and *St Patrick*. Capable of 22½ knots when required.
1913 May: Sold to CPR as a replacement for *Prince Rupert* (115). Digby-Saint John, NB service
across the Bay of Fundy. **1914** Spring: Entered service.
1917 May: Returned to the UK for use as a cross channel hospital ship, her service being
maintained by *Prince Rupert* and *Empress* (152).
1919 June: Sold to the Great Eastern Railway Co. Harwich-Hook of Holland route. Modified
by having her forward main deck accommodation enclosed, to provide more over-night berths.
1929 Oct: Sold for breaking up by Hughes, Bolckow & Co., Blyth.

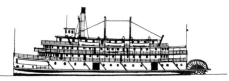
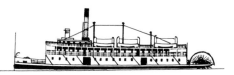

NASOOKIN   *NASOOKIN, rebuilt*

125 NASOOKIN
B 1913 Assembled by J.M. Bulger, CPR, Nelson. **T** 1,869g.
D 200.5/61.11 x 39.85/12.14 x 7/2.13.
E Sternwheeler, 2 cyl horizontal direct acting. By hull builder.
H Steel. 1 dk. **P** 400, later 550.
1913 The hull was prefabricated by Western Dry Dock Co., Port Arthur, and transported by
rail to Nelson where it was assembled. The upperworks were then added (Nelson could not
build steel hulls). Apr 30: Launched. June 1: Maiden sailing. She replaced *Kuskanook* (93).
Her name is Red Indian for 'Queen of the Lakes'. She was the largest sternwheeler in British
Columbian waters. **1930** Dec 31: Final passenger sailing.
1932 Sold to the Government of British Columbia. Modified forward to carry vehicles, her
accommodation was also cut down (as drawn). Used as a ferry across Lake Kootenay.
1942 The boiler from *Bonnington* (117) was installed.
1946 Withdrawn from service and laid up.
1947 Taken over by the Navy League of Canada for use as a cadet training and club ship.
1948 During floods she broke free, ran aground and was wrecked.

126 NARAMATA

B 1913 Assembled by J.M. Bulger, CPR, Okanagan Landing. **T** 150g, 74n.
D 89.9/27.36 x 19.5/5.94 x 8/2.44.
E Sgl scr, 2 cyl comp, 27 rhp, 8 kts. By Western DD Co., Port Arthur. **H** Steel. 1 dk.
1913 Tug boat. Like *Nasookin* the hull was built at Port Arthur and taken, in sections, by rail to Okanagan. Towing services on Lake Okanagan. Naramata being a township on the lake near to Penticton. **1970** Sold to J.L. Keffer, Victoria. Trace lost.

127 NELSON (II)

B 1913 J.M. Bulger, CPR, Nelson. **T** 25g.
D 61/18.59 x 11/3.35 x 4/1.22. **E** Sgl scr, 6 rph. **H** Wood.
1913 Kootenay Lake service, towing railway waggon flats.
1919 Laid up out of service. Trace lost.

MISSANABIE, METAGAMA

128 MISSANABIE

B 1914 Barclay, Curle & Co., Glasgow. **T** 12,469g, 7,660n.
D 520/158.50a, 500.3/152.5 x 64.2/19.56 x 37.9/11.,53.
E Tw scr, quad exp, 2 x 4 cyl, 9,000 ihp, 215 psi, 8 blrs. 15½ kts. By builder.
H Steel. 3 dks, 7 holds. **B** 240/73.15. Coal: 2,380 tons at 150 tpd. C: 400,000/11,326.8cu.
P 520 cabin, 1,138 3rd.
1914 June 22: Launched. She was among the first major vessels to have a cruiser stern. Named after the town of Missanabie near Lake Superior. Oct 7: M/v Liverpool-Quebec-Montreal. The pair were specifically designed for 'Cabin Class'. They replaced *Lake Erie* and *Lake Champlain* (67/68). **1916** Used as a troopship Canada-UK-Europe.
1918 Sept 9: Enroute to Montreal, torpedoed by *UB 87* 52 miles south-east of Daunt's Rock, Kinsale, Eire. She was being operated by CPR on commercial service with Cabin passengers and 57 troops in third. 48 lives lost.

129 METAGAMA

As *Missanabie*. **T** 12,420g, 7,653n.
1914 Nov 19: Launched.
1915 March: M/v Liverpool-Saint John, NB. Remained in company service.
1916-18 On most eastbound voyages she carried troops in third class.
1923 May 26: Collided with Hogarth's *Baron Vernon* in the Clyde.
1924 June 19: Collided with *Clara Camus* (Nav. Gen. Gerolimich) off Cape Race.
1929 May: Placed on the Antwerp-Southampton-Cherbourg-Quebec-Montreal route.
1930 Laid up during the depression and never came back into service.
1934 Apr 3: Sold to P & W McLellan, Bo'ness for scrap.

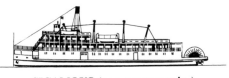

SICAMOUS (as a cargo carrier)   **NITINAT**

130 SICAMOUS
B 1914 Assembled by J.M. Bulger, CPR, Okanagan Landing. **T** 1,787g.
D 200.85/61.19 x 40.1/12.22 x 8/2.44.
E Stern-wheeler, 2 cyl comp horizontal direct acting. 17 kts. By hull builder.
H Steel. 20 snag-rooms. 1 dk. **P** 400.
1914 As built she was a sister to *Nasookin* (125). The hull was prefabricated by Western Dry Dock Co., Port Arthur and taken by rail to Okanagan Landing where it was re-assembled and the upperworks added and the vessel launched sideways in the usual manner. Cost $180,000. Sicamous is a main line town on Lake Shuswap.
1930 Rebuilt as a cargo carrier. The accommodation being cut down as drawn.
1931 April: All sternwheeler operations, on Lake Okanagan, except that of *Sicamous* ended.
1936 Withdrawn from service. Laid up. **1949** Sold for $1 to the Gyro Club of Penticton.
1951 Apr 30: Became a museum ship at Penticton. Still there.

131 NITINAT
B 1885 J. Readhead & Co., South Shields. **T** 332g, 58n.
D 149/45.41 x 26.2/7.97 x 14/4.27.
E Sgl scr, 2 cyl comp, 164 nhp, 9 kts. By builder. **H** Iron. 1 dk. 2 funnels.
1885 Built as *William Joliffe* for W.T. Joliffe, Liverpool. She was then the world's most powerful tug.
1907 Sold to British Columbia Salvage Co. and fitted out as a salvage vessel. Same name.
1914 Purchased by CPR. R/n *Nitinat*. Barge towing and salvage duties.
1924 Sold to Pacific Salvage Co. R/n *Salvage Chief*.
1925 Feb 7: Wrecked on Merry Island, Welcome Pass.

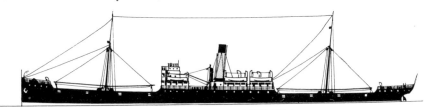

MATTAWA / BERWYN, MEDORA

132 MATTAWA / BERWYN
B 1912 A. McMillan & Sons, Dumbarton. **T** 4,874g, 3,058n.
D 401/122.2 x 52.1/15.87 x 27.3/8.31.
E Sgl scr, tpl exp, 458 nhp, 3 sgl blrs, 9 furn, 180 psi. 10 kts. By D. Rowan & Co., Glasgow.
H Steel. 2 dks. F 48/14.63. B 126/38.4. P 36/10.97.
1912 Build at *St Hugo* for the British & Foreign SS Co. (Rankin, Gilmour & Co's Saint Line).
1915 Feb 6: Sold to the Palace Shipping Co., Liverpool, Macvicar, Marshall managers. R/n *Franktor*. Sept 10: Acquired by CPR. Made one voyage as *Franktor*. Oct 21: R/n *Mattawa*.
1920 Apr: Transferred via the Suez Canal for the Vancouver-Singapore route with *Methven*.
1922 Placed on the Canada-West Indies service.
1923 May 16: R/n *Berwyn* by CPR when all the cargo ships were given 'B' names.
1928 Jan 30: Sold for £30,000 to Kintyre SS Co., Liverpool. R/n *Kingarth*. McMurchy & Greenlees managers. **1932** July: Sold to G & F Bozzo, Italy. R/n *Beppe*.
1942 Oct 19: Torpedoed by HM Submarine *Unbending* off Lampedusa Island.

133 **MEDORA**

Details as *Mattawa* except: **B** 1912 Russell & Co., Port Glasgow. **T** 5,135g, 3,460n.
D 410/124.97.
1912 Apr 26: Launched as *Frankmount* for Palace Shipping Co. Macvicar, Marshall & Co.,
managers. **1915** May 18: Acquired by CPR. R/n *Medora*.
1917 May 21: Bound Montreal-London, off the Lizard, missed by a torpedo from *UB-31*.
1918 May 2: Enroute Liverpool-Montreal, torpedoed by *U-86* 11 miles off the Mull of
Galloway. Master and 2 others taken prisoner.

MOOSE, ELK / WAPITI

134 **MOOSE**

B 1915 H & C Grayson, Garston, Liverpool. **T** 208g, 87n.
D 100.9/30.71 x 25.1/7.65 x 12.6/3.84.
E Sgl scr, tpl exp, 96 rhp. 9 kts. By Crabtree & Co., Great Yarmouth. **H** Steel. 1 dk.
1915 Being built for CPR's Mersey Towing Co. but taken over by the Admiralty. Apr: Saw
war service in the Dardanelles.
1917 Served in north Russian waters: Murmansk and Archangel.
1919 Oct 20: Returned to CPR. Tug service at Liverpool.
1945 July 28: Sank in the Mersey after collision with *Kawartha Park*, Park S.S Co.
Aug 2: Refloated.
1946 Feb 1: When CPR closed down Mersey Towing the pair were sold to the Liverpool Screw
Towing Co., Harold Edwards managing owner. With them went the CPR contract for
Liverpool towage. R/n *Prairie Cock*. The only change to the profile was the addition of the
gaff which all 'Cock' tugs bore. **1959** May: Sold for demolition at Passage West, Cork.

135 **ELK / WAPITI**

As *Moose*.
1915 Built as *Elk* but also taken over for parallel war service alongside her sister.
1919 June 12: Returned to CPR. R/n *Wapiti*.
1945 Sold with her sister to the Liverpool Screw Towing Co. R/n *Weather Cock*.
1959 Aug 16: Arrived at Barrow-in-Furness, in tow of Rea's *Rosegarth*, for breaking up.

CANADIAN PACIFIC OCEAN SERVICES LTD

*This concern was formed in 1915 to amalgamate the CPR and Allan services. The following
sixteen Allan Line ships, in alphabetical order (except for sisters) being transferred on January
10 1916 with the staff, assets and goodwill being officially handed over on July 16 1917. Some
were not officially handed over until later in the war.*

Drawing on page 85

136 **ALSATIAN / EMPRESS OF FRANCE (I)**

B 1914 Wm Beardmore & Sons, Glasgow. **T** 18,481g, 10,747n.
600 o/a **D** 571.4/174.17 x 72.4/22.07 x 41.7/12.7.
E Quad scr, 4 stm turbs, 21,400 shp, 18 kts (20 max). By builder.
H Steel. 3 + shelter dk. **F** & **B** 460/140.21.
P 263 1st, 504 2nd, 848 3rd. Crew 500. (Note: Pass. recordings varied)
1913 Mar 22: Launched for the Allan Line. She was the first transatlantic liner to be given a
cruiser stern.

1914 Jan 17: M/v Liverpool-Halifax-Saint John, NB. Allan Funnel: Red, white band touching the black top. May: With the thaw, transferred to the Montreal service. Sept: Requisitioned for use as an Armed Merchant Cruiser (AMC). 8 x 6 in guns, 2 x 12 pounders. Joined the 10th Cruiser Squadron (from Dec 24) as Flagship of Admiral de Chair. Served in 'A' patrol =Faroes-northwards to the ice cap. Sept 8: Took part in the rescue of the naval crew off White Star's *Oceanic* which was ashore and lost on Foula Island, Shetland. *Alsatian* patrolled between Iceland and Norwegian territorial waters. Covered 266,000 miles and examined 15,000 ships; she also escorted Atlantic convoys.
1917 July 16: Officially transferred to CPR ownership. **1918** Dec: Decommissioned.
1919 Feb: Returned to her builder for reconditioning at Dalmuir. Apr 4: R/n *Empress of France*. **T** 18,357. Sept 26: Emerged with a black hull and white band, as drawn. Signal yard and second crowsnest on foremast. Liverpool-Quebec service.
1920 Achieved a record Liverpool-Quebec crossing in 5 days, 23 hours.
1922 May: First voyage Hamburg-Southampton-Le Havre-Quebec. Off season she took a 4-month round the world cruise for Clarks Tourist Agency, New York.
1923 The Prince of Wales (Edward VIII) travelled in her to Quebec as an 'ordinary' passenger 'so that he might join in the fun'. Winter: repeated the round the world cruise for Clarks. After this CPOS operated and marketed all its own cruises.
1924 Converted to oil burning by builder. Bunkers 3,600 tons, sufficient for the round voyage. The stoke hold crew fell from 117 to 34. June 14: Resumed service. Broke the record with 19.3 kts out and 19.4 home
1927 Oct: Hamburg dropped. Southampton became her terminal.
1928 Oct 31: Left Southampton for Vancouver. Spent a year on the trans-Pacific service. White hull yellow band.
1929 Reverted to Liverpool-Halifax-Saint John service.
1931 Sept 2: Last sailing. Sept 29: Laid up in the Clyde.
1934 Oct 20: Sold to W.H. Arnott Young for £35,000. Nov 24: Arrived Dalmuir for scrap.

137 **CALGARIAN**

As *Alsatian* except: **B** 1914 Fairfield SB & E Co., Glasgow. **T** 17,515g.
P 280 1st, 500 2nd, 900 3rd.
1913 Apr 19: Launched. She was 9ft/2.74m shorter than her sister. Her funnels were also slightly more oval so that they looked a little thinner and taller from all angles except broadside on.
1914 May 8: M/v Liverpool-Quebec. Sept: Joined her sister as an AMC with the 10th Cruiser Squadron. Used to blockade the River Tagus and Lisbon where several German ships were hiding ready to break out. Her companion was HMS *Vindictive* of later Zeebrugge fame.
1915 Employed on the Atlantic with troops and passengers but still as an AMC.
1917 July 16: Officially transferred to CPR but did not ever sail for them commercially.
1918 Mar 1: Guarding a convoy of 30 ships she was torpedoed four times by *U-19* off Rathlin Island. 49 lost.

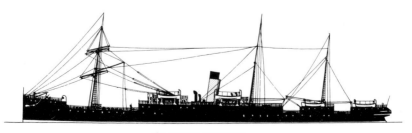

CARTHAGINIAN

138 CARTHAGINIAN

B 1884 Govan SB Co., Glasgow. **T** 4,444g, 2,559n. **D** 386.3/117.75 x 45.3/13.79 x 28.7/8.74.
E Sgl scr, 2 cyl comp inv, 520 nhp, 80 psi, 11 kts. By J & J Thomson & Co., Glasgow.
H Steel. 3 dks. **P** 64 1st, 32 2nd, 500 3rd.
1884 Oct 9: Launched. Dec 6: M/v Glasgow-Boston.
1914 Because of her age she remained on company service. **1916** Jan 10: Transferred to CPOS.
1917 Jun 14: Enroute Liverpool-Montreal struck a mine 2½ miles northwest of Inishtrahull Light, Co. Donegal. No lives lost. The mines were laid by *U-79*.

CORINTHIAN, SICILIAN / BRUTON

139 CORINTHIAN

B 1900 Workman,Clark & Co., Belfast. **T** 6,227g, 5,621n.
D 430/131.06 x 54.2/15.9 x 28.2/8.58.
E Sgl scr, tpl exp, 447 nhp, 14 kts. By builder.
H Steel. 2 dks. **F** 47/14.33. **B** 162/49.38. **P** 44/13.41. **P** 140 1st, 200 2nd, 600 3rd.
1900 Mar 19: Launched. May 24: M/v Liverpool-Quebec-Montreal.
1908 Converted to 2nd and 3rd class only. **T** 7,333g.
1914 Aug: Carried troops of the First Canadian Expeditionary Force to Liverpool.
1916 Jan 10: Taken over with the fleet by Canadian Pacific Ocean Services.
1918 Dec 14: Wrecked in the Bay of Fundy on Brier Island. Efforts to salvage her were abandoned after a month.

140 SICILIAN / BRUTON

Sister of *Corinthian* except: **B** 1899. **T** 6,224g, 3,968n.
1899 Aug 28: Launched. Oct 28: Upon completion taken over for Boer War transport duties. Thus, although completed first, she entered service after her later sister.
1901 Feb 28: M/v for Allan Line Liverpool-Portland, Maine.
1914 Sept: Made one Canadian Expeditionary Force trooping voyage and then reverted to Company service. **1916** Jan 10: Taken over by CPOS.
1919 Feb: Used to repatriate Belgian refugees from England and France.
1921 Dec: Placed on the Saint John-West Indies service. **1922** Laid up at Falmouth.
1923 Made 3 trips Libau, Latvia-Southampton with emigree Mennonites, who then carried by normal passage. Then reduced to cargo only. The six slung lifeboats removed. R/n *Bruton*. She was in service for only six months before being laid up.
1925 May 8: Sold for breaking up to F. Gregorini, Italy.

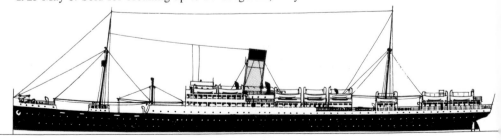

CORSICAN / MARVALE

141 CORSICAN / MARVALE
B 1907 Barclay, Curle & Co., Glasgow. **T** 11,419g, 7,272n.
D 500.3/152.4 x 61.2/18.64 x 38.1/11.58.
E Tw scr, 2 x tpl exp, 917 nhp, 17 kts. By builder.
H Steel. 3 dks. **F** 56/17.07. **B & P** 350/106.68. **P** 208 1st, 298 2nd, 1,000 3rd.
1907 Apr 29: Launched. Nov: M/v Liverpool-Saint John, NB.
1912 A glancing blow against an iceberg caused only slight damage.
1914 May: Glasgow-Montreal route. Aug 8: Requisitioned as a troopship.
1915 Trooped to India. **1916** Jan 10: Taken over by CPOS with the Allan fleet.
1917 Back in Company service.
1918 Nov: Taken over to repatriate Canadian troops, then went to the London-Canada berth.
1922 One of the ships chartered to take British troops to stand between the fighting Greeks
and Turks. Nov 16: Converted into a one-class vessel at Liverpool and r/n *Marvale*.
1923 May 21: Enroute Quebec-Glasgow she was caught in fog and wrecked on Freel Rock,
Cape Pine, Newfoundland, 20 miles west of Cape Race. All saved.

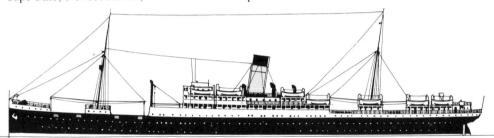

142 GRAMPIAN
B 1907 Alex Stephen & Sons, Glasgow. **T** 9,603g, 6,712n.
D 485.7/147.03 x 60.2/18.34 x 38.1/11.61.
E Tw scr, 2 x tpl exp, 825 nhp, 17 kts. By builder.
H Steel. 2 + shelter dk. **F** 58/17.68. **B & P** 341/103.94.
P 210 1st, 250 2nd, 1,000 3rd.
1907 M/v Glasgow-Quebec-Montreal. Her sister was *Hesperian*. The final Stephen ships built
for Allan. Notably they reverted to triple expansion (see *Virginian* 151)
1914 Aug: One trooping voyage from Canada before returning to winter Company service.
1915 Served for a year as a troop ship. **1916** Jan 10: Taken over with Allan by CPOS.
1921 Mar 14: Caught fire and burnt out while refitting at Antwerp.
1926 Broken up by F. Rijsdyk at Rotterdam.

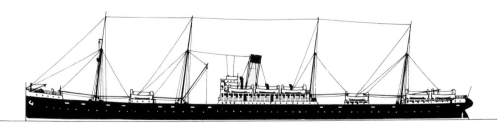

143 IONIAN
B 1901 Workman, Clark & Co., Belfast. **T** 8,268g, 5,323n.
D 470/143.26 x 57.6/17.53 x 37/11.28.
E Tw scr, 2 x tpl exp, 604 nhp. 14 kts. By builder.
H Steel. 3 dks. **F** 56/17.07. **B** 103/31.39. **P** 132 1st, 160 2nd, 800 3rd.

1901 Sept 12: Launched. Replaced Allan's *Castilian* (wrecked Mar 11, 1899).
Nov 21: M/v Liverpool-Halifax-Saint John, NB.
1905 Transferred to the Glasgow-Montreal route.
1906 After the loss of their *Bavarian* in November 1905 *Ionian* reverted to the Liverpool berth.
July: Reverted to Glasgow. **1914-18** Company service.
1916 Jan 10: Taken over by Canadian Pacific Ocean Services. **P** 325 Cabin, 800 3rd.
1917 Mar 24: Missed, off Prawle Point in the English Channel, by a torpedo fired by *UC-17.*
Oct 21: Leaving Milford Haven in ballast for Plymouth she was torpedoed off St Govan's Head
by *UC-51.* Seven lives lost.

Note: Allan's *Mongolian* was sold to the Indian & Peninsular SS Co. in 1914 prior to the CP
take over - although at the time CPR beneficially owned Allan.

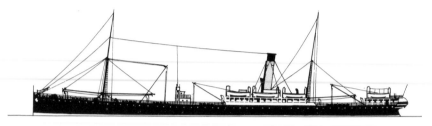

144 **POMERANIAN**

B 1882 Earle's SB & E Co. Hull. **T** 4,364g, 2,832n.
D 394/120.09 oa, 381/116.13 x 43.8/13.33 x 33.1/10.08.
E Sgl scr, 2 cyl comp inv, 550 nhp, 12 kts. By builder.
H Iron. 2 + awning dk. **P** 40 1st, 60 2nd, 1,000 3rd.
1882 Built as *Grecian Monarch* for the Monarch Line, (The Royal Exchange Shipping Co.).
Four masted profile.
1887 Acquired by Allan Line. R/n *Pomeranian.* Sept 8: First sailing London-Montreal.
1889 Transferred to the Glasgow-Montreal route.
1893 Feb: The vessel ran into a severe storm and huge waves carried away the bridge,
charthouse and fore deck saloon, killing 12 people. The ship had to return to Glasgow where
she was repaired and her masts reduced to two, the jigger being replaced by a pair of derrick
posts. Retained her rather stumpy funnel.
1900 Used as a mule transport to the Boer war. Wooden stalls were erected from the foremast
to funnel superstructure.
1902 Returned to Allan. Triple expansion fitted by Denny Bros, Dumbarton. 316 nhp, 12 kts.
The deck stalls were removed. Given a taller funnel (as drawn).
1908 Passenger accommodation reduced to 2nd and 3rd class only.
1914-18 Remained on Company service. **1916** Jan 10: Taken over by CPOS.
1918 Apr 15: Enroute London-Saint John, NB, torpedoed by *UC-77* 12 miles off Portland Bill.
55 lost.

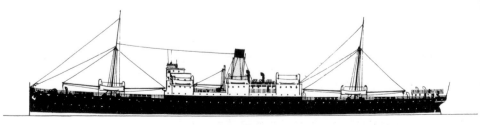

PRETORIAN

145 **PRETORIAN**

B 1901 Furness, Withy & Co., West Hartlepool. **T** 6,508g, 4,076n.
D 436.9/133.15 x 53.1/16.18 x 29.8/9.04.
E Sgl scr, tpl exp, 447 nhp, 14 kts. By Richardsons, Westgarth & Co., Middlesbrough.
H Steel. 2 dks. **F** 47/14.33. **B** 162/49.38. **P** 140 1st, 200 2nd, 600 3rd.
1900 Dec 22: Launched. **1901** Aug 8: M/v Liverpool-Quebec-Montreal.
1914-18 Remained on Company service.
1916 Jan 10: Taken over by CPOS. March: Taken over under the Liner Requisition Scheme.
1917 Apr 30: Chased by a German submarine off south-west Ireland. Turned into the rough of the sea and escaped by speed.
1919 Repatriated Belgian refugees. She then took troops to Archangel during the Bolshevik revolution. They withdrew when, in 1920, the British blockade of Russia ceased and Britain recognised the new Russia - the first by a major power. (The USSR dates from 1924).
1921 Converted to cabin class only. **T** 6,948. **1922** Mar 9: Laid up in the Gareloch.
1926 Feb 20: Sold, for £11,000 to J.J. King, Garston, Liverpool and broken up.

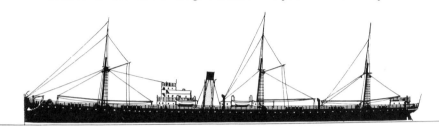

146 **SARDINIAN**

B 1875 Robert Steele & Son, Greenock. **T** 4,349g, 2,788n.
D 370.95/113.06 x 42.2/12.85 x 35.6/10.85.
E Sgl scr, 2 cyl comp inv, 600 hp, 13 kts. By Macnab & Co., Greenock.
H Iron 2 dks. **P** 100 1st, 850 3rd.
1874 Jun 3: Launched. **1875** July 29: M/v Liverpool-Quebec-Montreal.
1878 May 10: Caught fire at Moville, Ireland, following an explosion. Scuttled to put out the blaze. Salved. Jun 26: Back in service.
1882 Liverpool-New York service. Also took sailings out of London and Glasgow on this run.
1897 Triple expansion fitted by Wm Denny & Bros, Dumbarton. 316 nhp.
1901 Nov 26: Left Liverpool with Guiseppi Marconi and his equipment to set up a wireless station at St Johns, Newfoundland. **1908** Reduced to 2nd and 3rd class only.
1914 The ship was too old for anything other than Company service.
1916 Jan 10: Taken over by CPOS.
1919 While awaiting the release of other vessels from national service she was put on the Avonmouth-Quebec-Montreal route but cargo only. Her speed was now down to 10 knots but otherwise the ship was in fine condition. Her crew accommodation was spartan and disliked.
1920 Sold to Astoreca Azqueta. Engines removed to become a hulk at Vigo, Spain.
1938 Jun 22: Sold and scrapped at Bilbao.

Drawing on page 69

147 **SCANDINAVIAN**

B 1898 Harland & Wolff, Belfast. **T** 12,099g, 7,416n.
D 550.3/167.74 x 59.3/18.08 x 35.9/10.92.
E Tw scr, 2 x 4 cyl tpl exp (2 low pressure), 8,700 ihp, 3 dbl + 3 sgl blrs, 15 kts. By builder.
H Steel. 3 dks. **P** 200 1st, 200 2nd, 800 Steerage. Coal: 3,680 tons at 160 tpd.
1898 Apr 7: Launched as *New England* for the Dominion Line. Three masted.
Jun 30: M/v Liverpool-Boston.

1903 Nov: Transferred to the White Star Line. R/n *Romanic*. Nov 19: Made White Star's first sailing to Boston then the Boston-Mediterranean service. Two masts. **T** 11,394g, 7,416n.
1912 Jan 3: Positioned Genoa-Glasgow when acquired by Allan Line. R/n *Scandinavian* (as drawn). Mar 23: Glasgow-Halifax-Boston. May: After the thaw Glasgow-Montreal service.
1914 Aug 22: Carried Canadian troops to Glasgow.
1915 Oct 1: The negotiations by CPR to amalgamate with Allan were concluded. Government ratification followed. **1916** Jan 10: Taken over by CPOS.
1917-19 Operated under the Liner Requisition Scheme. **1920** May 18: Antwerp-Canada routes.
1922 July: Laid up at Falmouth due to the general surplus of tonnage.
1923 July 9: Sold to F Rijsdyk for scrapping. July 16: Resold to Klasmann & Lentze, Emden. Broken up at Hamburg.

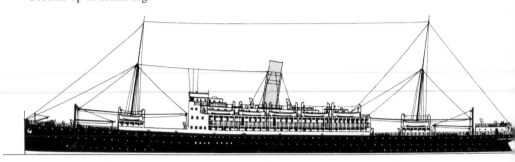

148 SCOTIAN / MARGLEN
B 1898 Harland & Wolff, Belfast. **T** 10,322g, 6,701n.
D 515.3/157.07 x 59.8/18.21 x 23.8/7.24.
E Tw scr, 2 x tpl exp, 1,126 nhp, 180 psi, 14 kts. By builder.
H Steel. 3 dks. Promenade dk 190/57.91. **P** 200 1st, 175 2nd, 1,000 Steerage. Crew 220.
1898 May 7: Launched as *Statendam* (I) for the Holland America Line. Rotterdam-New York.
1911 Mar 23: Acquired by Allan Line. R/n *Scotian*. Glasgow-Montreal service.
1914 Aug: Used for trooping duties. **1916** Jan 10: Taken over by CPOS.
1917-19 Operated under the Liner Requisition Scheme. Returned to CPOS; refitted.
P 304 Cabin, 542 3rd.
1922 Nov 16: Back in service. R/n *Marglen* to conform with the Cabin Class nomenclature.
1925 Oct 14: Chartered for three winter round voyages to Bombay.
1927 Dec 30: Sold for £23,000 to D.L. Pittaluga, Genoa, for breaking up.

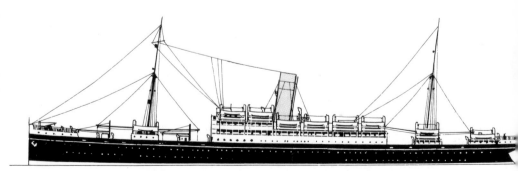

149 TUNISIAN / MARBURN
B 1900 Alex Stephen & Sons, Glasgow. **T** 10,576g, 6,802n, 17,500dwt.
D 500.5/152.55 x 59.2/18.03 x 39.9/12.14.

E Tw scr, 2 x tpl exp, 871 nhp, 16 kts. By builder. Coal: 2,400 tons at 160 tpd.
H Steel. 4 dks. F 54/16.46. B 177/53.95. P 40/12.19. C: 9,000 tons.
P 240 1st, 220 2nd, 1,000 3rd.
1900 Jan 17: Launched. Apr 5: M/v Liverpool-Halifax-Portland, Maine. her sister was *Bavarian*, wrecked Nov 3, 1905.
1903 Made a then record crossing of 6 days, 7 hours, 15 minutes Rimouski-Liverpool.
1914 Sept 16: Requisitioned for trooping following a single voyage to Canada. Then used, first, for four months as a p.o.w. accommodation ship (mainly German seamen taken in British ports when the war commenced)
1915 March: In the Dardanelles campaign and then, via the Suez canal, to Mesopotamia.
1916 Jan 10: Taken over by CPOS with the Allan fleet.
1917 Returned to her owners for the Canadian service out of Liverpool and Glasgow.
1919 Placed on the London-Canada route.
1920 Refurbished and re-engined by D & W Henderson. T 10,743g. P 310 Cabin, 736 3rd.
1922 Mar 25: Made the first Belfast call when this port was added to the Glasgow route. Nov 16: As a Cabin Class ship r/n *Marburn*.
1927 July 5: Laid up off Southend.
1928 Apr 6: Made her final sailing Antwerp-St Johns, Newfoundland. Sept 17: Sold for breaking up to Soc. Anon. Cooperativa Ligure Demolitori, Genoa. This firm acted for a number of ship breakers and *Marburn* was then allocated to the one ready to break her up.

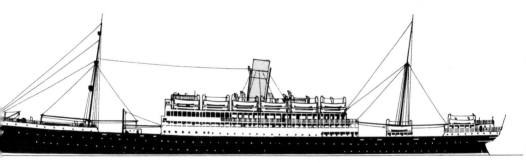

VICTORIAN / MARLOCH, VIRGINIAN

150 **VICTORIAN / MARLOCH**
B 1905 Workman, Clark & Co., Belfast. **T** 10,645g, 6,747n.
D 520/158.5 x 60.4/18.41 x 38/11.58.
E Tpl scr, 3 Parson's steam turbs, 15,000 shp, 18 kts. By builder.
H Steel. 3 dks. F 68/20.73. B 211/64.31. P 56/17.06. **P** 346 1st, 286 2nd, 1,000 3rd.
1905 Aug 25: Launched for tha Allan Line. Her managers were, like the rest of the fleet at this time, Allan Bros & Co UK Ltd. She and her sister were the turbine ships and the first triple screw on the North Atlantic. Achieved 19½ knots on trials.
1905 May 23: M/v Liverpool-Saint John, NB. Thence, in spring, onto the Montreal route.
1914 Sept: Taken over as an Armed Merchant Cruiser and joined the 10th Cruiser Squadron.
1916 Jan 10: Taken over by CPOS but not actually transferred due to her Admiralty requisition.
1917 July 16: The transfer to CPOS was completed.
1921 Used on trooping services to Bombay. Dec: At the end she was taken to Fairfield SB & E Co., Glasgow, converted to oil burning and given new turbines. Speed reduced to 14½ kts for an intermediate role. Her profile changed, the fcsle now extending to the foremast.
1922 Dec 11: Returned to service as the Cabin Class *Marloch*.
1924 Sank *Whimbrel* (British & Continental SS Co.) off Flushing.
1925 Laid up and used only as a reserve vessel during overhaul periods.
1929 Apr 17: Sold to Thos W Ward and broken up at Pembroke Dock, South Wales.

151 **VIRGINIAN**

As *Victorian* except: **B** Alex Stephen & Sons, Linthouse, Glasgow. **T** 10,757g, 6,827n.

1904 This ship was ordered from Workman, Clark but switched to Stephens due to the change to turbine drive which might have delayed her. Dec 22: Launched. Ident: Had no bridge deck opening aft.

1905 Apr 6: M/v Liverpool-Saint John, NB., then onto the Montreal route. The direct acting turbines in these two ships gave initial trouble. They drove three small propellers, 9.5ft/2.89m in diameter, at the high speed of 280 rpm. This caused cavitation and a strumming vibration aft. The efficient speed of the turbine was far too fast for the propeller and the design of the hull, as a result coal consumption was excessive. The effect can be gauged by the fact that the following Stephen's pair *Grampian* (142) and *Hesperian* returned to reciprocating engines. But note that for the designed Cunard flyer *Mauretania* the turbine speeds were perfect for her speed and propellers. June 16: Did Cape Race-Moville in 4 days 4 hrs - a record. Sept: Due to smoke from a forest fire she went gently ashore on Cape St Charles, St Lawrence, but came off safely.

1912 Apr 14: When *Titanic* sank *Virginian* was one of the ships which heard her SOS and headed for the scene but proceeded on passage when Cunard's *Carpathia* signalled that she was only 57 miles away.

1914 Aug: Taken over for trooping but, Nov 13, transferred to AMC service, converted and attached to the 10th Cruiser Squadron with her sister.

1916 Jan 10: Allan Line taken over by CPOS. *Virginian* remained with the Government.

1917 July 16: On the Liner Requisition Scheme she was officially transferred to CPOS.

1918 Dec 23: Returned to Stephen's for refurbishing. Declared surplus and put up for sale.

1920 Feb 14: Sold to the Swedish America Line. R/n *Drottningholm*. May: Gothenburg-New York service.

1922 De Laval single reduction 10,500 shp geared turbines installed at Gothenburg. These made her economic to operate at 17 kts.

1923 Resumed service. **P** 532 Cabin, 854 3rd. Her bridge deck was extended to the main mast.

1937 Given a white hull which became fleet livery.

1940-46 Used, with *Gripsholm* (same owner), by the International Red Cross for the exchange of diplomatic personnel, civilians and wounded prisoners of war. She was one of the only vessels which sailed the seas fully illuminated. In all she made 30 passages and carried 25,000 people.

1945 With the advent of a replacement, *Stockholm*, she was sold with current commitments to Home Lines, in whom Swedish America Line had a half share.

1948 Delivered to the Home Lines, Panama. R/n *Brasil*. July 27: First sailing Genoa-Rio de Janeiro service. Officially her Home Line owners were South Atlantic Lines Inc. Her consort was *Argentina* (ex-*Bergendfjord*).

1950 Naples-New York route during Holy Year.

1951 Modernised in Italy. R/n *Homeland*, same owners. **T** 10,043g. **P** 96 1st, 846 Tourist. June 16: Hamburg-Southampton-Halifax-New York service. Her managers were Hamburg America Line.

1952 Reverted to a Genoa-Naples-Barcelona-New York route. Now owned by the subsidiary Mediterranean Lines Inc.

1955 Mar 29: Arrived at Trieste and scrapped by Sidarma, aged 51.

EMPRESS

DOLA

152 EMPRESS

B 1906 Swan, Hunter & Wigham Richardson, Newcastle. **T** 1,342g, 612n.
D 235/71.63 x 34.2/10.41 x 20/6.1.
E Tw scr, 2 x tpl exp, 366 nhp, 160 psi, 12 kts. By builder.
H Steel. 1 + awning dk. **P** 600.
1906 Completed for the Charlottetown S.S. Co, Prince Edward Island. Used on the Charlotteville-Pictou service.
1916 Acquired by CPR to replace *Yarmouth* (116).
1919 After the sale of *Prince Rupert* (115) and the non return of *St George* (124) she maintained the Bay of Fundy service on her own.
1926 May: Her superstructure was damaged and the interior smashed and flooded during a severe gale.
1930 Replaced by *Princess Helene* (200).
1931 Her accommodation was gutted by fire while she lay at Saint John, NB.
1932 Became a coal hulk based at Saint John and owned by the Dominion Coal Co. Trace lost.

153 DOLA

B 1907 Wallace SB & DD Co., Vancouver. **T** 339g, 112n. **D** 93.3/28.45 x 21.8/6.63 x 10.85/3.3.
E Sgl scr, tpl exp, 39 rhp, 1 sgl blr, 180 psi. By McKie & Baxter, Glasgow. **H** Wood. 1 dk.
1907 Built for the Vancouver Tug & Barge Co., Vancouver. **1917** Acquired by CPR. Same name.
1933 Sold to Dola Tug-Boats Ltd., Vancouver.
1953 Oct 28: Sunk in Howe Sound, B.C., in collision with Union SS Co's *Lady Cynthia*.

ISLAND PRINCESS

CY PECK

154 ISLAND PRINCESS

B 1913 at Tacoma. **T** 339g, 203n. **D** 116.2/35.41 x 25.1/7.65 x 8.5/2.59.
E Sgl scr, tpl exp, 43 rhp, 1 sgl blr, 9 kts. By S.F. Hodge, Detroit. **H** Wood. 1 dk. **P** 140.
1913 Built as *Daily* for McDowell & Co., Puget Sound. Operated by the Merchant's Transportation Co. Her consorts were *Daring, Dart* and *Dove*. Black hull. Seattle-(West Passage)-Tacoma run.
1918 Purchased by CPR. R/n *Island Princess*. Placed on the Gulf Islands service.
1930 Sold to Sam Matson's Gulf Island's Ferry Co. R/n *Cy Peck*. Named after the distinguished British Columbia soldier Colonel Cyrus W. Peck VC DSO. As drawn.
1951 Her owners were taken over by Gavin Mouat. Same name and service.
1961 Sept 1: Taken over by British Columbia Ferries, including the terminal and equipment, for $249,823.
1966 Sold, for $5,000, to J.H. Todd & Sons. **1968** Scrapped.

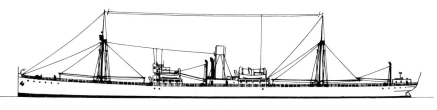

MINIOTA

155 MINIOTA

B 1913 Wm Gray & Co., West Hartlepool. **T** 6,422g, 3,971n.
D 420.2/128.07 x 55/16.76 x 32.3/9.86.
E Sgl sct, tpl exp, 490 nhp, 3 sgl blrs, 180 psi; 12 kts. By Central Marine Eng'g Works, Hartlepool. **H** Steel. 1 + shelter dk. **P** 12.
1913 Built as *Hackness* for Pyman Bros' London & Northern Shipping Co.
1916 Sept 28: Purchased by CPR. R/n *Miniota*; a war loss replacement vessel. Oct 20: First sailing from Glasgow.
1917 Aug 31: Inbound ex-Montreal, torpedoed by *U-19* thirty miles off Start Point. 3 dead.

156 MELITA

B 1914 Barclay, Curle & Co., Glasgow. **T** 13,967g, 8,526n.
D 546/166.42 oa, 520/158.5 x 67.2/20.47 x 41.8/12.73.
E Tpl scr, 2 x tpl exp with lp turb to centre shaft, 11,000 shp, 5 dbl blrs, 30 furn, 215 psi. By Harland & Wolff, Belfast. Coal: 170 tpd.
H Steel. 3 + awning dk. **F & B** 413/125.88. **P** 46/14.02. 2 sets Babcock & Wilcox gantry davits.
P 490 Cabin, 1,300 Tourist.
1914 Both were laid down for Hamburg America Line's North Atlantic Pool Organisation.
1917 Apr 21: Launched as *Melita* for CPR. June 2: Towed to Belfast for engine installation and finishing.
1918 Jan 25: M/v Liverpool-Canada. remained in Company service for the Ministry of Shipping. July 26: In the Atlantic she was attacked by gunfire from *U-140*; escaped by return of gunfire. Nov: Used for troop repatriation including India-Canada.
1921 May: Antwerp-Southampton-Quebec-Montreal route.
1926 Modernised by Palmers' Co., Jarrow. Given superheaters. **P** 206 Cabin. 545 Tst, 588 3rd.
1935 June: Sold and towed by Smit's *Zwarte Zee* to Genoa for breaking up. Taken over by the Italian Government for the Abyssinian war. R/n *Liguria*. Operated by Lloyd Triestino; white hull and yellow funnels.
1940 July: Damaged off Tobruk by British torpedo bombers.
1941 Jan 22: Set on fire and sunk at Tobruk. **1950** Raised, taken to Savona and scrapped.

157 MINNEDOSA

Sister of *Melita*. **T** 13,973g, 8,630n.
1917 Oct 17: Launched.
1918 May 2: Arrived at Belfast for finishing like her sister. Nov 21: Delivered to CPR but under Government requisition. Her finish was a utility nature. Dec 12: M/v Liverpool-Quebec. Used to repatriate Canadian troops.
1924 Rammed and damaged while berthed at Antwerp.
1925 Sent to Cammell, Laird, Birkenhead, for engine overhaul and the fitting of superheaters. However at the end of the season it was decided to modernise her like her sister. Went to Hawthorn, Leslie & Co., Newcastle. While there a fire in the officers quarters caused £5,000 of damage.
1926 July: Transatlantic radio was still to come. When 1,550 miles away contact was made by radio with Cape Race. Then a record. **1931** Laid up at Glasgow.
1935 Put on the disposal list. Sold to Ricuperi Metallici, Turin, for scrap. Towed to Genoa. Taken over by The Italian Government and commissioned as the troopship *Piemonte* for the Abyssinian war, with Lloyd Triestino as managers.
1938 Placed on Lloyd Triestino's Far East service.
1942 Nov: Torpedoed near Messina and badly damaged but survived. Taken into Messina.
1943 At Messina she was hit several times by Allied bombs and, May 4, settled, half submerged on her starboard side, in shallow water.
1949 Raised. July 27: Left Messina in tow for Spezia and scrapped.

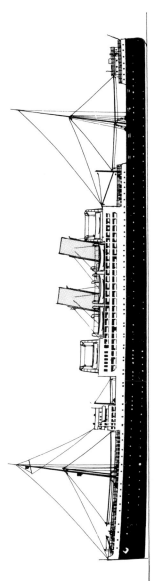

MELITA, MINNEDOSA

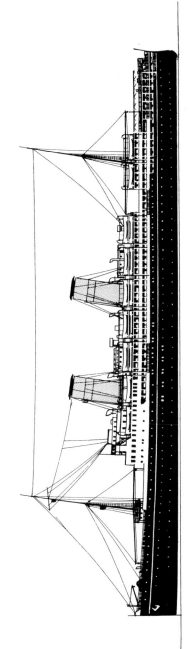

136-137 ALSATIAN / EMPRESS OF FRANCE (I), CALGARIAN

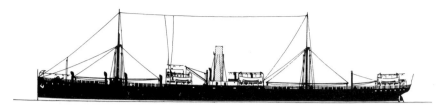

158 **METHVEN / BORDEN**

B 1905 D & W Henderson & Co., Glasgow. **T** 4,928g, 3,042n.
D 390/118.87 x 52.7/16.05 x 27.1/8.25.
E Sgl scr, tpl exp, 469 nhp, 3 sgl blrs, 9 furn, 12 kts (14 max). By builder.
H Steel. 2 + shelter dk.
1905 Dec 1: Launched as *Heliopolis* for the Alliance Steam Ship Co. Harris & Dixon managers.As drawn. **1906** Jan 6: Delivered.
1908 Mar 4: Transferred to Century Shipping Co., Harris & Dixon managers.
1913 Mar 17: Because of her reserve of speed she was purchased by the Admiralty for conversion into a naval hospital ship. It was then intended to name her *Mediator* because there was already a hospital ship *Maine* (II) ex-*Swansea*. Note: In 1899 *Maine* (I) came from Atlantic Transport Co. as the gift of Bernard H. Baker.
1914 July 6: When, due to stranding, the hospital ship *Maine* had to be replaced *Heliopolis* was completed *Maine* (III) and used as a supply ship.
1916 Mar 7: Her speed was not sufficient for naval fleet work. Reverted to *Heliopolis* and Harris & Dixon. Owned by Alliance Steam Ship Co.
1917 May 15: Acquired by CPR for service across the Pacific. Aug 20: R/n *Methven*.
1919 Oct: Inaugurated the new Vancouver-Singapore route.
1923 Mar 22: Transferred to the Atlantic station. R/n *Borden*.
1926 Oct 26: Sold, for £12,000, to Perseus S S Co. R/n *Perseus*. Her managers became Rethymis & Kulukundis. **1928** Owned by E.G. Culucundis & S.C. Costomeni, Syra.
1929 Transferred to the Atlanticos S.S. Co., Syra. Same owner.
1933 Broken up at Genoa by Febo Amadeo Bertorello.

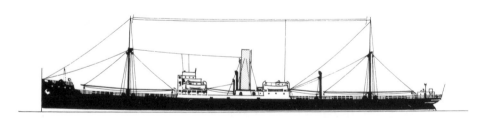

159 **MONTCALM (II) / BOLINGBROKE**

B 1917 Northumberland SB Co., Newcastle. **T** 6,608g, 4,145n.
D 420.1/128.04 x 53.45/16.28 x 36.3/11.07.
E Sgl scr, tpl exp, 662 nhp, 3 sgl blrs, 12 furn, 180 psi, 11 kts. By North East Marine Eng'g Co., Newcastle. **H** Steel. 2 + shelter dk. F 34/10.36.
1917 June 7: Launched for CPR. Oct 12: M/v London-Quebec-Montreal.
1920 Aug 25: R/n *Bolingbroke*. **1929** Laid up at Falmouth.
1933 Dec 27: Sold to W.H. Arnott, Young & Co. for scrap. **1934** Feb: Broken up at Troon.

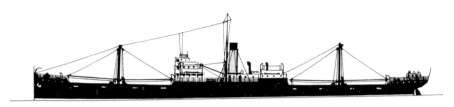

160 MONTEZUMA (II) / BEDWYN / BALFOUR

B 1917 Robert Duncan & Co., Glasgow. **T** 5,038g, 3,187n.
D 405.3/123.55 x 53/16.15 x 27.4/8.36.
E Sgl scr, tpl exp, 538 nhp, 3 sgl blrs, 9 furn, 180 psi, 12 kts. By J.G. Kincaid, Glasgow.
H Steel. 2 dks. F 46/14.02. B 126/38.4. P 43/13.11.
1917 Mar 28: Launched as *Camperdown* for Glen & Co., Glasgow. Acquired by CPR before completion. R/n *Montezuma*. Managers: Canadian Pacific Steamships.
1918 May 23: M/v to Canada.
1923 May 14: R/n *Bedwyn*. Made one voyage with this name. June 19: R/n *Balfour* for the Montreal-West Indies route. **1926** North Atlantic service.
1928 Feb 4: Sold, for £40,000, to Lyle Steamship Co., Glasgow. R/n *Cape Verde* (II). The cash being raised, Jan 16, by the sale of investments.
1935 June: Sold to Fan Shien Ho., Shanghai. R/n *Shang Ho*.
1938 July: Taken over by Mayachi Kisen K.K. R/n *Kizan Maru*.
1943 Sept 27: Destroyed by Allied underground forces at Singapore. When captured the men involved were beheaded, not shot. A Japanese sign of honour for bravery

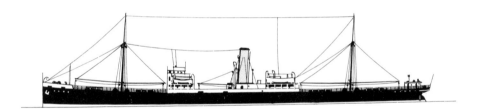

161 MOTTISFONT / BAWTRY

B 1917 W.Dobson & Co., Newcastle. **T** 5,692g, 4,228n.
D 412.5/125.73 oa, 400.5/122.07 x 52/15.85 x 33/10.06.
E Sgl scr, tpl exp, 455 nhp, 3 sgl blrs, 9 furn, 12 kts. By North East Marine Eng'g Co., Newcastle. **H** Steel. 1 + shelter dk.
1916 Nov 11: Launched.
1917 Mar 15: Delivered as *Mottisfont*. to Harris & Dixon, London. Carried wheat cargoes River Plate then USA-UK. Expeditionary Force supply ship Canada-France.
1918 June 5: Acquired by CPR. First sailing: Barry Docks-Canada with a cargo of coal.
1923 Mar 22: R/n *Bawtry*.
1927 Feb 22: Sold, for £40,000, to N.G. Livanos, Piraeus. Owned by his Arbor Shipping Co. R/n *Archangelos*. **1935** May: Transferred to Theofano Maritime Co. Same owners.
1950 June: Sold to Kemal Sadikoglu, Galata, Turkey. R/n *K. Sadikoglu* (as drawn).
1957 Late: Laid up with damage. **1961** Sept: Broken up at Kalafatyeri, Turkey.

HOLBROOK / BREDON / BRANDON, DUNBRIDGE / BRECON

162 HOLBROOK / BREDON / BRANDON
B 1917 J.L. Thompson & Son, Sunderland. **T** 6,655g, 4,155n.
D 412.3/125.68 x 55.5/16.92 x 34.4/10.49.
E Sgl scr, tpl exp, 558 nhp, 4 sgl blrs, 12 furn, 12 kts. By Blair & Co., Stockton.
H Steel. 1 + shelter dk. F 34/10.36.
1917 July 17: Launched for Century Shipping Co. as *Holbrook*. Harris & Dixon managers.
Nov: Delivered; used as a military nitrate carrier. As drawn. Later altered, resembled
Mottisfont but with a pair of derrick posts aft.
1918 June 24: Acquired by CPR. First sailing from Liverpool.
1923 Mar 2: R/n *Bredon*. Did not sail with this name. May 19: R/n *Brandon*.
1928 Mar 3: Sold, for £44,000, to Christian Salvesen. Their largest vessel to date. Entered the
grain trade Hudson's Bay or River Plate - UK.
1939 Dec 8: In ballast Cardiff-Port Everglades, torpedoed by *U-48* 150 miles off Land's End.
9 dead, 43 saved by the escort.

163 DUNBRIDGE / BRECON
Sister of *Holbrook*. **T** 6,650g, 4,157n.
1917 Oct 1: Launched as *Dunbridge* for Century Shipping Co.
1918 Feb: Delivered. June 10: Acquired by CPR. Aug 9: First sailing from Barry Docks.
1923 Feb 24: R/n *Brecon*.
1928 Mar 15: Sold, for £40,000, to Goulandris Bros., Andros. R/n *Frangoula B. Goulandris*.
1940 June 26: Enroute Cork-St Thomas in ballast, torpedoed by *U-26* south west of Cape Clear.
U-26 did not report the sinking and was herself sunk next day by HMS *Gladiolus*. However
she was the only U-boat in the area at the time. 6 crew lost and 32 picked up by a Spanish
fishing boat and taken into San Sebastian.

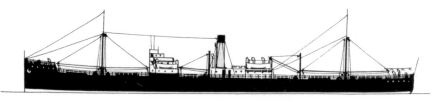

BOSWORTH, BOTHWELL

164 BOSWORTH
B 1919 J.L. Thompson & Sons, Sunderland. **T** 6,672g, 4,140n.
D 412.3/125.68 x 55.5/16.92 x 34.4/10.49.
E Sgl scr, tpl exp, 619 nhp, 3 sgl blrs, 12 furn, 180 psi, 12 kts. By J. Dickinson & Sons,
Sunderland. **H** Steel. 1 + shelter dk. F 36/10.97.
1918 Dec 31: Launched, for the Shipping Controller as *War Peridot*, standard 'F' type.
1919 Mar 7: Acquired by CPR. Mar 15: M/v to Canada. **1920** June 14: R/n *Bosworth*.
1928 Mar 5: Sold to H.M. Thomson & Co., same name.
1944 Sept 4: Sunk as a part of the Mulberry Harbour storm replacements, Normandy.
1949 Raised and towed to Dalmuir where she was scrapped by W.H. Arnott, Young & Co.

165 BOTHWELL

As *Bosworth* except: **B** 1918 W. Doxford & Sons, Sunderland. **T** 6,723g, 4,094n.
1918 Dec 7: Launched as *War Pearl*, Shipping Controller.
1919 Apr 14: Acquired by CPR. Apr 25: M/v Sunderland-Canada.
1920 June 23: R/n *Bothwell* after G.M. Bothwell, Chairman of Pacific Ocean Services, London.
1929 July 10: Laid up at Falmouth after 62 Atlantic voyages.
1933 Nov 27: Sold to Tramp Shipping Development Co.
1934 Mar 23: Next to Tower Shipping Co., Sheriff & Brownlie managers. R/n *Tower Crown*.
1937 Oct: Purchased by Kulukundis Shipping Co. R/n *Mount Ossa*, Piraeus.
1939 Apr: Bought by Robert Bornhofen GmbH., Hamburg. R/n *Robert Bornhofen*.
1940 Became the German naval supply ship *Sperrbrecher III*, later *Sperrbrecher A* then *Sperrbrecher 14*. **1942** Sept 9: Sunk by a mine off Honningsvaag, Norway.

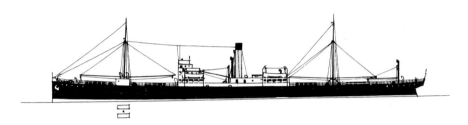

166 BATSFORD

B 1914 J.L. Thompson & Sons, Sunderland. **T** 4,782g, 2,906n.
D 388.7/118.36 x 54.1/16.49 x 26/7.92.
E Sgl scr, tpl exp, 455 nhp, 3 sgl blrs, 9 furn, 12 kts. By J. Dickinson & Sons, Sunderland.
H Steel. 1 + shelter dk.
1913 Dec 12: Launched for Century Shipping Co. Harris & Dixon managers. Grain carrier.
1914 Feb 20: Delivered. Used as an Admiralty collier (No.427) and then similarly used by the French Government; Army Transport D.816.
1918 June 11: Acquired by CPR. Sept 26: Sailed from Weymouth on her first CPR voyage.
1924-26 Spent much of her time laid up.
1927 Jan 18: Sold, for £40,000, to Turnbull Coal & Shipping Co., Cardiff. R/n *Hamdale*.
1933 The owners were re-styled Turnbulls (Cardiff) Ltd.
1937 Apr 12: Sold to Barry Shipping Co., Cardiff. B & S Shipping Co. managers. Apr 29: R/n *St Mellons*. Aug: Became *Tozan Maru* of Seiichi Okada, Osaka.
1938 Her owners were restyled Okada Gumi K.K., Japan. Mar 6: Wrecked in fog on Goto Island enroute Yawata-Keelung in ballast.

---

167 COLUMBIA (II)

B 1920 CPR, Nakusp. **T** 90g.
D 72/21.95 x 15/4.57 x 7/2.13. **E** From *Columbia* (I), (16). **H** Wood. 1 dk.
1920 Barge tug. Built for the Arrow Lake service. **1948**. Sold and became a houseboat.

---

168 KELOWNA

B 1920 CPR Okanagan Landing. **T** 96g.
D 89/27.13 x 19/5.79 x 8/2.44. **E** Sgl scr 2 cyl comp, 27 rhp; from *Whatshan* (99). **H** Wood.
1920 Tug on Okanagan Lake. **1956** Withdrawn and laid up. Trace lost.

169 MONTREAL (II)

B 1906 Blohm & Voss, Hamburg. **T** 9,720g, 5,611n. **D** 475.7/144.98 x 55.3/16.87 x 30.95/9.42.
E Tw scr, quad exp, 2 x 4 cyls, 1,204 nhp, 3 dbl + 1 sgl blr, 21 furn, 16 kts. By builder.
H Steel. 2 + shade dk. **P** 229 1st, 240 3rd. Crew 108.
1904 Ordered for the Far East route but which was now taken over by Norddeutscher Lloyd. **1906** July 4: Launched for the Hamburg America Line as *Konig Friedrich August*. Placed on the South American service.
1920 Nov 6: Purchased from the Reparations Commission, London. R/n *Montreal*.
1921 Feb 5: Went for refitting at Antwerp. Forward well removed. June 1: First CPR sailing Antwerp-London-Quebec-Montreal.
1923 Cabin Class only. **1927** May 22: Laid up off Southend.
1928 May 4: Sold to Cyprien Fabre, Marseilles (Cie Française de Nav à Vapeur Cyprien Fabre & Cie). R/n *Alesia*. Marseilles-Syria-New York route. Note: CPR records give 1928. Hamburg America say 1929. **1931** Oct: Laid up at Marseilles.
1933 Nov 3: Arrived at Genoa for scrapping.

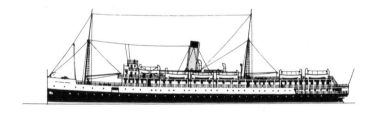

170 PRINCESS LOUISE (II)

B 1921 Wallace SB & DD Co., Vancouver. **T** 4,032g, 2,449n.
D 317.2/96.67 x 48.1/14.66 x 34.6/10.54.
E Sgl scr, tpl exp, 310 nhp, 17½ kts. By builder.
H Steel. 2 dks. **P** 1,000 + 14 motor cars.
1921 Aug 28: Launched for the Vancouver-Alaska service. Named after the daughter of King Edward VII. **1950** Used a a cruise vessel to the Alaskan fjords.
1963 Intended for use as a restaurant at the British Columbia Ferry terminal at Tsawwassen but sold and used for the same purpose at Los Angeles. She later moved to San Pedro.
1989 Oct: Sank at her moorings after capsizing. Raised and scrapped.

171 EMPRESS OF CHINA (III) / EMPRESS OF INDIA (II) / MONTLAURIER / MONTEITH / MONTNAIRN

B 1907 J.C. Tecklenborg A.G., Tecklenborg. **T** 17,282g, 9,785n.
D 590.1/179.86 x 68.3/20.85 x 38.6/11.76.
E Tw scr, 2 x 4 cyl quad exp, 1,416 nhp, 19 kts. By builder.

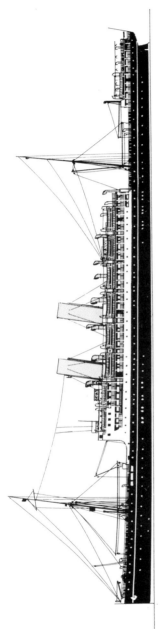

171 EMPRESS OF CHINA (III) / EMPRESS OF INDIA (II) / MONTLAURIER / MONTEITH / MONTNAIRN

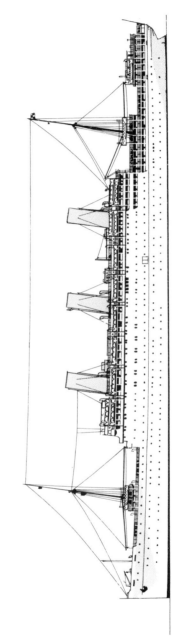

172 EMPRESS OF CHINA (II) / EMPRESS OF AUSTRALIA (I)

H Steel. 2 dks. **F** 123/. **P** 425 1st, 338 2nd, 1,756 3rd. Crew 400.

1907 Oct 12: Launched for Norddeutscher Lloyd, Bremen, as *Prinz Friedrich Wilhelm*.

1908 June 8: M/v Bremerhaven-New York.

1912 Apr 12: She sent out an ice report which had it been acted upon would have saved White Star's *Titanic*.

1914 Aug 2: Cruising to Norway at the outbreak of war. Trying to slip back to Germany she grounded and had to take refuge in the Norwegian port of Odda.

1916 Broke out of internment and sailed for Germany but went ashore on the coast of Denmark. Salvaged and returned to Kiel.

1919 Ceded to Great Britain. Used to repatriate US troops.

1920 Reconditioned at Liverpool. Managed for the Shipping Controller by Canadian Pacific Ocean Services. Operated to Canada carrying troops home. Made one voyage Bombay-Canada.

1921 May 13: Purchased from the Reparations Commission by CPR. Aug 2: R/n *Empress of China* but this name had already been allocated (and was in the process of registration) to the *Tirpitz* purchased a few days earlier. Oct 12: R/n *Empress of India*. Refurbished. Used mainly as a reserve ship.

1922 June 23: First sailing, as an intermediate vessel, Liverpool-Cobh-Quebec. Had yellow funnels, black top. Made one trooping voyage to Turkey when the Greeks were unexpectedly routed and British forces were interposed to keep the peace leading to the Treaty of Lausanne. Dec 13: R/n *Montlaurier* following the policy of giving the intermediates names commencing with 'M'.

1925 Feb 26: Stranded at Cobh after rudder damage. Repaired at Cammell, Laird, Birkenhead. Her well deck was planked over. As drawn. June 18: R/n *Monteith* but did not sail under this title. July 2: R/n *Montnairn* for the Antwerp-Quebec route.

1928 Oct 7: Arrived at Southampton and laid up off Netley.

1929 Dec 23: Sold for breaking up by Soc. Anon. Co-operativa Ligure Demolitori Navi, Genoa.

172 **EMPRESS OF CHINA (II) / EMPRESS OF AUSTRALIA (I)**

B 1913 Vulkan Werke A.G., Stettin. **T** 21,498g, 11,749n.

0/46 15 **D** 589.8/179.76 x 75.2/22.91 x 41.5/12.65.

E Tw scr, 2 stm turb with 2 Foettinger hydraulic gearings, 16,000 shp, 4 wt blrs, 17 kts. By builder. **H** Steel. 5 dks. **B** 282/85.95. **P** 370 1st, 190 2nd, 415 3rd. Crew 500.

1913 Dec 20: Launched as *Admiral von Tirpitz* for the Hamburg America Line. One of three virtual sisters (the others being, finally, *Resolute* and *Reliance*)

1914 Feb: Her name was shortened to *Tirpitz*. Aug: Work ceased when war broke out. Held by many as being the most graceful ship ever built in Germany. She was designed to be Germany's most luxurious ship and was to have had a special suite for the Kaiser. Later in the war she was fitted out as a Royal Yacht aboard which the Kaiser intended to lead in the surrendered British Fleet.

1919 Mar: Handed over to the British as part of war reparations. At Hamburg work to complete her recommenced; being delayed at one stage by a fire. One odd thing: The gap between the second and third funnels was 8ft/2.43m greater than between the first and second. The space can also be seen in the gap between the sixth and seventh lifeboats. An engine room access hatch being responsible.

1920 Arrived at Hull with her consort *Kaiserin Auguste Victoria* (173). Engaged on garrison troop replacement work with P & O as managers. Then laid up at Immingham for some months.

1921 July 25: Acquired by CPR. R/n *Empress of China*. Aug 20: Returned to Vulcan Werke, Hamburg for a refit of the engines. Then to John Brown & Co., Clydebank for fitting out to CPR requirements.

1922 June 2: R/n *Empress of Australia*. **T** 21,860g. June 16: Sailed from the Clyde via Panama to take up her Pacific service. Black hull white band.

1923 Sept 1: She was on the point of leaving Yokohama, with about 2,000 aboard, when the earthquake occurred. This destroyed the embarkation pier and the ship was buffeted by tsunami tidal waves. In an attempt to free herself she went astern but her screws caught up in the anchor chains of another ship and this left her powerless to manoeuvre. After twice colliding with the Japanese *Lyons Maru* (Nippon Yusen K.K.) she was at the mercy of burning surface oil spreading across the harbour. The coastal tanker *Iris* (Petroleum Maats.'La Corona'), also abandoning the anchorage, answered her S.O.S, put a line aboard and towed the bows of *Empress of Australia* round to seawards and took her clear of the oil. Away from the danger the liner anchored and gave aid. Over 3,000 people were then rescued by the ship's boats.

1926 Aug: Her slow, 16½ kts, original engines were replaced with a pair of srg Parsons's turbines at Fairfield SB & Eng'g Co. 20,440 shp, 6dbl + 1 sgl Scotch blrs, 220 psl. 19 kts (20.34 on trials). Oil: 150 tpd. To preserve the lovely accommodation the fitting of the boilers was via No. 2 hold with the intervening bulkheads being temporarily cut. They went in with 1¼ inches/3.17 cm to spare. P 400 1st, 150 2nd, 630 3rd.

1927 Emerged with a white hull. Placed on the Atlantic express service. June 25: Carried the Prince of Wales (Edward VIII), Prince George (George VI) and Prime Minister Stanley Baldwin Southampton-Quebec, *via Sherbourg.*

1933 P 387 1st, 394 Tst, 358 3rd.

1939 May 6: At his personal choice, she carried King George VI and Queen Elizabeth from Portsmouth to Quebec. Sept: Requisitioned for trooping duties. She continued in this service for the remainder of her career.

1952 May 7: Sold to British Iron & Steel Corporation and scrapped by Thos W. Ward at Inverkeithing.

Drawing on page 95

173 EMPRESS OF SCOTLAND (I)

B 1905 Vulkan Werke A.G., Stettin. **T** 24,581g. 14,968n.
D 677.5/206.5 x 77.3/23.57 x 50.2/15.29.
E Tw scr, 2 x 4 cyl quad exp, 2,992 nhp, 8 dbl blrs, 51 furn, 17 kts. By builder.
H Steel. 4 + shelter dk. F 84/25.6. **P** 652 1st, 286 2nd, 216 3rd, 1,843 Steerage. Crew 593.

1904 Laid down as *Europa*. A development of the Harland & Wolff built *Amerika*.

1905 Aug 29: Launched by the Kaiserin for the Hamburg America Line and r/n *Kaiserin Auguste Victoria* in her honour; the largest ship in the world until *Mauretania* of 1907.

1906 May 10: M/v Hamburg-New York. Rather a piled up looking vessel, perhaps with one deck too many. She had a tendency, in a cross sea, to hesitate at the end of a roll - as if unable to make up her mind whether to recover or not - but was very steady steaming into a seaway.

1914 Aug: Laid up at Hamburg for the duration of the war but was modified for possible use as a troop transport and was kept ready for sea service.

1919 Ceded to Great Britain; Shipping Controller. March: Arrived at Hull (See 172). Chartered by the U.S. Shipping Board and used to repatriate United States troops.

1920 Chartered to Cunard. Feb 14: First sailing Liverpool-New York.

1921 May 13: Acquired at Liverpool. R/n *Empress of Scotland*. Returned to Vulcan Werft, Hamburg, for overhaul. Converted to oil burning. T 25,037g. P 459 1st, 478 2nd, 536 3rd.

1922 Jan 22: First CPR voyage Southampton-New York to take, Feb 2, a New York-Mediterranean cruise on charter to a New York travel agency. Then Southampton-Quebec; she could not get up to Montreal.

1923 June: Collided at Hamburg with the steamer *Bonus*, Red. Johannes Ick.

1927 Brought back the Prince of Wales' party from Quebec-Southampton.

1930 Dec 2: Sold to Hughes, Bolckow, Blyth, for scrapping. Dec 10: Caught fire and gutted and finally sank at her berth.

1931 May: Raised. June 1: Broke in two while being moved to her place of final demolition.

Drawing on page 95

174 MONTCALM (III)

B 1920 John Brown & Co., Clydebank, Glasgow. **T** 16,418g, 9,789n.
D 549.5/167.49 x 70.2/21.38 x 40.2/12.24.
E Tw scr, 2 x 2 srg Brown-Curtis stm turbs, 2,476 nhp, 10 sgl oil fired blrs (coal fired if needed). 17½ kts. By builder.

H Steel. 2 + shelter dk. F & B 490/149.35. Upper B 265/80.77.
P 542 Cabin, 1,286 3rd. Crew 370.
1920 Originally five, possibly six, were intended but building costs were so high that the order was restricted to three. Constructed with gun mountings installed in the hull - hence the instant call up of the trio on 1939. July 3: Launched. Cost £1,800,000 each. The standard of the Cabin Class accommodation was the best yet seen.
1922 Jan 17: M/v Liverpool-Halifax-Saint John. During the voyage she rescued 23 out of the 32 crew of the Norwegian steamer *Mod*, Ivarans Rederi, inbound on her first voyage. Heyn's *Melmore Head* was also there.
1928 Dec 6: Arrived at Harland & Wolff, Belfast for re-engining with six sgl reduction geared turbines, 10 sgl brs, 215 psi, 2,390 nhp.
1929 Mar 16: First sailing Southampton-Saint John, NB. Then placed on Antwerp-Southampton-Saint John and later Antwerp-Southampton-Montreal.
1930 Made one of CP's only two calls at Reykjavik.
1932 Used for cruising out of Liverpool.
1939 Aug 25: Taken over; converted into an Armed Merchant Cruiser. 2 x twin 6 inch guns. R/n HMS *Wolfe* to avoid confusion with the French cruiser of the same name.
1941 Nov: Used as a trooper.
1942 Jan: Converted into a submarine depot ship. Given the vertical rig of the era, as drawn. May 22: Purchased by the Admiralty. Served with the 3rd Submarine Flotilla.
1943 Used as a destroyer depot ship. Complement 1,302. By now she had 52 light AA guns. There were other modifications; ie derricks replaced the lattice girder cranes.
1944 Transferred to the Eastern Fleet, Trincomalee.
1950 Laid up in the reserve fleet still as HMS *Wolfe*.
1952 Nov 7: Sold to Metal Industries (Salvage) Ltd and towed to Faslane for breaking up.

175 MONTMORENCY / MONTROSE (II)

As *Montcalm* except: **B** Fairfield SB & Eng'g Co., Govan. **T** 16,402g, 9,824n.
D She was 1 foot/.3m shorter. Ident: *Montrose*, only, had bulwarks from the bow to the fore deck-house which also had the first six feet/1.83m plated.
1919 Laid down as *Montmorency*. **1920** Dec 14: Launched as *Montrose*.
1922 May 5: M/v Liverpool-Quebec-Montreal. **1929** May 29: First sailing Hamburg-Montreal.
1931 Re-engined like her sister at Harland & Wolff, Belfast. Employed as a cruise ship.
1939 Sept 3: Requisitioned the day war broke out for use as an Armed Merchant Cruiser. Became HMS *Forfar*. 8 x 6 inch guns, 2 x 3 in AA. Crew 190. Deployed on the Northern Patrol out of Scapa Flow and Loch Ewe.
1940 Dec 1: Torpedoed by *U-99* 500 miles off the coast of Ireland. The ship sank the following day. 36 officers, including her Captain N.A.C. Hardy, and 136 ratings were lost. Only 3 officers and 15 ratings were rescued.

176 METAPEDIA / MONTCLARE

Details as *Montcalm* except: **B** 1921. **T** 16,314g, 9,724n.
1919 Laid down as *Metapedia*.
1921 Dec 17: Her launching ceremony had to be postponed due to high winds. Dec 18: Launched as *Montclare*. **1922** Aug 18: M/v Liverpool-Quebec-Montreal.
1928 July 26: Landed over 100 pilgrims at Westport, Co. Mayo. The largest ever to call.
1929 Jan: Re-engined like her sisters at Belfast. She was the second of the trio to be done. All three engines having been ordered at the same time with the vessels going to Belfast as each set of turbines became available. May 22: Re-entered service on the Antwerp-Saint John, NB service.
1930 Mar 20: First sailing Hamburg-Saint John. It should be remembered that Saint John was the Atlantic coast terminal of CPR.
1931 Aug 21: Left Glasgow on the final ex-Allan Line direct Glasgow-Montreal sailing.
1933 Cruising until the advent of war.
1939 Aug 28: One of the 56 liners requisitioned for use as an Armed Merchant Cruiser.

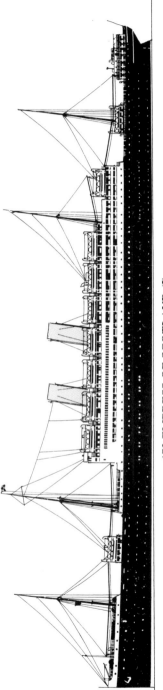

173 EMPRESS OF SCOTLAND (I)

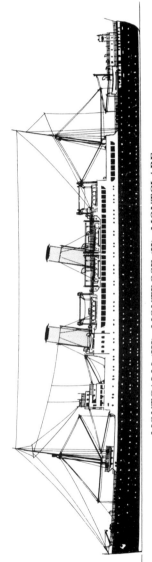

MONTCALM (III), MONTROSE (II), MONTCLARE

1942 Converted, like *Montrose*, into a submarine depot ship. Her design and appearance being the same. May: On completion acquired by the Admiralty as HMS *Montclare*.
1944 Became the flagship of Rear-Admiral Fisher's Pacific fleet supply train.
1946 Acted as submarine mother ship at Rothesay.
1954 Oct 12: After de-commissioning towed to the Gareloch in reserve.
1955 Transferred to Portsmouth for care and maintenance. Feb 4: During the voyage she broke adrift from the Admiralty tugs *Warden* and *Enforcer* 25 miles west of the Scillies but was recovered. Sept: Placed on the disposal list.
1958 Jan: Towed by *Englishman* and *Merchantman* (both United Towing) to Inverkeithing where she was scrapped by Thos W. Ward.

177 EMPRESS OF CANADA (I)

B 1922 Fairfield SB & Eng'g Co., Govan. **T** 21,517g, 12,811n.
D 627/191.11 x 77.7/23.67 x 42/12.8.
E Tw scr, 2 x 3 Curtis-Brown drg turbs, 23,000 shp, 8 dbl + 1 sgl blr. 18 kts. By builder. Oil: 2,475 tons at 220 tpd.
H Steel. 4 + shelter dk. C 377,000/10.675.5cu g + 15,900/450.24cu ref in 7 chambers specially designed to carry silk.
P 488 1st, 1-06 2nd, 288 3rd, 926 Steerage for Asiatics only. Crew 530.
1920 Aug 17: Launched by Mrs G.M. Bosworth, wife of the Chairman. Cost £1,700,000. At her launch the economics were detailed. She had to earn £60,000 per round voyage more than would have occurred pre-war. Working expenses having gone up by 350% while fares had risen only by 185%.
1922 Her completion was delayed by strikes. May 5: M/v Falmouth-Suez Canal-Hong Kong then onto the transpacific service.
1923 Sept 1: At Yokohama when the earthquake struck and rendered assistance. See 172.
1924 Jan 30: Left New York on CPR's first Round-the-World cruise.
1927 March: Collided with the Japanese steamer *Kinsho Maru*, Mewa Kisen, at Shanghai.
1928 Re-engined by builder, 26,000 shp, 21 kts. Given a buff strake at bridge deck level.
1929 Sept 18: Made one round voyage Southampton-Quebec then proceeded back, via the Panama Canal, to her Vancouver berth.
1932 Nov 7: Collided with the Japanese *Yetai Maru* on passage Kobe-Shanghai.
1939 Nov 29: After completing 200 Pacific crossings the ship was requisitioned for trooping duties. **1941** Aug: Took part in the Spitsbergen Raid.
1943 Mar 1: Left Durban with 1,800 aboard including 200 Poles (released by Russia when Germany invaded) and 400 Italian p.o.w's, in the forward hold - locked up only at night - plus several hundred naval personnel. Because of her speed she proceeded out of convoy and, to avoid the usual U-boat threatened route, sailed south towards the Antarctic before circling northwards round Tristan da Cunha Island. Mar 12: The *Empress of Canada* was ordered into Takoradi to pick up another 300 Italians. Mar 13: 23.45 hrs, torpedoed 1,000 miles off the coast of Africa by the Italian submarine *Leonardo da Vinci*. Mar 14: 12.50 hrs, a second torpedo struck and, while still being abandoned, at 13.15 hrs, the ship sank quickly. 392 lives lost (340 passengers, 8 gunners and 44 crew) including half the Italians aboard. A Catalina aircraft found the scattered boats and the destroyer HMS *Boreas* and the sloop HMS *Petunia* arrived to pick up the survivors taking them into Freetown. Here they were re-kitted aboard the base ship *Edinburgh Castle* (Union-Castle) and then put aboard *Mauretania* (Cunard) for the remainder of the journey to the UK.

MOTOR PRINCESS

MOTOR PRINCESS (1955)

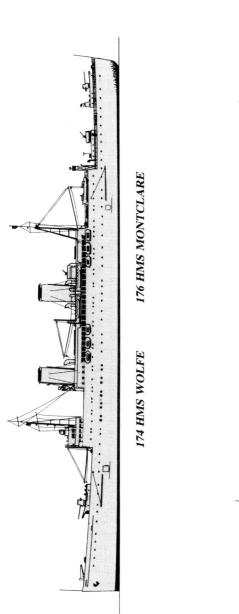

174 HMS WOLFE

176 HMS MONTCLARE

177 EMPRESS OF CANADA (I)

178 **MOTOR PRINCESS / MOTOR PRINCESS** (1955)

B 1923 Yarrows Ltd, Esquimalt, Victoria, B.C. **T** 1,243g, 779n.
D 165/50.29 x 43.5/13.26 x 9/2.74.
E Tw scr, oil. 2 x 6 cyl, 4s.sa, 318 nhp, 14 kts. By McIntosh, Seymour & Co., Auburn, N.Y.
H Wood (Douglas fir and Spruce). Car ferry. **P** 250/370 (2 staterooms only). Cars: 45 (32 main deck + 13 upper deck aft reached by a ramp.
1923 Jan 10: Keel laid. Mar 31: 13.30 hrs. Launched. May 15: Delivered. The first motor vessel built for CPR. Had forward vehicle side loading doors. Cost $243,517. May 23: Daily Bellingham (Washington State) (Dep 08.30)-(Arr 11.30) Sydney (Victoria Island) service (Dep 15.30, 18.30 arr at Quackenbush Dock). Operated by British Columbia Coast Steamship Services (B.C.C.S.S.)
1924 Vancouver-Nanaimo route with *Princess Patricia* (101). Two trips daily.
1929 Replaced by *Princess Elaine* (191). June 15: Transferred to the twice daily Sydney-Steveston summer run. **1942-46** Her service was discontinued due to war shortages.
1949 Following the loss, by fire, of *Noronic* (Canadian National) her passenger certificate was withdrawn. Used for freight only.
1955 Jan: Sold for $1,000 to Gavin C. Mouat, Ganges, Salt Spring Island, B.C. Owned by the Gulf Islands Ferry Company (1951) Ltd. Re-engined and remodelled by the Victoria Machinery Depot Ltd. Given two Fairbanks-Morse 525 hp engines. As drawn.
1956 June 30: Four times daily Fulford Harbour, Salt Spring Is.-Swartz Bay, Vancouver Island, service. **1961** Sept 1: Her owners were acquired by British Columbia Ferry Corp.
1963 R/n *Pender Queen*. Used as a relief ferry.
1979 Autumn: Laid up, out of service, at Dea Dock, Fraser River.
1981 Sold for £75,300 to Clark & Small, Salt Spring Island, for use as a floating hotel at Rivers Inlet for fishermen. Trace lost.

179 **KYOQUOT**

B 1919 J. Crichton & Co., Saltney, Cheshire. **T** 419g, 9n.
D 135.2/41.2 x 29.1/8.86 x 13.6/4.14.
E Sgl scr, tpl exp, 123 nhp, 10 kts. By Fawcett, Preston & Co., Liverpool.
H Steel. 1 dk. F 35/10.67.
1919 Completed as the tug *St Florence* for the Admiralty; one of the 'Rescue Class', all with 'St' names, of which 15 were (eventually) retained by the Royal Navy. The surplus being progressively put up for sale as post-war duties were finalised.
1924 Acquired by CPR. R/n *Kyoquot* after a small port on Vancouver Island.
1925 Jan 25: Left Leith for Victoria via the Panama Canal. Mar 21: Arrived. Used for towing and salvage duties, based Victoria.
1931 Dec: Ran aground at Porlier Passage while towing a barge from Vancouver to Ladysmith.
1932 Feb 26: Salvaged. Repaired with a short modern funnel and a fore mast only.
1957 Laid up at Victoria.
1962 July 11: Arrived for scrapping by General Shipbreaking Co., Vancouver. CPR's last Pacific coast tug.

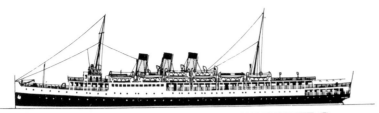

PRINCESS KATHLEEN, PRINCESS MARGUERITE (I)

180 PRINCESS KATHLEEN
B 1925 John Brown & Co., Clydebank. **T** 5,875g, 2,719n.
D 350.1/106.71 x 60.1/18.31 x 17.1/5.21.
E Tw scr, 2 x 2 srg turbs, 2,642 nhp, 22½ kts. By builder.
H Steel. 3 + promenade dk. **P** 600 berthed, 900 dk. 3 vehicles.
1924 Sept 27: Launched by Lady Mount Stephen.
1925 Jan 15: M/v Clyde-Panama-Vancouver. Feb 13: Arrived. Employed on the Vancouver-Victoria-Seattle triangular route.
1939 Sept: Taken up for trooping work which lasted five years.
1946 Operated as a troop transhipment vessel in the eastern Mediterranean. She came alongside the larger troop ships to take off men, up to battalion strength. Grey livery but with black topped funnels. The day that the war ended the crew had painted the funnels back into Canadian Pacific colours and she carried on trooping.
1947 June 22: Resumed her Vancouver-Seattle-Victoria triangular route. **P** 1,800 deck. Made 24 knots after her refit. **1949** June 15: Transferred to the Alaska service.
1951 Aug 30: Collided with Canadian National Rly's *Prince Rupert*. Because *Princess Kathleen* was taking in water her passengers were transferred; both ships made port safely.
1952 Sept 7: Bound Vancouver-Skagway with 300 passengers she went aground, during a gale and at low tide, on Lena Point, Favorite Channel, 31 miles north of Juneau. This left her fore part well up the shore line. When the tide rose it swamped her stern, filling it with water. As the ship started to become bouyant she slid off into deep water to become a total loss. No lives were lost.

181 PRINCESS MARGUERITE (I)
Details as *Princess Kathleen*.
1924 Nov 29: Launched by the Hon. Miss Marguerite Shaughnessy after whom she was named.
1925 Mar 25: M/v Clyde-Panama Canal-Vancouver.
1939 May 29: Carried King George VI and Queen Elizabeth Vancouver-Victoria.
1940 Used as a troop ship in tandem with her sister.
1942 Aug 17: Enroute Port Said-Famagusta, Cyprus, torpedoed, north of Port Said, by *U-83*. She was carrying about 1,000 troops but only 49 lives were lost.

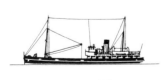

KIPAWO

NOOTKA

182 KIPAWO
B 1925 Saint John Dry Dock & SB Co., Saint John, NB. **T** 200g, 84n.
D 122.9/37.45 oa, 113/34.44 x 26/7.92 x 9/2.74.
E Tw scr, oil. 2 x 4 cyl, 2s.sa, 138 nhp, 10 kts. By Fairbanks, Morse & Co., Beloit, Wisconsin.
H Steel. 1 dk. **P** 127. 8 vehicles.

1925 Built to replace *Prince Albert* (114) on the Kingsport-Parrsboro-Wolfville service.
1940 At the end of the season the service was withdrawn and after a short lay up the ship was requisitioned by the Canadian Government and used as a coastal military supply ship.
1947 Sept 20: Purchased by Crosbie & Co., St Johns, Newfoundland.
1952 Nov 20: Owned by the Terra Nova Transportation Co. with Crosbie & Co. as managers. Used as a car ferry.
1953 Fitted with a Ruston & Hornsby, Lincoln, srg 6 cyl, 4s.sa, oil engine. Operated on the St Johns-Conception Bay interport routes. **1973** Laid up with survey overdue.
1975 June: Owned by Bonavista Bay Boat Tours Ltd, Trinity Bay, NF. Excursion steamer, summer only. **1982** Became part of a floating theatre complex at Wolfsville, NS.

183 NOOTKA

B 1919 Port Arthur SB Co., Port Arthur, Lake Superior. **T** 2,069g, 1,201n.
D 251.3/76.61 x 43.9/13.36 x 20.3/6.2. **E** Sgl scr, tpl exp, 256 nhp, 11 kts. By builder.
H Steel. 1 dk. **F** 25/7.62. **B** 64/19.51. **P** 26/7.92.
1919 Built as the standard ship *Canadian Adventurer*. Owned by the single ship company of the same name and one of over 60 war-built ships operated (unprofitably) by the Canadian Government Merchant Marine Ltd.
1925 R/n *Emperor of Port McNicoll* by Richard's Marine & Transportation Co., Montreal.
1926 Purchased, for £25,000, by CPR for cargo services out of Vancouver along the BC coast. R/n *Nootka*. Converted to oil fuel. She was also given a 171,000 gallon/778,500 litre olive oil cargo tank for serving the pilchard fish canning industry. Later, when she began to carry workers to and from the canneries, she was fitted with three lifeboats on her port side and two to starboard.
1950 Nov 12: Sold to Enrique Echecopar, Lima. R/n *Iquitos*.
1957 Sold to Cia de Nav. y Comercio Amazonas, Lima. Reverted to *Nootka*. **1962** Broken up.

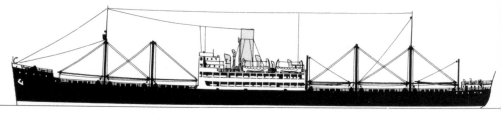

BEAVERBURN (I), BEAVERFORD (I), BEAVERDALE, BEAVERHILL, BEAVERBRAE (I)

184 BEAVERBURN (I)

B 1927 Wm Denny & Bros, Dumbarton. **T** 9,874g, 5,930n, 10,500dwt.
D 503/153.31 x 61.8/18.82 x 37/6/11.46.
E Tw scr, 2 x 3 three-stage srg (24.5:1) Parsons stm turb, 1,516 nhp, 8,000 shp (all five ships), 2 sgl Scotch (for use in port) + 4 Yarrow water tube blrs with Erith-Roe mechanical stokers, 252 psi, 6 furn, 15 kts. Installed by builder. Coal: 2,500 tons.
H Steel, ice strengthened. 2 dks. **F** 48/14.63. **C**: 570,000/16,140.7cu g + 80,000/2,265.3 refrig. in 6 holds. Fuel: 1,308 tons coal. **P** 12. Crew 79.
1926 June 25: Ordered as the prototype for the class of five. Specified to maintain 14½ knots in all weathers on a London-Canada weekly service. Of Denny design - but the order was given to three Yards for speed of delivery. At the time they were notable for having all accommodation amidships and above the main deck.
1927 Sept 27: Launched. She was the first ship to be fitted with Erith-Roe automatic stokers. Cost £262,823. Dec 24: M/v Glasgow-Canada.
1940 Feb 5: In convoy OA.84 (= Southend-Outwards, America), torpedoed by *U-41* in the North Atlantic. The U-boat was then sunk by the convoy escorts.

185 BEAVERFORD (I)

As *Beaverburn* except: **B** 1928 Barclay, Curle & Co., Glasgow. **T** 10,042g, 6,060n.
1927 Oct 28: Launched. **1928** Jan 21: M/v Glasgow-Canada.
1940 Feb 22: Requisitioned by the Admiralty for the carriage of vital war cargoes. Nov 5: *Beaverford* was a member of the 38 ship convoy HX 84 inward bound across the Atlantic. The commodore was Rear-Admiral H.B. Maltby flying his flag in Reardon Smith's *Cornish City*. The escorting auxiliary cruiser was *Jervis Bay*, Captain E.S. Fogarty Fegen. At 17.00 hrs, 1,000 miles east of Newfoundland, the convoy was attacked by the German 'Pocket Battleship' - Heavy Cruiser - *Admiral Scheer*. The range was ten miles and *Jervis Bay's* 6-inch guns could not strike back at the enemy's 11 inch main armament; nevertheless she steamed at the enemy and for an hour, still unable effectively to reply, bore the brunt of the attack until, with every gun out of action, she sank with the loss of 180 dead, including her captain who received a postumous Victoria Cross. 65 were picked up by a Swedish ship (Capt Sven Olander) which, with extraordinary bravery turned back. During the *Jervis Bay* action the enemy's 5.9 inch guns fired upon *San Demetrio* (Eagle oil) setting the ship on fire but her escape to safety is another epic. The faster *Admiral Scheer* now set off in pursuit of the convoy, overhauling *Beaverford* at some 12 miles distance. The scattering ships were now given more time to escape into the darkness by *Beaverford*, Capt. E. Pettigrew, which, knowing that she was doomed anyway, courageously steamed straight for the attacking German before being sunk with the loss of all 77 hands. *Beaverford* was only armed with two 4-inch guns, one forward and one aft. But the *Admiral Scheer* was unaware of this and cautiously held off, using only her big guns. *Beaverford's* action enabled most of the remainder of the convoy to escape. Only six ships out of the 38 were lost. The other five were: *Fresno City* (Readon Smith - one killed), *Kenbane Head* (G. Heyn), *Maidan* (Brocklebank – all 90 lost), *Mopan* (Elder & Fyffes – 68 taken prisoner. She was ahead of the convoy and was stopped by *Admiral Scheer* before HX.84 was reached) and *Trewellard* (Hain). This action underlines the differing naval strategies. The German was to 'maintain a fleet in being' and her surface warships were not permitted to endanger themselves. British policy has always been 'attack any enemy, anywhere, anytime'. In this case, also, the standard British 'attack' strategy had caused the German to use up over a third of his ammunition in the first week of his 160 day sortie (Home: Kiel Apr 1 1941).

186 BEAVERDALE

Sister of *Beaverburn* except: **B** and **E** 1928 Sir W.G. Armstrong, Whitworth & Co., Newcastle. **T** 9,957g, 6,005n.
1927 Oct 12: Launched. Her Babcock & Wilcox blrs were hand fuelled.
1928 Feb 1: M/v Newcastle-Antwerp-Saint John, NB.
1939 Sept 13: Requisitioned for the carriage of vital war cargoes.
1941 Apr 1: Torpedoed in convoy SC.26 (= Sydney-UK, assembly port New York) and then shelled by *U-48* in the North Atlantic. 21 dead and 37 wounded. In all 14 ships were sunk by seven U-boats.

187 BEAVERHILL

Details as *Beaverburn* except: **B** 1928 Barclay, Curle & Co., Glasgow. **T** 10,041g, 6,060n.
1927 Nov 8: Launched. **1928** Feb 18: M/v Glasgow-Canada.
1940 May 3: Requisitioned for the carriage of vital war cargoes.
1941 Fitted for the austerity carriage of 138 passengers.
1944 Nov 24: Went aground on Hillyard's Reef, Saint John, NB, where she remained fast and broke in two.
1946 Dec 11: The stern half was refloated and towed into Saint John where it sank at its berth. After refloating it was towed out to sea and scuttled off Grand Manan Island.

188 BEAVERBRAE (I)

Details as *Beaverburn* except: **B** 1928 Sir W.G. Armstrong, Whitworth & Co., Newcastle.
1927 Nov 24: Launched. **1928** Mar 15: M/v Newcastle-Antwerp-Halifax-Saint John.
1940 Mar 1: Requisitioned by the Admiralty for war service cargoes.
1941 Mar 25: Sunk by enemy aircraft in the North Atlantic, position 60.12N 09.00 W.

---

189 GRANTHALL

B 1927 Canadian Vickers, Montreal. **T** 164g. **D** 92/28.04 x 24.1/7.34 x 10.3/3.14.
E Sgl scr, tpl exp, 9 kts. By builder. **H** Steel. 1 dk.
1927 Tug. After construction dismantled and carried west by rail on ten flat cars.
1928 Mar 7: Launched at Nelson, BC. Mar 10: Trials. Service: Towing barges Kootenay
Landing-Proctor. **195**7 Laid up when Ivan Horie took over the work for CPR.
1964 Sold to the Yellowknife Transportation Co. in service at New Westminster. Not seagoing.
Trace lost.

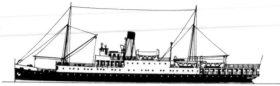

190 PRINCESS NORAH / QUEEN OF THE NORTH / PRINCESS NORAH

B 1928 Fairfield SB & Eng'g Co., Govan, Glasgow. **T** 2,731g, 1,519n.
D 250.1/76.23 x 48.1/14.66 x 23/7.01.
E Sgl scr, tpl exp, 437 nhp, 16 kts. By buildcer.
H Steel. 2 dks. **P** 450. 9 vehicles.
1928 Sept 27: Launched, Dec 20: M/v Glasgow-Panama Canal-Vancouver.
1929 Jan 23: Arrived. Placed on the West Coast ports of Vancouver Island service.
1942 Used for two years as a US troopship between Seattle and Alaska.
1949 Transferred to Vancouver-Alaskan ports route.
1955 Sept: R/n *Queen of the North* for the Portland Canal-Kitimat joint service with Canadian National Railways.
1957 When the service was discontinued she reverted to *Princess Norah*. Put up for sale.
1958 July: Sold to the Northland Navigation Co., Vancouver. R/n *Canadian Prince*. Coastal cargo and passenger service out of Vancouver.
1964 Her engines were removed and she was towed to Kodiak for use as a restaurant and dance hall. Oct: R/n *Beachcomber*. Trace lost.

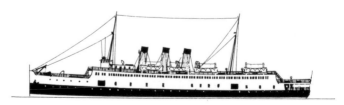

191 PRINCESS ELAINE

B 1928 John Brown & Co., Clydebank. **T** 2,027g, 725n.
D 291.4/88.82 x 48.1/14.66 x 13.4/4.09. **E** Tpl scr, 3 srg Brown-Curtis stm turbs, 934 nhp, 2 Yarrow wt blrs, 200 psi, oil fuel, 19½ kts. By builder.
H Steel. 2 + promenade dk. **B** 280/85.34. **P** 1,200. Vehicles: 60.

1927 Oct 26: Launched. CPR's first ship designed with the carriage of motorcars in numbers. The vehicles were side loaded over special gangways onto the car deck. The doors were situated fore and aft so that a drive through flow could be used. One vehicle turn-table was also installed.
1928 Mar 17: M/v Clyde-Panama Canal-Vancouver. May 7: Replaced *Princess Patricia* (101) on the 40 mile/64.37 km Nanaimo service.
1955 Oct: Damaged her stem when she hit the barge *VT 25* in Vancouver harbour entrance. Continued her voyage.
1960 Jan 11: Collided with the coaster *Alaska Prince*, British Columbia S.S. Co.
1963 Dec 30: Towed to Blaine, Washington State to become a floating restaurant.
1967 Moved to Seattle and dismantled ten years later.

192 ROSEBERY (I)
B 1928 CPR, Rosebery. **T** 133g, 6n. **D** 92/28.04 x 20/6.1 x 7/2.13.
E Sgl scr, 2 cyl comp, 27 rhp. By Collingwood SB Co., Ontario. **H** Wood. 1 dk.
1928 Tug on Lake Slocan.
1943 Withdrawn from service. Replaced by *Rosebery* (II) (202)

Profile on page 105

193 DUCHESS OF BEDFORD / EMPRESS OF FRANCE (II)
B 1928 John Brown & Co., Clydebank. **T** 20,123g, 11,887n, 8,750dwt.
D 581.9/177.34 x 75.2/22.91 x 41.7/12.7.
E Tw scr, 2 x 3 Parsons 2,000 rpm stm turb, srg to 120 rpm, 3,557 nhp, 20,000 shp, 6 Yarrow wt blrs, 370 psi, 6 furn. 17½ kts (19 kts max). By builder. Oil: 2,725 tons.
H Steel. 4 dks. F & B 520/158.5. Prom dk 325/99.06.
P 580 Cabin, 480 Tst, 510 3rd. Crew 510.
1928 Jan 24: Launched by Mrs Stanley Baldwin, wife of the Prime Minister. June 1: M/v Liverpool-Quebec-Montreal.
1933 Feb: Chartered by Furness, Withy to run alongside the new *Monarch of Bermuda* pending the arrival of the *Queen of Bermuda*.
1939 Aug 29: Requisitioned for trooping with voyages to Bombay.
1942 Aug 9: Credited with sinking a U-boat but none identified.
1943 Trooped West Africa-Burma with colonial regiments.
1947 Decommissioned. Mar 2: Left Liverpool for Govan. Mar 3: Arrived at Fairfield SB & E Co. for refitting. Initially she was to have been r/n *Empress of India* but because of independence the name was not bestowed. Emerged as *Empress of France* as drawn.
1948 Sept 1: First sailing Liverpool-Quebec-Montreal. **T** 20,448g. **P** 400 1st, 482 tst.
1958 Pepper pot funnels fitted as inset drawing.
1960 Dec 19: Left Liverpool to be broken up by John Cashmore, Newport, Mon. Her Empress Bar is now in the Barry Hotel, Barry, Glamorgan.

194 DUCHESS OF ATHOLL
As *Duchess of Bedford*. **B** 1928 Wm Beardmore & Co., Dalmuir. **T** 20,119g, 11,872n.
D 582/177.39.
1927 Nov 23: Launched by the Duchess of Atholl. The first of the four. While fitting out a sling snapped and a vital part of her machinery fell and smashed. Completion was thereby delayed and she was the second to enter service.
1928 July 13: M/v Liverpool-Quebec-Montreal.
1935 Dec 30: Lost her rudder and arrived at Liverpool three days late having used her screws as steerage. **1939** Dec 30: Taken over for trooping duties.
1942 May 5: As part of convoy WS 17 (WS = Winston's Specials) she took part in the Madagascar landings at Courier Bay, Diego Suarez intended to stop the Japanese from cutting

the vital lifeline to the Middle East. The three other troopships were *Oronsay* (Orient), *Sobieski* (Gdynia America) and *Winchester Castle* (Union-Castle) plus the assault ships *Karanja, Karen* (both British India), *Royal Ulsterman* (Burns & Laird) and *Bachaquero* (Lago Shipping). They were escorted by 27 warships including the battleships *Ramillies* and *Malaya*, the aircraft carriers *Illustrious* and *Indomitable*, the cruisers *Devonshire* and *Hermione* plus the 12th Destroyer Flotilla. *Atlantis* (Royal Mail) was their hospital ship.

Oct 10: Torpedoed by *U-178* some 200 miles north of Ascension Island. 4 killed.

195 DUCHESS OF RICHMOND / EMPRESS OF CANADA (II)

As *Duchess of Atholl* except: **B** 1929. **T** 20,022g, 11,821n.

1928 June 18: Launched. **1929** Jan 26: M/v was a cruise to the Canary Islands.

1932 Nov: Collided with Cunard's *Alaunia* off Sorel, Quebec.

1935 Jan 25: Carried the Duke and Duchess of Kent on their honeymoon cruise.

1940 Feb 14: Requisitioned for trooping. Her first sailing was Liverpool-Mediterranean-Suez (Italy only came into the war on June 10).

1946 May: At Fairfield, Glasgow, for refurbishing. **T** 20,325g. **P** 397 1st, 303 Tst.

1947 July 12: Returned to service as *Empress of Canada*. White livery (Drawing 195A).

July 16: First post-war sailing Liverpool-Quebec-Montreal. Departures were every third Wednesday. Winter was to Saint John, NB.

1953 Jan 25: Caught fire and capsized onto her berth at Gladstone Dock, Liverpool. Work to right the ship was commenced immediately by the Mersey Docks & Harbour Board salvage team but the ship lay on her side until March 1954. Masts, funnels and superstructure had to be cut away. Tall inverted 'V' shaped spars were welded to the upper side of her hull at main deck level. Each of these was connected by wire ropes to a static winch on the far side of the dock. All the remaining openings in the hull were sealed.

1954 March: The water was pumped out of the hull while, at the same time, the winches took up the strain and commenced to haul the hull upright. Mar 6: Righting finished. The work had cost £450,000. June 30: Moved into Gladstone Dry Dock where she was made watertight (and condemned). Aug: Sold to Cantiere di Portovenere, Genoa, for scrap. Sept 1: Left in tow of Smit's tug *Zwarte Zee*. Oct 10: Arrived at La Spezia for demolition.

196 DUCHESS OF CORNWALL / DUCHESS OF YORK

Sister of *Duchess of Atholl* except: **T** 20,021g, 11,822n.

1927 The ship was ordered as *Duchess of Cornwall*. There being, at the time, no such person it was decided to rename her after a living Duchess.

1928 Sept 9: Launched by the Duchess of York. The Southampton, Isle of Wight & South of England Royal Mail S.P. Co. (Britain's longest owner's title) had a *Duchess of York*. To free the name they renamed their vessel *Duchess of Cornwall*.

1929 Mar 22: M/v Liverpool-Saint John. **1931** Jan-May: Cruised New York-Bermuda.

1940 Mar 7: Requisitioned for trooping. June 21: Carried 500 German p.o.w's plus 1,700 German seamen and 400 internees to Canada. Enroute one sailor was killed when a crowd, told to go below, panicked and a shot was fired by a guard. A British officer was court-martialled.

1943 July 11: Enroute with troops Clyde-Freetown when off the coast of Morocco, she was set on fire by air attack from long range bombers. The fire could not be brought under control and the troops were taken off by the escorting destroyers *Douglas* and *Iroquois* plus the frigate *Moyola*. 11 lives lost. Mar 8: 12.45 hrs, the hulk was torpedoed.

Profile on page 107

197 EMPRESS OF JAPAN (II) / EMPRESS OF SCOTLAND (II)

B 1929 Fairfield SB & Eng'g Co., Govan, Glasgow. **T** 26,032g, 15,725n.

666 **D** 644/196.29 x 83.8/25.53 x 44.5/13.56.

ofl. **E** Tw scr, 2 x 3 srg stm turbs, 6,475 nhp, 6 wt blrs, 425 psi. 22 kts. By builder.

H Steel. 3 dks. F & B 578/176.17. Upper B 443/135.03.

P 399 1st, 164 2nd, 100 3rd, 510 Steerage. Crew 579.

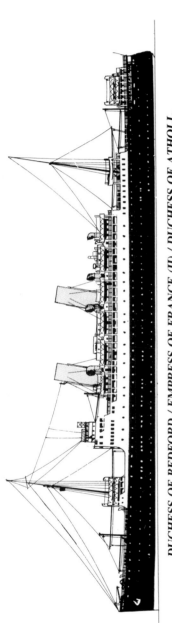

DUCHESS OF BEDFORD / EMPRESS OF FRANCE (II) / DUCHESS OF ATHOLL,
DUCHESS OF RICHMOND / EMPRESS OF CANADA (II), DUCHESS OF YORK

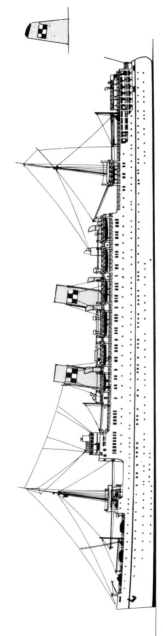

EMPRESS OF FRANCE (II) / EMPRESS OF CANADA (II)

1929 Dec 17: Launched. She had an open promenade deck for Pacific weather (as drawn).
1930 June 14: M/v Liverpool-Quebec-Southampton. July 12: Southampton-Suez-Hong Kong. Aug 7: Hong Kong-Yokohama-Vancouver. White livery - she never had a peacetime black hull. The fastest and finest vessel on the route. **1939** Nov 26: Requisitioned for trooping duties.
1940 Nov 9: Dive bombed off Ireland but she managed to evade the sticks aimed at her.
1942 Oct 16: Ten months after the attack on Pearl Harbor she was r/n *Empress of Scotland* due to protests about the continued use of an enemy name. At the time changes of name were prohibited; in this case said Churchill 'it is a nonsense'.
1948 May 2: Arrived at Liverpool at the end of her trooping work. She had steamed 600,000 miles and her log recorded that she had berthed 138 times. Oct: Went, when her turn came, for refitting to her builder. It was intended to return her to the Pacific but circumstances in the Far East dictated otherwise. She emerged with her promenade deck glassed in for Atlantic service. T 26,313g. P 458 1st, 250 Tst. Crew 480.
1950 May 9: First post-war sailing Liverpool-Greenock-Quebec. In winter she cruised New York-West Indies.
1952 Apr: Her masts were shortened to allow the ship to pass under Quebec Bridge and to sail up to Montreal which had now been dredged to her draught. May 13: First sailing.
1957 Nov 25: At the season's end laid up at Liverpool. Later dry docked at Belfast.
1958 Jan 13: Sold to the Hamburg Atlantic Line. Managers: Hamburg America Line. Jan 19: Left for delivery to Hamburg as *Scotland*, flying the German ensign. Jan 22: Arrived at Hamburg. R/n *Hanseatic*. At Hamburg she was rebuilt, modernised and given two funnels which detracted from her classic profile. T 30,030g. D 673/205.2 oa. P 85 1st, 1,167 Tst, July 21: First sailing Cuxhaven-Le Havre-Southampton-Cobh-New York. She went cruising during the off season.
1966 Sept 7: Caught fire, in the engine room, at New York. Sept 23: Left New York for Hamburg in tow of the Bugsier tugs *Atlantic* and *Pacific*. Delivered to Howaldtswerke Shipyard but found to be beyond economic repair. Dec 2: Sold for scrap to Eckhardt & Co. Broken up by Eisen & Metall A.G., Hamburg.

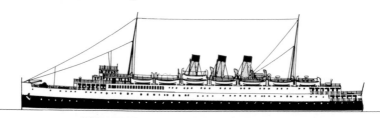

PRINCESSS ELIZABETH / PRINCESS JOAN

198 **PRINCESS ELIZABETH**
B 1930 Fairfield SB & Eng'g Co., Govan. **T** 5,251g, 3,023n.
D 353.3/107.7 x 52.1/15.87 x 25.2/7.67. **E** Tw scr, 2 x 4 cyl quad exp, 622 nhp, 16 kts. By builder.
H Steel. 2 + car deck. **F** & **B** 307/95.57. **P** 1,000. Cars: 48.
1930 Jan 16: Launched. Mar 27: M/v Clyde-Panama Canal-Victoria. May 3: Arrived. Placed on the Vancouver-Victoria route.
1960 Dec: Sold to Epirotiki S.S. Co., Piraeus. R/n *Pegasus*. A single modern funnel was fitted and she was given a curved stem. Used on the Venice-Patras-Corinth Canal-Piraeus service. She later went onto cruising. Owned by Epirotiki's Hellenic Mediterranean Cruises & Car Ferry Co.
1973 Feb 14: Left Piraeus. Chartered to Brown & Root Inc., Houston, for service as an accommodation ship at Niggs Bay, Cromarty Firth, for North Sea oil workmen who were building an oil exploration platform. Mar 3: Arrived. R/n *Highland Queen*.
1975 Sold by Epirotiki to Highland Shipping Co.
1976 Mar 26: Left the River Tees in tow for Zeebrugge. Broken up, at Bruges, by Bruges Scheepssloperij N.V..

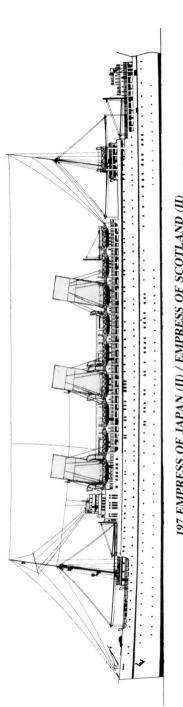

197 EMPRESS OF JAPAN (II) / EMPRESS OF SCOTLAND (II)

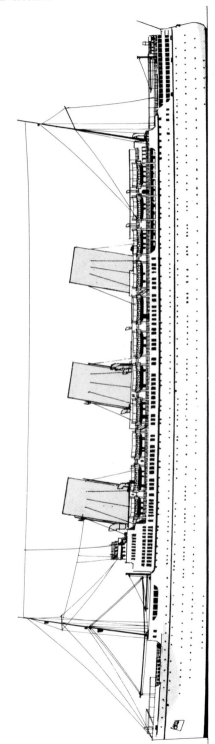

201 EMPRESS OF BRITAIN (II)

199 PRINCESS JOAN
As *Princess Elizabeth*.
1930 Mar 4: Launched. Apr 15: Delivery voyage to Victoria. May 16: Arrived. Joined her sister on the Victoria-Vancouver route.
1959 Feb 24: Made her final crossing at the end of 29 years service. Mar 27: Laid up.
1960 Dec: Sold, with her sister, to Epirotiki. R/n *Hermes*. Rebuilt like her sister and placed on the same weekly service which was extended to Haifa. Operated by Hellenic Maritime Transports Co. S.A., Piraeus.
1970 Sold for $525,000 to the Government of Nigeria. To be used as a floating hotel.
Sept 28: Arrived at Lagos. Later her owners became L. Dupes & Associates, Cyprus.
1973 Oct 22: Became an accommodation vessel at Niggs Bay alongside her sister.
1974 Owned by Loima Shipping Co. Same name. Aug 29: Arrived at Inverkeithing and broken up by Thos. W. Ward.

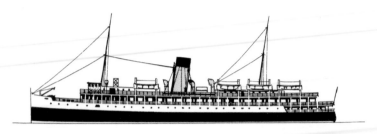

200 PRINCESS HELENE
B 1930 Wm Denny & Bros., Dumbarton. **T** 4,055g, 2,022n.
D 320.1/97.56 x 50.6/15.42 x 24.3/7.42.
E Tw scr, 2 x 3 stage sgr stm turb, 1,123 nhp, 2 Johnston wt blrs (the first to be fitted), 265 psi. 19 kts. By builder. Fuel: 367 tons oil.
H Steel. 2 dks. F & B 256/78.03. **P** 1,000 (114 berthed) + 45 cars. Crew 48.
1929 July 11: Ordered. Sept 27: Keel laid. Her building was superintended by Canadian Pacific Steamships for CPR. Cost £224,940.
1930 May 12: Launched. Aug : Trials, 19.42 knots at 6,305 bhp and 217.45 rpm. Aug 13: Delivered. Aug 22: Arrived at Saint John, NB, for the 3-hour Saint John-Digby service which she did twice daily six days per week. Her departures being connected to train arrival times. The ship was designed with an extra Scotch boiler for use only when in port.
1963 Feb: Withdrawn from service. May: Sold to Marvic Navigation Co., Liberia. July 11: Left Saint John for the Mediterranean as *Helene* for use as a car ferry. Sold to Chandris Lines. R/n *Carina II*. (They had *Carina* ex-*Mona's Queen*, I.O.M.S.P. Co.) Given a curved stem, fore mast only and white livery. Funnel Blue, black top and white X
1967 Nov: R/n *Carina* when the other *Carina* was r/n *Fiesta*; owned by the Chandris subsidiary International Cruises S.A., Piraeus.
1977 Mar 7: Sold for breaking up to Kyriazi Bros., Perama. Mar 15: Work commenced.

Drawing on page 107

201 EMPRESS OF BRITAIN (II)
B 1931 John Brown & Co., Clydebank. **T** 42,348g, 22,545n.
D 760.6/231.84 oa, 733.3/223.52 x 97.8/29.79 x 56/17.07.
E Quad scr, 12 srg Curtis-Brown stm turbs, 62,500 shp, 9 wt blrs (8 Yarrow + 1 Johnson; he was their Chief Superintendent Engineer), 24 kts. By builder.
H Steel. 4 dks. F & B 649/197.82. Upper B 545/166.12.
P 465 1st, 260 Tst, 470 3rd. Crew 740.
1930 June 11: Launched by Edward, Prince of Wales. CP's largest passenger ship and the largest ever in service to Canada.

1931 Apr 13: Trails. Averaged 25.27 over the measured mile. May 27: M/v Southampton-Cherbourg-Quebec. Her departure being witnessed by the Prince of Wales. Her crossing in 4 days, 19 hrs, 35 mins Cherbourg-Father Point was a record. Dec 3: Her first world cruise of the winter was from New York during which she became the, then, largest vessel to go through the Suez Canal. For her winter work her two outer propellers were removed and two turbines shut down.
1932 July 18: Collided, superficially, with *Briarwood* (Joseph Constantine) off Saguenay River. Neither vessel being delayed.
1934 Aug 9: Arrived at Cherbourg after a record crossing from Belle Isle of 4 days, 6 hrs, 58 mins.
1935 June 16: In fog in the St Lawrence she was in collision with *Kafiristan* (Common Bros) which suffered three fcsle dead and several injured. *Beaverford* (208) took *Kafiristan* in tow. *Empress of Britain* was able to continue.
1939 June 15: King George VI and Queen Elizabeth boarded at Halifax for their return from Canada to Southampton (arr. May 22). Sept 2: Left Southampton on her final commercial service. She remained at Quebec. Nov 25: Requisitioned for trooping. Made two crossings Halifax-Clyde with troops, on each occasion escorted by destroyers.
1940 Mar 17: Left Southampton for Australia and New Zealand to bring back troops. May 12: Left Fremantle in a troop convoy with *Empress of Canada* (177), Cunard's *Queen Mary, Aquitania* and, *Mauretania* (II) plus Royal Mail's *Andes* (II). Aug 6: Left Liverpool in convoy WS2 (= Winston's Specials. UK-Middle East) via the Cape for Suez. She then set off back, leaving Cape Town with 643 persons aboard, but was destined never to arrive. Oct 26: Off the west coast of Ireland, the ship was set on fire by attack from a long range Focke-Wulf Condor aircraft. The blaze was soon out of control and abandon ship was ordered except for a skeleton crew. She was next taken in tow by the Polish destroyer *Burza* joined by the tugs *Marauder* and *Thames*. But her position was known and *U-32* made for her, stalking her for nearly 24 hours. Oct 28: Torpedoed twice by *U-32* (a third exploded prematurely). *Empress of Britain* sank with the loss of 45 lives, most of whom were killed in the initial air attack. *U-32* was sunk by the destroyer *Harvester* two days later. *Empress of Britain* was the largest liner sunk during World War II.

---

202 ROSEBERY (II)

B 1943 CPR, Montreal. **T** 166g, 80n.**D** 97.7/29.77 x 20.2/6.15 x 7.4/2.29.
E Sgl scr, 2 cyl comp, 10 kts. By Collingwood SB Co., Collingwood, Ontario. **H** Steel. 1 dk.
1943 Prefabricated at Montreal and then transferred by rail to Rosebery where the tug was re-assembled for service on the lake. Designed for wood burning, hence the steam engine.
1957 Laid up and then scrapped.

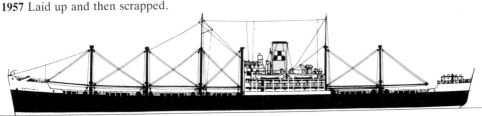

BEAVERDELL / MAPLEDELL / BEAVERDELL, BEAVERGLEN, BEAVERLAKE, BEAVERCOVE / MAPLECOVE

203 BEAVERDELL / MAPLEDELL

B 1946 Lithgows Ltd, Port Glasgow. **T** 9,901g, 5,875n.
D 497.5/151.54 oa, 476/145.08 x 64.3/19.61 x 40/12.19.
E Sgl scr, 2 stm turbs connected by 3 x 225 watt generators (one standby) with electric drive to the shaft, 1 wt blr of 850 psi superheated. 16 kts. By C.A. Parsons & Co., Newcastle.

H Steel. 2 dks. F 41/12.5. P 33/10.06. C: 9,000 tons of which 160,000/4,530cu was refrigerated in 18 chambers.
1945 Aug 27: Launched. The first of a class of four and the only one with a deck house on the poop, as drawn. Replacements for the earlier 'Beaver' class.
1946 Feb 28: M/v Liverpool-Saint John then, Apr 11, London (Royal Albert Dock)-Montreal, the route for which the four had been designed. Their winter service being to Saint John.
1952 Aug 28: Transferred to a new (unsuccessful) Pacific service Vancouver-Japan-China-Manila. R/n *Mapledell* due to there being no oriental word for 'Beaver'.
1954 June 24: Left Vancouver for London where she was switched to the North Atlantic.
1956 Dec 21: Reverted to *Beaverdell*.
1963 Jan 11: Sold to Giacomo Costa fu Andrea, Genoa. R/n *Luisa Costa*. The name of her owners was later changed to Costa Armatori (= Shipowners) S.p.A.
1971 Mar 24: Arrived at La Spezia. Mar 29: Handed over, payment having been cleared, for scrapping and broken up (January 1972) by Terrestre Marittima S.p.A.

204 BEAVERGLEN
Sister to *Beaverdell*. **T** 9,824g, 5,818n.
1945 Dec 10: Launched. **1946** May 24: M/v Liverpool-Canada.
1963 Sept 29: Sold to Hibiscus Ltd, Hamilton, Bermuda. R/n *Bermuda Hibiscus* of London.
1965 April: Sold to Teh-Hu S.S. Co., Hong Kong. R/n *Ping An*. Nov 24: Went aground near to the Hook of Holland and broke her back. Sold to H.P. Heuvelman N.V. and broken up 'as lay'.

205 BEAVERLAKE
Sister to *Beaverdell*. **T** 9,824g, 5,818n.
1946 May 20: Launched. Oct 25: M/v Liverpool-St Lawrence.
1962 Jun 18: Sold to Lloyd Tirrenico S.p.A., Genoa. R/n *Bice Costa*. This Costa subsidiary operated from the same address; the other Costa ship registered with them was the passenger liner *Federico C.*
1964 Owned by Giacomo Costa fu Andrea and then, later by Costa Armatori S.p.A.
1971 Apr 23: Arrived at La Spezia for breaking up by Cantieri Navali Santa Maria where she berthed alongside the cut down hulk of her sister *Giovanni Costa* (206)

206 BEAVERCOVE / MAPLECOVE
Details as *Beaverdell* except: **B** 1947 Fairfield SB & Eng'g Co., Govan. **T** 9,824g, 5,819n.
1946 July 16: Launched. **1947** Sept 3: M/v from London.
1952 July 22: R/n *Maplecove* when she was transferred to the Pacific route. May 13: First sailing from Vancouver. Dec 8: Lost her rudder in a storm and towed to safety by *Island Sovereign* (Island Tug & Barge Co.).
1956 Dec 1: Reverted to *Beavercove* when she returned to the London route.
1963 Aug 19: Became *Giovanni Costa* of Giacomo Costa fu Andrea. Later owned by Costa Armatori S.p.A.
1971 Mar 24: Sold for demolition to Cantieri Navali Santa Maria, La Spezia.

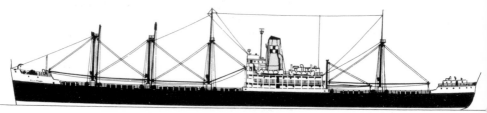

BEAVERBURN (II), BEAVERFORD (II), BEAVERLODGE

207 BEAVERBURN (II)

B 1944 Caledon SB & E Co., Dundee. **T** 9,875g, 7,110n, 12,000dwt.
D 497.5 oa, 475.8/145.01 x 64.4/19.63.
E Sgl scr, 2 drg steam turbs, 2 wt blrs, 490 psi. 15 kts. By C.A. Parsons & Co., Newcastle.
H Steel. 2 dks. F 40/12.19 P 34/10.36. C: 719,650/20,378.3cu g. **P** 35.
1944 Feb 25: Launched as *Empire Captain* for the Ministry of War Transport. A Standard Fast
Cargo Liner; designed by Furness SB Co., these had facilities for the carriage of large or bulky
items of war and had 1 x 80 derrick, 1 x 50 ton, 1 x 30 ton + 11 lesser lift derricks. Six yards
built them and, in all, only 12 were built for M.O.W.T. - and with three different funnel types
(a: Tall with cowl. b: Normal. c: Squat for motorships). The lead ship being *Empire Chieftain*
(*Loch Ryan*, Royal Mail). Other ships of the hull type were licensed to be built by private
owners. The *Beaverdell* (203) class being an example. Dec: Entered service with T & J Harrison
as managers.
1946 May 15: Acquired by CPR. R/n *Beaverburn*. Funnel was as drawn. May 19: First sailing.
1948 March: Her passenger accommodation was reduced to 12.
1960 Mar 25: Sold to Wm. Thomson's Ben Line. R/n *Bennachie*. July 7: Caught fire and towed
into Singapore. Sept: Sold to the Atlantic Navigation Co., New York. R/n *Silvana*.
1969 Owned by Outerocean Nav. Co., Kaohsiung, Taiwan but her survey lapsed in 1965.
1971 Apr 15: Arrived at Kaohsiung and scrapped.

208 BEAVERFORD (II)

Details as *Beaverburn*. **T** 9,881g, 7,109n. **E** By Metropolitan Vickers Co., Manchester.
1944 Aug 18: Launched as *Empire Kitchener* for the M.O.W.T. Tall funnel type.
Dec: Entered service, Canadian Pacific Steamships as managers.
1946 June 12: Acquired. R/n *Beaverford*. June 16: First CP sailing from Liverpool.
1948 March: Passenger accommodation reduced to 12.
1956 Sept 6: Requisitioned at Liverpool for the Suez crisis which followed the unilateral
nationalising of the canal by President Nasser of Egypt. British and French troops then landed
but later withdrew. Sept 18: Released.
1962 Aug 26: Laid up at Antwerp. Dec 3: Bought by Alliance Marine Corp., Hong Kong.
R/n *Hulda*. **1966** Her owners were the International Marine Development Corp., Monrovia.
1969 Aug 18: Driven ashore outside Gulfport, Mississippi, by hurricane Camille and abandoned
as a total loss. Nov 24: Sold, as lies, to Coastal Metal Processors Inc. Broken up by P & W
Industries Ltd.

209 BEAVERLODGE

As *Beaverburn* except: **B** 1943 Furness SB. Co., Haverton Hill-on-Tees. **T** 9,904g, 7,165n.
1943 July 17: Launched as *Empire Regent* for the M.O.W.T., the second ship of the class.
Normal funnel type. Nov 25: Completed, Furness, Withy & Co. managers.
1946 Aug 13: Purchased by Furness, Withy's Rio Cape Line. R/n *Black Prince*.
1949 May 19: Placed on long term charter with Shaw, Savill & Albion, part of the group, and
r/n *Zealandic*. **1952** Oct 3: Acquired by CPS. R/n *Beaverlodge*.
1960 Mar 16: Sold to the Ben Line, Wm. Thomson & Co. managers. R/n *Benhiant*.
1970 R/n *Venus* by Witty Cia Naviera S.A., Limassol.
1971 July 14: Arrived at Kaohsiung and broken up by Chuang Kuo Steel & Iron Works.

OKANAGAN (II)

210 OKANAGAN (II)

B 1947 West Coast Shipbuilders, Vancouver. **T** 204g, 139n.
D 110/33.53 x 23.7/7.21 x 10.6/3.23.
E Sgl scr, oil, 8 cyl. 4s.sa, 10 kts. By Washington Engine Works, Seattle. **H** Steel. 1 dk.
1947 Tug. Built at Vancouver and shipped on rail cars to Vernon, British Columbia for re-assembling. Used for towing on Lake Okanagan: Okanagan Landing-Penticton-Kelowna. The method was to moor the tug between two barges, carrying railway wagons, which were fastened together at their fore end to prevent splaying. Their combined speed was 9 kts.
1972 May 31: The service ceased. Laid up and then sold to Fintry Estates.
1980 Sold to Payco Holdings Ltd. Trace lost.

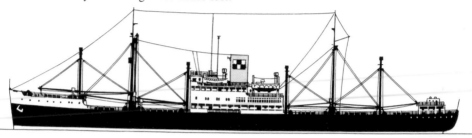

211 BEAVERBRAE (II)

B 1939 Blohm & Voss, Hamburg. **T** 9,034g, 5,902n.
D 487.5/148.59 oa, 469.1 x 60.3/18.39 x 35.4/10.8.
E Sgl scr, oil. 3 engines: 2 x 8 cyl, 2s.sa, + 1 x 6 cyl with electric drive to screw. 16 kts. By builder. Fuel: 1,098 tons oil. **H** Steel. 3 dks. **F** 81/24.69. **P** 33/10.06. **C**: 555,000/15,706.5cu g. **P** 35 - 58 (as built and according to season). Crew 27.
1938 Dec 15: Launched as *Huascaran* for Hamburg America Line's Gulf of Mexico-Panama Canal-South American service. Her sister was *Osorno*.
1939-45 Served in the German Navy as a submarine Werkstattschiff = Workshop ship.
1945 Nov 14: Ceded to Great Britain. Taken over by the Canadian War Assets Corporation as war reparations. Managed, for the Canadian Government, by the Park S.S. Co.
1947 Sept 2: Acquired by CPS. Rebuilt at Sorel. Fitted with 775 berths for the carriage of emigrants Europe-Canada. R/n *Beaverbrae*.
1948 Feb 2: First sailing Saint John-Antwerp-Hamburg, her regular terminus.
1954 Jan 11: Sold to Compagnia Genovese d'Armamento, Genoa. R/n *Auralia*. Emigrant service to Australia. Rebuilt with extra passenger accommodation and more lifeboats.
1970 Sold to Chandris' International Cruises S.A., Panama. R/n *Romanza*. One of four vessels purchased to expand cruising. She was modernised at Perama.
1979 Transferred to Armadores Romanza S.A., Panama. Still in Chandris colours. Oct 17: While cruising grounded on Dhenousa Island, Aegean, in fog. Her passengers were evacuated. Oct 19: Refloated and towed into Syros for repairs of damage forward.
1985 Her cruising became seasonal with intervening lay up at Scaramanga.
1991 R/n *Romantica* by New Ambassador Leisure Cruises, Cyprus.

PRINCESS MARGUERITE (II), PRINCESS PATRICIA (II)

212 PRINCESS MARGUERITE (II)

B 1949 Fairfield SB & Eng'g Co., Govan. **T** 5,911g, 2,379n.
D 359.5/109.58 x 48.1/14.66 x 23/7.01.
E Tw scr, 2 stm turbs to 2 electric motors. 23 kts. By British Thomson-Houston, Rugby.
H Steel. 2 dks. **P** 2,000. Vehicles: 50.
1948 May 26: Launched.
1949 Mar 6: M/v Clyde-Panama Canal-Victoria, 9,600 miles. Apr 6: Arrived. Placed on the Victoria-Seattle day service.
1963 Summer service only. Laid up at Victoria in winter.
1971 Ownership transferred from Canadian Pacific Railway Co. to Canadian Pacific Ltd.
1974 Sept: At the end of the summer the service was withdrawn.
1975 There was, however a need for the route and to avoid a subsidy the ship was bought, April, by the British Columbia S.S. Co (1975) Ltd. Operated by the Province of British Columbia Department of Transportation. Same name and route.
1979 Dec 31: The service was cancelled. **1980** Taken over by British Columbia S.S. Co. (1975) Ltd. Owned by the Minister of Transport & Communications - B.C. Ferries.
1988 July: Sold to the British Columbia Stena Line who sent out *Scandanavica* r/n *Crown Princess Victoria* (ex *Patricia*) for the Vancouver-Seattle service. *Princess Marguerite* being used as a summer excursion vessel. The third ship being *Vancouver Island Princess*.
1990 Nov 17: The service ceased following U.S.legislation banning offshore gambling. All but 30 minutes of the 5 hour crossing being in U.S. waters. Sold to Mykris Hotels plc. To be towed to Bristol, England, for use as a hotel and conference ship. The venture was halted when the ship was arrested on behalf of the Canadian Merchant Service Guild who were in dispute with the previous owners over severance pay.
1991 The arrest order was lifted but problems at Bristol remain.

213 PRINCESS PATRICIA (II)

1948 Oct 5: Launched. The deep toned whistle off *Princess Victoria* (66) was installed.
1949 May 10: M/v Clyde-Panama-Esquimalt, Victoria. June 3: Arrived. Placed on the Vancouver-Victoria-Seattle 'Tri-City' day service.
1963 Converted for cruising. May-Sept: Summer cruising to Alaskan waters.
1966 Chartered to Princess Cruises for a Los Angeles-Acapulco winter service. Summer: Alaskan cruises. **1968** Winter lay up was followed by Alaskan cruises in summer.
1971 Owned by Canadian Pacific Ltd.
1979 May 15-Sept 28: Her final season of 18 weekly cruises Vancouver-Ketchikan-Wrangell-Glacier Bay-Skagway-Juneau-Tracy Arm-Prince Rupert-Alert Bay-Vancouver.
1980 American requirements came into force which required all vessels entering American waters to have self contained waste disposal systems. The cost of conversion was uneconomic. CPR gave up further plans for new ships.
1985 Sold to Hampstead Holdings Ltd (Fox, Morgan & Co.), Vancouver. Grey hull.
1987 Chartered to Great American Cruise Lines.
1989 Sold by Hampstead Holdings. Apr 19: Left Vancouver and towed by *Baltic Rescuer* (North Atlantic Towage & Salvage, Cyprus), to Kaohsiung. June 8: Arrived. Broken up.

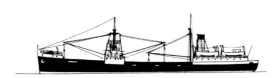

214 YUKON PRINCESS

B 1946 North Van Ship Repairs (now Pacific Drydock Co.), North Vancouver. **T** 1,334g, 761n.
D 224.2/68.34 oa, 214.1/65.25 x 36.7/11.18 x 19.8/6.02.

E Sgl scr, 3 cyl tpl exp, 10 kts. By Canadian Allis-Chalmers, Montreal.
H Steel. 2 dks. F 30/9.14.
1945 Nov 28: Launched as *Ottawa Parapet*, one of two sisters. She was a British Type B standard vessel (of which 7 were built). **1946** Government operated.
1947 Sold to Clarke S.S. Co. R/n *Island Connector*.
1950 Dec: Acquired by CPR. R/n (Jan 1951) *Yukon Princess* for coastal BC work Skagway-Vancouver, mainly with asbestos concentrates. She was then given a deck crane for handling containers at small ports. **1956** Laid up.
1958 Apr: Sold to Westley Shipping Co. R/n *West Princess*.
1961 Feb: R/n *Rosita* by La Lutz Mines Ltd., Monrovia.
1963 June 21: Grounded on Cape Gracias, Nicaragua. Constructive total loss. Sold to Southern Scrap Metals Co. **1964** Broken up at New Orleans.

215 PRINCESS OF NANAIMO / PRINCESS OF ACADIA / PRINCESS OF NANAIMO / HENRY OSBORNE

B 1950 Fairfield SB & Eng'g Co., Govan. **T** 6,787g, 3,409n.
D 357.95/109.09 oa, 343.9/104.8 x 62.1/18.92 x 26.4/8.05.
E Tw scr, 4 srg stm turbs, 20½ kts. By builder.
H Steel. 2 dks. B 223/67.97. **P** 1,500. Vehicles: 130.
1950 Sept 15: Launched.
1951 May 2: M/v Clyde-Panama-Esquimalt, Victoria. Incidentally, for these delivery voyages Vancouver ships had all their windows boarded up. June 11: Arrived. June 27: Entered the Vancouver-Nanaimo service. **1962** Sept: Ended the summer service and laid up.
1963 Transferred to the Saint John-Digby route. R/n *Princess of Acadia*.
Apr 24: First sailing.
1971 May 27: Replaced by *Princess of Acadia* (II) (245). Placed in lay up and reverted to *Princess of Nanaimo*. Owned by Canadian Pacific Ltd.
1972 Stripped of most of her passenger accommodation and converted to a car ferry for 225 vehicles. Route: Saint John, NB-Halifax-St Johns, Newfoundland.
1973 May 16: Stranded outside Saint John, NB, in fog. Abandoned to the Underwriters. Nov 14: R/n *Henry Osborne*. She never traded under this name. Dec: Sold to Union Pipe & Machinery Co., Montreal. Remained at Saint John.
1974 Jan 29: Arrived at Bilbao in tow of *Hansa* (Petersen & Alpers) and broken up.

216 TRANSFER NO. 4

B 1946 U.S. Navy Yard, Boston and Yarrows Ltd, Victoria. **T** 1,593g, 1,521n.
D 308/93.88 x 53/16.15 x 19/5.79. **E** As built: Tw scr, oil, 12 kts. By builder.
H Steel. 1 dk. F 27/8.23. 33 trucks or 24 rail cars.

1946 Built as a landing craft.
1952 Acquired by CPR. Taken to their Victoria Machinery Dept. and converted into a towed rail car ferry. Engines and screws removed. Placed on the Vancouver-Nanaimo service. All the barges on this route were named *Transfer No.xx*; there were ten in all. Other CPR barges were named *C.P.R. Barge No.xx.*. **1957** Out of Lloyd's Register. Trace lost.

---

217 TRANSFER No. 9

B 1929 Canadian Vickers Ltd., Montreal. **T** 1,396g.
D 278.5/ x 44.7/ x 8.3/. **H** Steel. 1 dk.
(Note: Out of chronological sequence in order to pair with the 216 entry)
1929 Completed as *C.P.R.Barge No. 16* for service on Kootenay Lake.
1941 Cut into sections and taken to the Victoria Machinery Dept.
1942 Reconstructed for 17 rail floats and lengthened by 27ft/8.23m as above. Placed on the Namaimo-Vancouver route.
1964 Dec: Sold to Island Tug & Barge Co.,Vancouver. Same name. No longer in Lloyds.

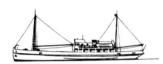

218 PRINCESS OF ALBERNI

B 1945 Martinolich SB Co., San Francisco. **T** 538g, 313n.
D 141.85/43.23 x 33.3/10.16 x 15.6/4.75. **E** Sgl scr, oil, 5 cyl, 2s.sa, 13 kts. By Fairbanks, Morse & Co., Chicago, Illinois. **H** Wood. 1 dk. **P** 30.
1945 Built for the US Navy as one of a class of boom defence vessels, hence her good turn of speed. Given wooden hulls as protection against magnetic mines.
1946 Became *Pomare* for South Seas S.S. Co., Honolulu. Modified as drawn; the fore mast originally being at the bridge front. Served the outer Hawaiian Islands as far as Guam.
1947 Used for fishing by Cia Pesquera "Ambas Costas" S.A., Mazatlan, Mexico.
1953 Bought by CPR. R/n *Princess of Alberni* for the Vancouver Island east coast service.
1958 Sold to Northland Navigation Co., r/n *Nootka Prince*.
1959 Acquired by Crown Zellerbach (Canada) Ltd., paper manufacturers. Converted into a tug and r/n *Ocean Crown* and operated by the Canadian Tugboat Co.. Used for towing log barges.
1962 Re-engined with a Nordberg diesel of 2,000 bhp.
1978 Apr: Owned by Techno Maritime Ltee., Quebec. R/n *Techno Crown* and used on fishing hydrographic work. The vessel is not recorded again in Lloyd's.

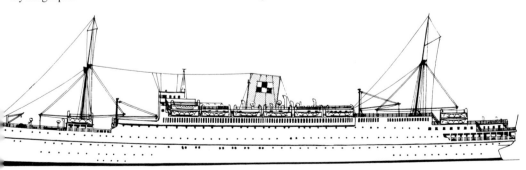

EMPRESS OF AUSTRALIA (II)

219 EMPRESS OF AUSTRALIA (II)

B 1924 Cammell, Laird & Co.,Birkenhead. **T** 19,379g, 10,296n.
D 552/168.25 x 71.1/21.67 x 41.5/12.65.
E Tw scr, 4 srg C.A.Parsons stm turbs, 13,000 shp. 16 kts. By builder.
H Steel. 4 dks. **P** 500 cabin.
1920 Mar 23: Laid down as *Suffren* for the French Line.
1924 Feb 23: Launched as *De Grasse*. Aug 4: Completed after being towed to St Nazaire because of a strike at Cammell, Laird. **P** 399 Cabin, 1,712 3rd. Crew 420.
1932 Refurbished to give more Cabin class. **T** 18,435g. **P** 536 Cabin, 410 3rd.
1940 June: Taken by German forces at Bordeaux. Used as an accommodation ship in the Gironde estuary off Blaye.
1941 Became a depot ship for the Italian submarines operating in the Atlantic.
1944 Aug 25: Sunk by German gunfire during their withdrawal from the city.
1945 Raised. Refitted by Chantiers & Ateliers de Saint-Nazaire-Penhoet. She was now given a single funnel. **1947** July 12: First post-war sailing Le Havre-New York.
1952 Transferred to the West Indies service. Apr 24: First sailing.
1953 Mar 26: Acquired by CPS to replace the burnt out *Empress of Canada* (195).
The 'Canada' was fully booked for the forthcoming coronation of Queen Elizabeth II and the purchase enabled these bookings to be honoured although the cost was high.
Apr 24: R/n *Empress of Australia* (there was press speculation that she would be named *Empress of France*). Apr 25: First sailing Liverpool-Quebec.
1955 Dec 12: Made her final CPS voyage. Laid up at Liverpool on the disposal list.
1956 Feb 16: Sold to Sicula Oceanica, Palermo (Grimaldi-Siosa). R/n *Venezuela*. Naple-La Guaira, Venezuela service.
1960 A raked stem fitted. **D** 604.3ft/187.2m. **T** 18,769. **P** 180 1st, 500 Tst, 800 3rd.
1962 Mar 17: Aground off Cannes. Apr 16: Refloated; assessed as beyond economic repair. Aug 16: Sold to Soc. Anon. Santa Roslaia, La Spezia, and broken up.

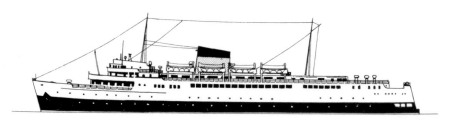

220 PRINCESS OF VANCOUVER

B 1955 Alex. Stephen & Sons, Linthouse, Glasgow. **T** 5,554g, 2,430n.
D 416/126.8 oa, 388/118.26 x 65.6/19.99.
E Tw scr, oil. 4 x 4 cyl 4s.sa srg with hydraulic couplings, 7,000 shp, 15½ kts. By National Gas & Oil Engine Co., Ashton-under-Lyme. Voith-Schneider bow thrust propeller.
H Steel. 1 dk + vehicle deck. F & B 379/115.52. **P** 1,200 as built, 770 as licensed. 115 vehicles or 28 rail cars on recessed rails.
1955 Mar 7: Launched. Apr 29: M/v Clyde-Panama-Vancouver. June 5: Arrived. Vancouver-Nanaimo service thrice daily. For this route she had a bow rubbing strake at upper deck level, as drawn. The large windows on the boat deck were the coffee shop.
1963 Apr: Overhauled at Yarrows yard, Victoria. Vehicle capacity increased to 170 by the installation of a mezzanine car deck.
1971 Transferred to Canadian Pacific Ltd ownership.
1972 Sept: Fitted at Burrard DD Co. with 4 x General Motors diesels, 8,600 bhp. 17 kts.
1979 Reduced to a freighter in winter with passengers summer only.
1982 Sold, with the route, to the Government of Canada (Department of Highways of the

Province of British Columbia), Vancouver. Same name.
1985 Transferred to the B.C. Ferry Corporation. Placed on the Comex-Powell River route. R/n *Vancouver Island Princess*. **1991** Apr: Laid up at Seattle.

Drawing on page 118

221 EMPRESS OF BRITAIN (III)
B 1956 Fairfield SB & Eng'g Co., Govan. **T** 25,516g, 13,706n.
D 640/195.08 oa, 600/182.88 x 85.2/25.96 x 48/14.63.
E Tw scr, 6 drg Pametrada stm turbs, 30,000 shp, 3 Foster-Wheeler wt blrs, 690 psi, 20 kts. By builder. Denny-Brown stabilisers.
H Steel. 3 dks. F & B 578/176.17. Upper B 487/148.44. **P** 160 1st, 894 Tst. Crew 464.
1955 June 22: Launched by HM Queen Elizabeth II. The ships cost £5,500,000 each. Both were air-conditioned throughout - reputedly the first on the Atlantic. It led to speculation that they were really designed for the Pacific. Another aspect was their ability to answer the helm at speeds as low as 5 knots - the St Lawrence being a hazardous waterway.
1956 Mar 2: Delivered to Liverpool; final inspection and repaint in Gladstone Graving Dock. Mar 8: Speed trials off Arran. Apr 20: M/v Liverpool-Quebec-Montreal.
1957 Jan 1: Left Liverpool. Among her passenger were 500 Hungarian refugees.
1963 Oct 10: Completed voyage 123 for CPS. Chartered to Max Wilson's Travel Savings Association (funded equally by CPS, Royal Mail and Union-Castle) for winter cruising.
Oct 25: Made her first TSA cruise. These were based on advance monthly subscription payments. Later she cruised in their summer from Cape Town to South America.
1964 TSA were unable, from members' subscriptions, to pay for the charter cost and the business was concentrated with Union Castle and *Reina del Mar*. Aug 22: Final arrival at Liverpool. Nov 16: Sold, for $8,000,000 to the Greek Line (Goulandris Group). R/n *Queen Anna Maria*. Registered as owned by Transoceanic Navigation Corporation, Andros. Sent to Mariotti Shipyard, Genoa, to be fitted with a Lido deck aft. **T** 21,716g. **P** 168 1st, 1,145 Tst. Crew 450.
1965 Mar 15: Officially named by Queen Anna Maria of Greece her second naming by a Queen. Mar 24: First sailing Piraeus-Naples-New York. Later on the Haifa-New York route.
1975 Jan 22: Laid up at Piraeus. Dec: Sold to Ted Arison's Carnival Cruise Lines Inc., New York, to become their second ship - see 223. R/n *Carnivale*. **P** 950.
1976 Given a $5 million face lift internally. Owned by the subsidiary Fairweather International Corp., Panama. Apr: Commenced cruising. During her first season she achieved a 94% load factor. Route: Miami-day at sea-Samana Bay, Dominican Republic-day at sea-San Juan, Porto Rico-St Thomas, US Virgin Islands-day at sea-Miami.
1991 Still in service.

222 EMPRESS OF ENGLAND
Sister of *Empress of Britain* except: **B** 1956 Vickers Armstrong (Shipbuilders) Ltd, Walker-on-Tyne. **T** 25,585g, 13,725n. **E** By C.A. Parsons at the builders yard.
1956 May 9: Launched by Lady Eden, wife of the Prime Minister. Ident: Had five windows, two-one-two, under the bridge at boat deck level, her sister had six in three pairs.
1957 March: Her delivery took place the day before a strike was to be called at her builders. Apr 18: M/v Liverpool-Quebec-Montreal. She released the *Empress of Scotland* (197) at the end of the season.
1962 Jan: Started the final cruising careers of the last CPS passenger ships. Dec: While in Gladstone Dock she broke adrift in a gale and collided with *Hindustan* (Common Bros). Both suffered damaged plating.
1963 Oct 23: Chartered to the Travel Savings Association. Oct 28: Her first TSA cruise then out of Cape Town with her sister.
1965 Apr 18: Off charter. Apr 28: With the re-opening of the St Lawrence, returned to the Liverpool-Montreal route. Nov 8: Damaged by collision with a Norwegian tanker in the St Lawrence estuary.

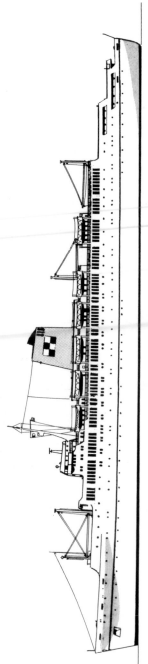

221/2 EMPRESS OF BRITAIN (III), EMPRESS OF ENGLAND

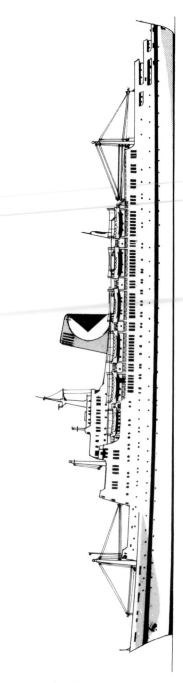

EMPRESS OF CANADA (III)

1970 Apr 1: Withdrawn. Apr 3: Sold to Shaw, Savill & Albion. R/n *Ocean Monarch*. Apr 11: Made one sailing Liverpool-Southampton-Australia and then went to Cammell, Laird, Birkenhead, for refitting as a one class vessel with lido decks and swimming pools. **T** 25,791g. **P** 1,372. No cargo capacity. Cost £2,000,000 but strikes cost another £2,000,000 in lost profit contribution (£12 million in lost revenue).
1971 Sept 17: Left the Mersey for Southampton. The ship was six months late and 12 summer cruises were cancelled. Oct 16: First (and last) cruise Southampton-Mediterranean. Nov 5: Took up her intended Auckland berth. Southampton-Barbados-Curacao-Panama-Acapulco-Los Angeles-Vancouver (her first visit despite being Canadian Pacific built)-Honolulu-Tokelau Island (to pick up children being taken to New Zealand for their education)-Fiji-Auckland.
1973 Pacific cruising out of Sydney. Her performance was marred by persistent breakdowns, staff trouble and a bad reputation. Returned to the UK.
1975 June: Withdrawn. June 13: Final sailing. July 17: Arrived at Kaohsiung for scrapping.

223 EMPRESS OF CANADA (III)

B 1961 Vickers-Armstrong (Shipbuilders) Ltd., Walker-on-Tyne. **T** 25,585g, 13,725n.
D 650/198.12 oa, 600/182.88 x 86.8/26.44 x 48/14.63.
E Tw scr, 6 Parsons' drg stm turb, 30,000 shp, 3 wt blrs, 690 psi. 20 kts. By builder.
H Steel. 3 dks. F & B 583/177.7. Upper B 465/141.73. **P** 192 1st, 856 Tst. Crew 470.
1960 May 10: Launched by Mrs Diefenbaker, wife of the Prime Minister of Canada.
1961 Apr 24: M/v Liverpool-Greenock-Quebec-Montreal.
1970 She became the last Canadian Pacific ocean liner in service but made only 13 transatlantic summer sailings per annum; the remainder of the time she went cruising.
1971 Nov 23: Arrived at Liverpool and the North Atlantic service ceased after 68 years.
1972 Jan: Sold to Ted Arison's Carnival Cruise Lines Inc., Panama. The first ship owned by the new company. R/n *Mardi Gras*. Feb 26: Made a delivery cruise Tilbury-Miami. **P** 906. Italian officers, mixed crew. One aspect is that, being an Atlantic ship, there are many more inside (but larger) cabins than on the more recent Caribbean ships; viz *Mardi Gras* has 193 inside ones.
1973 The Company progressively introduced the 'Fun Ship' concept. Over eighteen months US$10 million was spent on converting the ship while she was actually in cruising service. This was done by closing off portions of the accommodation during the refurbishing. A 60% load factor resulted. She was given red and white livery and much modernised internally with bright lights and vivid colours plus casinos and several discos. The prices were also virtually the cheapest in the Caribbean cruise market. Route: Every Saturday (16.00 hrs) Miami-(day at sea)-Cozumel-(day at sea)-Grand Cayman-Ocho Rios-(day at sea)-Miami although Nassau was frequently substituted for Cozumel.
1974 The ship was marketed nation-wide in the USA and Canada and sailed with occupancies of over 100% - due to children's berths. A second ship was sought - see 221. Incidentally Carnival's third ship, stemming from such success, was to be the ex-Union Castle *Transvaal Castle* rebuilt as *Festivale*.
1980's Two overhauls with modernisation and extra cabins added. **1991** Still in service.

224 BEAVERFIR

B 1961 Sarpsberg Mek. Vekstad A/S, Greaker, Oslofjord. **T** 4,539g, 2,532n.
D 344.5/105 x 50.6/15.42 x 32.1/9.78. **E** Sgl scr oil, 6 cyl, 2s.sa, 3,100 bhp, 14½ kts. By Burmeister & Wain, Copenhagen. **H** Steel. 2 dks. F 40/12.19.

1960 Oct 25: Keel laid.
1961 March: Acquired by CP. The first of five ships acquired to serve the Great Lakes via the new St Lawrence Seaway. Mar 22: Launched as *Beaverfir.* July 7: M/v Antwerp-Quebec-Montreal. Sept: Her sailings were extended to Toronto and she became the first CP ocean going vessel to visit the Lakes.
1972 Apr 21: R/n *Arion* by Arion Shipping Corp., Monrovia.
1975 Nov: Became *Manaure II* of Linera Manaure Cia. Anon., Venezuela.
1981 R/n *Anden* by Kabat Enterprises Overseas Ltd, Grand Cayman.
1982 Owned by Intercontinental Maritima S.A., Peru. Sept 20: Dragged her anchor during a storm while lying off Acajutla. Blown ashore on Barra de Santiago. Sixteen out of 26 lost.

BEAVERPINE

C P EXPLORER

225 BEAVERPINE / C P EXPLORER
B 1962 Burntisland SB Co., Burntisland, Firth of Forth. **T** 4,514g, 2,437n.
D 345/105.16 x 52.6/16.03 x 30.5/9.3.
E Sgl scr oil, 6 cyl turbo-charged Fairfield-Sulzer 2s.sa, 4,000 bhp, 14 kts. By Fairfield SB & E Co., Govan. **H** Steel. 2 dks. 4 holds. **F** 32/9.75. Transom stern. Crew 39.
1962 June 18: Launched. Oct 23: M/v London-Montreal. Operated on the Great Lakes service.
1971 Converted into a container ship. **T** 4,766g. Dec 13: R/n *C P Explorer.*Europe-Canada-Great Lakes service.
1973 Dec: Sold to Arion Shipping Corp., Monrovia, to join 224. R/n *Moira.*
1981 Became *Trade Container* of Kien Hung Shipping Co., Panama.
1986 Dec 29: Arrived at Kaohsiung for demolition.

226 BEAVERELM
B 1960 Moss Vaerft & Dokk A/S., Moss, Norway. **T** 3,964g, 2,243n.
D 331.3/100.99 x 48.7/14.83 x 25.4/7.76. **E** Sgl scr, oil. 7 cyl 2s.sa, 3,600 bhp.
14 kts. By Burmeister & Wain, Copenhagen. **H** Steel. 2 dks. 5 holds.
1960 May 5: Launched as *Roga* for Akties. Asplund, Moss. Rönneburg & Galtung managers; their fleet then became two ships. Sept: M/v Riga-Conakry.
1962 Aug 9: Acquired by CP. R/n *Beaverelm.* Sept 1: First sailing Antwerp-Bremen-Hamburg-Montreal-Toronto on the Great Lakes service; a joint route with Ellerman's Wilson Line.

1971 Sept 28: R/n *Hengshan*, Nan Yang Shipping Co., Mogadishu. Somali flag. Macao owned.
1976 Owned by Fortune Sea Transport Corp. (Panama) S.A., Panama. Same name.
1977 Sold to China Ocean Shipping Co, People's Republic of China. R/n *Yong Kang*.
1991 Still registered but not necessarily in service.

227 BEAVERASH
B 1958 A/B Ekensberg Varv., Stockholm. **T** 4,529g, 2,3342n.
D 344.5/105 x 50.6/15.42 x 23.6/7.19.
E Sgl scr, oil. 7 cyl 2s.sa, 3,600 bhp, 15 kts. By Burmeister & Wain, Copenhagen.
H Steel. 2 dks. 4 holds. Refrigerated (1963).
1958 May 19: Launched as *Mimer* for M. Thorviks Rederi A/S., Oslo.
1963 Jan 10: Acquired by CP. Fitted with 6,000/1,699cu ref. R/n *Beaverash*. Feb 17: First sailing Zeebrugge-Bremen-Hamburg-Saint John. Summer: she was on the Great Lakes route.
1968 Made one voyage to the West Indies on charter to Thos & Jas Harrison.
1969 To the Friendship Shipping Co. S.A. Managers Prodromos Lines, Piraeus. R/n *Zanet*.
1977 Owned by the Zanet Navigation Co., Piraeus.
1980 Apr: Sold to A. Zacharis, Greece. R/n *Agios Nikolaos*.
1982 Aug: Bought by Anvagim Maritime S.A., Piraeus. Same name. Her agents were Saint Michael Shipping Co. **1991** Still registered.

NOTE In 1964, while CP built their own ships, two vessels, the *Anders Rogenaes* and *N.O. Roganaes* were chartered from Nils Roganaes, Haugesund, to pioneer the containers service to the Great Lakes. R/n *Medicine Hat* and *Moose Jaw* they were painted in CP colours. Each carried normal cargoes plus 12 containers on deck.

BEAVEROAK

C P AMBASSADOR (I)

228 BEAVEROAK / C P AMBASSADOR (I)

B 1965 Vickers-Armstrong (Shipbuilders) Ltd., Walker-on-Tyne. **T** 6,165g, 3,078n.
D 408.2/124.41 oa, 376.2/114.66 x 57.7/17.58 x 33.5/10.21.
E Sgl scr, oil. 6 cyl turbo charged Clark-Sulzer 2s.sa, 6,500 bhp, 16 kts. By G. Clark & North East Marine, Sunderland.
H Steel. 2 dks, 3 holds. Refrig. F 93/28.35. P 112/34.14. 134 TEU's. Stayless masts.
1965 Mar 3: Launched. Sept 7: M/v Antwerp-London-Montreal-Great Lakes.
1967 Apr 10: carried the Pacific class locomotive 'Dominion of Canada' to the Canadian Railroad Museum, Montreal. A centenary gift.
1970 July: Lengthened by Boeles Scheepswerven, Rotterdam, and converted into a proper container ship for 332 20 x 40ft TEU's. **D** 432.5/131.83. She was Boeles 50th such conversion. Oct 5: Returned to service as *C P Ambassador*. Placed on the Liverpool-Wolf Cove, Quebec container service operated in conjunction with Head-Donaldson Line's *Inishowen Head*. Too small in service compared with the third generation container ships entering commission. These had squarer hulls to give extra container space.
1973 May 4: After developing an engine room leak, she arrived in tow at St Johns, Newfoundland, after being abandoned, as a precaution, by all her crew except the Captain and Chief Engineer. Dec 24: The third CP ship to be sold to the Arion Shipping Corp. R/n *Atalanta* (In Jan 1974). **1980** On charter to Zim Lines. R/n *Zim Atalanta*; same owner.
1981 Became *New Penguin* of Sin Chiao Shipping (Pte) Ltd., Singapore. She was then sold to Ming Chiao Shipping (Pte) Ltd, Singapore with Sin Chiao as managers.
1982 Sold to Island Ship Management (Pte) Ltd., Singapore. R/n *Flamingo*.
1984 Apr 30: Arrived at Karachi for breaking up at Gadani Beach.

Note: All subsequent ocean going ships were owned by **Canadian Pacific (Bermuda) Ltd.** unless shown otherwise.

229 R.B. ANGUS

B 1958 Brodogradiliste, Split, Jugoslavia. **T** 9,371g, 5,438n.
D 502.4/153.14 x 61.95/18.87 x 29.9/9.11.
E Sgl scr,oil. 6 cyl 2s.sa. 15 kts. By S.A."Fiat' SGM, Turin.
H Steel. 2 dks. F 35/10.67. P 120/36.58.
1958 Nov 2: Launched as *Sunrise* for Alf Torgersen & Co., Oslo. One of several standard sisters built at Split. She was contracted on a 5 year charter to Saguenay Terminals Ltd., Montreal,-hence the 'Sun' name.
1963 Aug 29: Taken by Saguenay Terminals. R/n *Modena*. Not one of their usual 'Sun' names.
1965 Nov 19: Acquired by Canadian Pacific (Bermuda) Ltd. R/n *R.B. Angus*. CP now broke with tradition and commenced to name their ships after leading men connected with the company's history. *R. Bruce Angus came from the Bank of Montreal when CPR was formed and was a director of CPR for 41 years.* Dec 3: First CP sailing Grimstad-Panama-Vancouver.
1966 Placed on the North Pacific route to Japan, mainly with paper pulp under charter to the shippers, MacMillan Bloedal.
1967 Nov 25: Left Chemainus for Tokyo. Dec 17: During a severe storm she developed a leak in Nos 3 and 4 holds. Abandoned, she sank 620 miles north east of Japan. Her crew were picked up by the 1,770g *Yasaka Maru No 18* (Kagoshima Yusen K.K.). Having no facilities to

aid the men two US doctors were parachuted from a US military aircraft. Jan 19: The crew and doctors were transferred to the Japanese Maritime Safety vessel *Natori* and taken into Yokohama. All 39 crew saved.

Profile on page 124

230 LORD MOUNT STEPHEN
B 1966 Mitsui Heavy Industries, Nagasaki. **T** 41,521g, 24,385n.
D 757.95/231.02 oa, 713.6/217.51 x 118.3/36.05 x 57.1/17.4.
E Sgl scr, oil. 9 cyl, 2s.sa, Sulzer type 9RD 90, 20,700 bhp at 119 rpm and 65 tpd oil. 16½ kts. By builder.
H Steel, bulbous bow. 1 dk. F 72.2/22. P 63/19.2. Crude oil carrier. 5 centre tanks and 10 wing tanks. C: 2,983,940/84,496.2cu liquid. 3 discharge pumps with cargo heating coils.
1966 Aug 3: Launched for Canadian Pacific (Bermuda) Ltd. Nov 10: M/v Nagasaki-Vancouver. She then went on long term wet-chartered to the Shell Petroleum Co. Persian Gulf-Japan. *Lord Mount Stephen*, *as George Stephen was the founding President of CPR.*
1985 May: Sold to Junior Cia Naviera S.A., Cyprus. R/n *Pedoulas*. **1991** Still in service.

231 LORD STRATHCONA (II)
Sister to *Lord Mount Stephen*.
1966 Nov 15: Launched. *Donald Smith, Lord Strathcona, drove the final spike into the CPR transcontinental line on Nov 7 1885. He remained a director until his death in 1914.*
1967 Feb 14: M/v Nagasaki-Vancouver. Placed on long term charter to British Petroleum. Persian Gulf, Mina al Ahmadi-Japan route.
1985 May: Sold to Acanthus Cia Naviera S.A., Cyprus. R/n *Breeden*. **1991** Still in service.

232 TRAILER PRINCESS
B 1944 Bethlehem Steel Corp., Bethlehem, Baltimore. **T** 2,689g, 2,258n.
D 307.7/93.79 x 56.5/17.23 x
E Tw scr, oil. 12 cyls,, 1,800 bhp. 10½ kts. By General Motors Corp., Detroit. Bow thrust propeller. **H** Steel. 2 dks. Rail car carrier, 4 tracks.
1944 June 29: Commissioned as *LST 1003* for the United States Navy. July 7: One of 59 such craft taken for conversion into an auxiliary repair ship for battle damage to landing craft. *LST 1003* by Bethlehem Key Highway Shipyard, Baltimore. Became the USS *Coronis* (ARL 10). Anti-aircraft armament only.
1966 July: Acquired by CPR. Converted into a rail car carrier with inlaid rails so that vehicles could also use the vessel. R/n *Trailer Princess*. Vancouver-Schwartz Bay service.
1978 Her owners listed as Canadian Pacific Ltd., Victoria.
1987 Taken over by the Government of British Columbia, Department of Ferries. Same name and service. **1991** Still in service.

Profile on page 124

233 H.R. MACMILLAN
B 1967 Mitsubishi Heavy Industries, Hiroshima. **T** 21,461g, 11,941n.
D 594/181.01 oa, 556.7/169.68 x 95.95/29.24 x 51.8/15.75.
E Sgl scr, oil, 7 cyl, 2s.sa, 10,500 bhp. 14½ kts.
H Steel. 1 dk. 6 holds serviced by three 18 ton Munk self-unloading gantry cranes. Strengthened for heavy cargoes with nos 2 and 4 holds empty. F 49.3/15. P 95.2/29.
C: 1,328,000 /37,605cu g.
1967 Oct 31: Launched. *Until 1957 H.R. MacMillan was Chairman of MacMillan Bloedal Ltd.*

230/231 LORD MOUNT STEPHEN, LORD STRATHCONA (II)

223/235 H.R. MACMILLAN, J.V. CLYNE, N.R. CRUMP

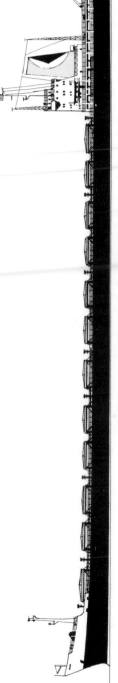

237/8 T. AKASAKA, W.C. VAN HORNE

Canada's largest forest products company and one of CP's largest customers.
1968 Jan 26: Delivery voyage to Vancouver in CP colours. Wood product bulk carrier for MacMillan Bloedal to whom the trio were on a ten year wet charter. Feb: Carried their funnel: White with, in red, an underlined letter 'M' (two inverted V's style).
1978 July: Sold to Pender Shipping Corp., Panama. R/n *Grand Reliance.*
1985 Oct 13: Arrived at Huangpu, China, for breaking up.

234 **J.V. CLYNE**
Sister of *H.R. MacMillan.* **B** 1968.
1968 Feb 2: Launched. Apr 26: Delivery voyage to Vancouver. She was the last vessel to have CP's yellow funnel and chequered house flag. May: MacMillan Bloedal funnel. *J.V. Clyne took over the Chairmanship of MacMillan Bloedal when H.R. MacMillan retired.*
1979 March: Sold to Korea Shipping Corp., Panama. R/n *West Sunori.* **1991** Still registered.

235 **N.R. CRUMP**
Sister to *H.R. MacMillan.* **B** 1969.
1969 Mar 8: Launched for C P Bermuda but managed by C P Steamships (one of only three). May 31: Delivery voyage to Nanaimo. The first CP ship to carry the new green designed funnel. *N.R. Crump became Chairman and Chief Executive of CPR in 1964.* July: MacMillan Bloedal funnel. **1979** Feb 27: Sold to Baruca (Panama) S.A., Panama. R/n *West Jinori.*
1980 Transferred to Korea Shipping Corp., Panama. Same name.
1980 R/n *Texistepec* by Azufrera Panamericana S.A.
1982 Owned by NAVIMIN (Cia Nav Minera del Golfo S.A. de C.V.), Coatzacoalcos. Same name.
1983 Damaged by stranding. Class suspended.
1986 Sold to Yoshita Shipping Corp., Panama. R/n *Yoshito Venture* (sic).
1991 Still registered.

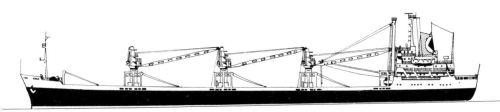

236 **PACIFIC LOGGER / FORT ST JOHN (I)**
B 1968 Sanoyasu Dockyard Co., Osaka. **T** 10,324g, 6,235n, 15,925dwt.
D 486.8/148.37oa, 459.6/140.01 x 69.9/21.29 x 39.9/12.15.
E Sgl scr, oil, 7 cyl 2s.sa Sulzer, 8,000 bhp, 15 kts. By Sumitomo SB & Machinery Co., Tamashima. **H** Steel. 1 dk. **F** 37/11.3. **P** 90.25/27.5. Log carrier. C:722,569.5 /20,461cu g. 4 holds, 7 hatches: 1,2,2,2 layout; opened by the deck cranes. 3 x 16 ton cranes, 1 x 16 ton derrick with one x 1 ton aft.
1969 July 8: Launched as *Pacific Logger.* Sept 5: M/v Osaka-Seattle.
1974 Dec 18: Disabled by engine failure in gale conditions. Towed to builder for repair.
1977 Mar 28: R/n *Fort St John.*
1981 Became *Shanta Rohan* of Hede Navigation (Pvt) Ltd., Bombay.
1988 Sept 5: Laid up off Bombay. **1989** July: Took a severe list, waterlogged.
1990 Abandoned to the Authorities. Scrapped locally.

237 T. AKASAKA
Drawing on page 124

B 1969 Nippon Kokan K.K., Yokohama. **T** 33,328g, 24,041n, 57,138dwt.
D 744.3/226.88 obb, 710.1/216.42 x 102/31.09 x 52/17.38.
E Sgl scr, oil, 7 cyl 2s.sa, B & W type 7K84EF, 17,500 bhp at 114 rpm. 15½ kts on 56 tpd. By Mitsui Zosen, Timano. **H** Steel. 1 dk. 7 holds. Strengthened for the carriage of ore with nos 2, 4 and 6 holds empty. **F** 57.1/17.4. **C:** 2,683,758.8/75,996cu g.
1969 Aug 15: Launched. The main mast was hinged for passing under bridges on her intended route. Ore carrier. *Named after the President of the builders.* Nov 21: Completed. Nov 22: M/v Yokohama-Vancouver-Dampier. Placed on charter with the Japanese firm of Marubeni-Lida Kabusiki Kaisya. **1986** Jan: Sold to Waterdiamond Marine Ltd., Cyprus. R/n *Seaboss*. **1991** Still in service.

238 W.C. VAN HORNE
Details as *T. Akasaka* except: **B** 1970.
1970 Mar 11: Launched. *Sir William Cornelius Van Horne was Chairman of CPR 1899-1910.* Completed June 9, two months late. June 10: M/v (delivery) Yokohama-Vancouver. Chartered to Marubeni-Lida K.K.
1986 March: Sold to Peninsula Shipping Co. Ltd., Hong Kong. R/n *Pratincole*. **1991** In service.

239 PORT HAWKESBURY
Drawing on page 128

B 1970 Nippon Kokan K.K., Tsu. **T** 133,699g, 98,669n, 257,028dwt.
D 1,109.25/338.11 obb, 1,050.1/320 x 170.2/51.87 x 87.6/26.7.
E Sgl scr, oil. 9 cyl 2s.sa, B & W type 9K98FF, 34,200 bhp at 103 rpm, 15½ kts. By Mitsui Zosen, Tamano. **H** Steel, all welded. 1 dk. **F** 77.1/23.5. Oil tanker; eight compartments, 13 tanks, 4 discharging pumps, driven by steam from one stm turb in the engine room. Unloading in 37 hrs including ballasting emptied tanks. As strengthening the hull's deck level edge was curved inwards.
1969 Oct 26: Launched. The new Tsu yard built ships on the Canalock system whereby the vessel was constructed outwards towards both ends at the same time. Delivered three months early despite the yard itself being completed during her construction.
1970 July 16: M/v Yokohama (in ballast)-Mina al Ahmadi, Persian Gulf. made three such voyages pending the completion of Nova Scotia's Point Tupper Refinery.
1971 Loaded oil for her regular service to the Point Tupper Refinery, Nova Scotia.
1986 May: Became *Porthmeus* of Mill Reef Shipping Ltd., Hong Kong. Her managers were Barber Ship Management. Nov: Sold to Popham Shipping Ltd., Hong Kong. R/n *Red Sea Pioneer*. Same managers. **1991** Still in service.

240 T.G. SHAUGHNESSY
Sister of *Port Hawkesbury* except: **B** 1971. **T** 133,701g, 98,647n, 252,831dwt.
1970 Apr 4: Launched. *(Lord) Thomas George Shaughnessy was head of CPR from 1899 to 1923.*
1971 Jan 29: Positioned to Mina-al-Ahmadi and loaded for her service to Point Tupper Refinery, Nova Scotia. **1982** Sold to Shinwa Kiaun K.K., Japan. R/n *Shin-en Maru*.
1986 R/n *Shining Star* by Aurica Shipping Ltd., managers Kappa Maritime Ltd., Cyprus. Nov: Became a store ship at Hormuz Terminal. Nov 25: While serving as a store ship struck by four bombs from Iraqi aircraft and set on fire at Larak Island. Extinguished next day.
1987 Oct 5: Struck by an Iraqi missile while still at Larak Island and severely damaged forward. Abandoned by her owners. **1991** Still abandoned at Larak.

241 I.D. SINCLAIR
Details as *Port Hawkesbury* except: **B** 1974. **T** 133,679g, 98,564n, 254,735dwt.
1974 Mar 23: Launched. *I.D. Sinclair was President and Chief Executive of CP in 1969.* July 20: Positioned in ballast to Dubai for service to the Point Tupper Refinery. Ident: Her lifeboats were above an island stanchioned deck. She also had fewer oil deck fitments

1986 May: Sold to Mill Reef Shipping Ltd., Hong Kong. R/n *Fidius*. managed by Barber Ship Management, Hong Kong.
1988 Apr: R/n *Happy Master* by K/S A/S Norman Tankers IX, Norway. **1991** Still in service.

C P VOYAGEUR, C P TRADER, C P DISCOVERER

242 C P VOYAGEUR

B 1970 Cammell Laird (Shipbuilders & Engineers) Ltd., Birkenhead. **T** 15,680g, 7,805n, 16,330 dwt **D** 548.1/167.06 oa, 502/153 x 84.1/25.6 x 50/15.25.
E Sgl scr, oil. 8 cyl 2s.sa, type 8K74EF, 15,000 bhp. 18 kts. By Harland & Wolff, Belfast.
H Steel. 1 dk. Geometric ram bow, transom stern. 4 holds, 7 longitudinally divided hatches. No cargo handling gear. Container ship 707 20ft/6.1m TEU's seven abreast in 6 hull tiers plus 204 in two tiers on the hatch tops. Crew 34.
1970 Aug 19: Launched for Canadian Pacific Steamships Ltd. Nov 29: M/v Liverpool-Canada then inaugurated a weekly container service Rotterdam-Tilbury-Quebec in conjunction with the Head-Donaldson Line. (The Liverpool section of the route being taken by *C P Ambassador* (228) and Head Line's *Inishowen Head*). The Canadian terminal being that of Canadian Pacific at Wolf's Cove, Quebec. The three cost $20 million.
1983 Jan: R/n *Andes Voyageur* by CPS for a chartered voyage then R/n *C P Voyageur* again. Very much the vogue these days - even for a single voyage.
1984 Transferred to Centennial Shipping Ltd., Hong Kong. R/n *Andes Voyageur* again. Her managers remained Canadian Pacific Bulkship Services Ltd.
1985 R/n *Louisiane* by Centennial then, during the year, r/n *Cedar Voyageur*; same owner. Managers still CP Bulkship Services.
1986 R/n *Bio Kovo*. Registered at Kingstown, St Vincent. Panama flag. Owned by Mid Atlantic Shipping with Jadranska Slobodna, Split, as managers. **1991** Still in commission.

243 C P TRADER

Details as *C P Voyageur* except: **B** 1971.
1971 Jan 28: Launched for Canadian Pacific Steamships. June 6: Due to a strike, towed to Verolme Dockyard, Cork, for completion. July: Joined her sister on Rotterdam-Quebec.
1983 R/n *Andes Trader* by CP Bulkship Services.
1984 Transferred to Centennial Shipping Ltd., Hong Kong Same name. Managers CP Bulkship Services.
1986 Nov: Sold to Island Navigation Corporation (Ship Management) Ltd., Hong Kong. R/n R/n *San Lorenzo*. **1991** Still in service.

244 C P DISCOVERER

As *C P Voyageur* except: **B** 1971
1971 Mar 26: Launched for Canadian Pacific Steamships. July 28: M/v Liverpool-Tilbury where she joined her sisters on the Rotterdam-Quebec route.
1978 July 17: Became the first ship to use the new Canadian Pacific 'allcomers' Racine Container Terminal, Montreal. **1983** R/n *Andes Discoverer* by CP Bulkship Services.
1985 Transferred to Centennial Shipping Ltd. R/n *Mississippi*. **1991** Still in service.

239/41 PORT HAWKESBURY, T.G. SHAUGHNESSY, I.D. SINCLAIR
(Scale 1:1800)

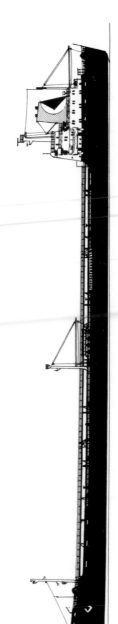

246/53 G.A. WALKER, W.A. MATHER, R.A. EMERSON, FORT MACLEOD, FORT STEELE, FORT EDMONTON, FORT KIPP, FORT COULONGE

255/57 E.W. BEATTY, D.C. COLEMAN, W.M. NEAL

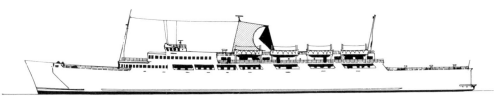

245 PRINCESS OF NOVA / PRINCESS OF ACADIA (II)

B 1971 Saint John SB & DD Co., Saint John, NB. **T** 10,109g, 6,199n.
D 480/146.3 oa x 67.3/20.51 x 15.3/4.66.
E Tw scr KaMeWa controllable pitch inward turning, oil. 2 x 2 16 cyl 'Vee' engines, type 16-645-E5 (the type used in CPR locomotives and thus interchangeable from stock; the whole unit being lifted out), 11,480 bhp, Service speed 15½ kts (Max 18 at 900 rpm) By General Motors Corp., Le Grange, Detroit. Bow thrust propeller.
H Steel, 2 dks. McGregor bow & stern doors. **P** 650. Cars 159 or 40 45ft/13.7m trailers in six traffic lines with a hanging car deck above the two wing roadways.
1971 Launched as *Princess of Nova*. The largest ferry then built in Canada yard.
R/n *Princess of Acadia* (II) while fitting out. Cost $8 million.
June 1: Entered the twice daily 2½ hour Saint John-Digby service. Replaced *Princess of Nanaimo* which carried too few vehicles.
1974 Dec 24: Sold to the Government of Canada. Operated by CPR. Same route.
1976 Sept 1: Transferred to the Government of Canada, Ministry of Transport. Operated by the East Coast Marine & Ferry Service. Same route.
1979 Sold to CN Marine Inc., Saint John. Same name and service.
1988 Owned by Marine Atlantic Inc., Canada. Same name. **1991** Still in service.

Drawing on page 128

246 G.A. WALKER

B 1973 Van der Giesen-de-Noord N.V., Krimpen, Netherlands. **T** 18,774g, 12,174n, 30,607dwt.
D 560/170.69 obb, 531.6/162.03 x 85.4/26.04 x 47.4/14.46.
E Sgl scr, oil. 6 cyl 2s.sa, type B & W 6K74EF, 12,200 bhp at 134 rpm and 43 tpd oil. 15 kts.
By Burmeister & Wain, Copenhagen.
H Steel. 1 dk. F 57.1/17.4. P 111.3/33.9. Square transom stern. Product carrier with 7 centre and 14 wing tanks; 12 compartments. C: 1,458,935/41,312.7cu liquid. Could carry four different products discharged by four centrifugal steam turbine pumps. Derricks: 2 x 10 ton amidships. 1 x 3 ton, machinery, at funnel and 2 x 3 ton, stores, aft.
1973 Mar 19: Handed over to Canadian Pacific (Bermuda) Ltd. Mar 20: M/v. A clean oil product carrier on charter to Esso Petroleum. Carried their funnel. *G.A. Walker was Chairman in 1948.*
1987 Dec: Sold to Alke Shipping Ltd, Isle of Man. R/n *Iver Alke*. Still on Esso charter. Managed by BCP Ship Management Ltd., Douglas Isle of Man. BCP = Barber Canadian Pacific. This unit progressively replaced Canadian Pacific Bulkship Services Ltd as ship managers.
1991 R/n *Alke*, same owner. Still in service.

247 W.A. MATHER

Sister of *G.A. Walker*.
1973 July 28: Handed over to CP (Bermuda) on charter to Shell Petroleum. C P funnel. *W.A. Mather was Chairman of CPS in 1948.*
1988 Transferred from Isle of Man Registry. R/n *Arma Trader* by CP Ships.
1990 Sold to Arma Shipping Ltd, Isle of Man. R/n *Arma*. **1991** Still in service.

248 R.A. EMERSON
As *G.A. Walker*.
1973 July: Launched; no date given. Owned by CP (Bermuda). Nov 2: Entered service. *R.A. Emerson was CPR president in 1964.*
1989 Sold to Ceres Hellenic Shipping Ltd, Piraeus. R/n *Clearventure L.* Owned by Elcoral Inc., Piraeus, a single ship co. **1991** Present fleet.

249 FORT MACLEOD
As *G.A. Walker* except: **B** 1974.
1974 Mar 1: Handed over to CP (Bermuda). Mar 4: Entered service, managed by CPSS.
1988 Dec: R/n *Osco Macle* by Macle Shipping Ltd. managers: BCP Ship Management Ltd, Douglas, Isle of Man. **1991** Still in service.

250 FORT STEELE
As *G.A. Walker* except: **B** 1974.
1974 Nov 28: Handed over to CP (Bermuda). Nov 30: Entered service.
1990 Apr: Sold to Elcrown Inc., Greece. R/n *Crestventure L.*
1991 Still in service. owned by Ceres Hellenic Enterprises Ltd., Piraeus.

251 FORT EDMONTON
As *G.A. Walker* except: **B** 1975. **T** 18,782g, 12,205n, 31,275dwt.
1975 Feb 28: Handed over to CP (Bermuda). Mar 1: Entered service. managed by CPSS.
1982 Oct 15: Chartered by the Royal navy as an oiler.
1988 Feb: Sold to Edmonton Shipping Co., Isle of Man. R/n *Edmonton.*
1989 R/n *Osco Edmo* by Edmo Shipping Ltd. Managers: BCP Ship Management, Douglas.
1990 Her name was shortened to *Edmo.* Still in service.

252 FORT KIPP
As *G.A. Walker* except: **B** 1975. **T** 18,782g, 12,205n, 31,275dwt.
1975 July 3: Handed over to CP (Bermuda).
1989 R/n *Iver Tiki* by Tiki Shipping Ltd. Managers BCP Ship Management, Douglas, I.O.M.
1991 R/n *Nike.* Same owners.

253 FORT COULONGE
As *W.A. Mather* except: **B** 1976. **T** 18,872g, 12,205n, 31,275dwt.
1976 Feb 20: Entered service for CP (Bermuda).
1987 R/n *Coulonge* by Coulonge Shipping Co., Isle of Man.
1988 R/n *Ulan Trader* of Ulan Shipping Ltd., Managers BCP Ship Management Ltd, Hong Kong. **1991** Still in service.

254 CARRIER PRINCESS
B 1973 Burrard DD Co., Vancouver. **T** 4,353g, 2,196n.
D 365.9/111.51 x 66.3/20.22 x 24/7.32.
E Tw scr, oil. 2 x 2 Vee 16 cyl locomotive engines which were interchangeable from stock and

no on board machinery maintenance, 2s.sa, 11,500 bhp, reverse reduction geared. 18 kts. By General Motors Corp, Le Grange, Detroit. Bow thrust propeller.
H Steel. 1 dk. B 138.2/42.1. **P** 260. Vehicles: 150 motor or 30 rail-cars.
1973 Feb 20: Launched. Roll on-roll off ferry. June 1: Entered the thrice daily Vancouver-Nanaimo service. **1987** Owned by CP Ships Ltd.
1989 Owned by Coastal Marine Operations (CP Rail) Ltd, Vancouver. Their only ship.
1991 Still in service.

Profile on page 128

255 E.W. BEATTY
B 1973 Nippon Kokan K.K., Tsu. **T** 69,904g, 44,473n, 123,137dwt.
D 853.1/260 obb, 813.6/247.99 x 136.7/41.66 x 77.8/23.7.
E Sgl scr, oil. 9 cyl 2s.sa, B & W type 9K 84EF, 23,300 bhp at 114 rpm and 84 tpd oil. 15 kts. By Mitsui SB & E Co.
H Steel. 1 dk. OBO (Oil-bulk-ore) carrier. 9 holds/hatches. C: 5,072,862/143,648.2cu bulk. Side rolling hatch covers each operated by an electro-hydraulic winch. Derricks: 2 aft.
1973 Sept 26: Completed for Canadian Pacific (Bermuda). *E.W. Beatty was Chairman of CPS in 1925.* OBO's were dual carriage in that they could carry two types of bulk cargo. Oil one way with ore inwards - but were restricted to areas where this feat is possible. Thus only a limited number were required in general fleets such as Canadian Pacific.
1988 Sold to Winsor Bulk Inc., Manila. R/n *Solita.* Owned by Philippine Transmarine Carriers Inc a subsidiary of Ugland Bros, Manila, which was in turn a subsidiary of Uglands of Grimstad, Norway. **1991** R/n *Apostolos Andreas 4* by Lakewood Shipping Co., Cyprus.

256 D.C. COLEMAN
Details as *E.W. Beatty* except **B** 1974. **T** 125,107dwt.
1974 Jan 17: Delivered to CP (Bermuda). *D.C. Coleman was Chairman of CPS in 1942*
1985 Apr: Sold to Dawn Sky Ltd, Hong Kong. R/n *Goldean Commander* then sold and r/n *Philippine Commander* by Crimson Navigation Co. S.A., Panama.
1988 R/n *Delantera,* Coresol Ventures Inc., Panama.
1989 Became *El Delantero* of Delantero K/S, managers Morton, Werrings Rederi, Tonsberg.
1991 Still in service.

257 W.M. NEAL
As *E.W. Beatty* except **B** 1974. **T** 125,107dwt.
1974 Aug 7: Handed over to CP (Bermuda). *W.M. Neal was Chairman of CPS in 1947.*
1987 Sold to Ocean Queen Maritime Corp., Manila. R/n *Channel Commander.*
1988 Became *Ladybird* of Bachelor Investments Soc. Anon., Manila. **1991** Still in service.

Profile on page 133

258 FORT NELSON
B 1975 Sanoyasu Dockyard Co., Osaka. **T** 21,894g, 13,623n, 35,414dwt.
D 603.6/185 obb, 570.95/174.02 x 92.25/28.1 x 50.5/15.4.
E Sgl scr, oil. 7 cyl 2s.sa, B & W type 7K67GF, 13,100 bhp at 145 rpm on 46 tpd oil, 15.7 kts. By Mitsui Zosen, Tamano.
H Steel. 1 dk. 5 holds, 9 hatches, side rolling operated from the deck cranes.
F 46.1/14.4. **P** 95.2/29. 5 x 15 tonnes Hagglund deck cranes. Bulk carrier, strengthened for heavy loads. Could carry lumber deck cargoes. C:1,575,929/44,625.6cu g + 619,266/17,535.7cu on deck. Carbon-dioxide fire extinguishers in holds.
1975 May 28: Launched for CP (Bermuda). Aug 12: Handed over. Registered at Hong Kong.
1989 R/n *Elso* by Elso Shipping Ltd. Managers: BCP Ship Management Ltd., Hong Kong.
1991 Still in service.

259 LEDA / FORT ST JOHN (II) / LEDA / FORT NANAIMO

Sister to *Fort Nelson*. **T** 19,498g, 13,023n, 35,974dwt.

1975 Laid down as *Leda* for the Canadian Pacific subsidiary Atalanta Ship Management Services Ltd., London. Sept 12: Launched. Dec 5: M/v as *Leda* although the ship was registered by Lloyd's under the name *Fort St John*.

1980 March: As *Leda* transferred to Canadian Pacific (Bermuda) Ltd. R/n *Fort Nanaimo*. Registered at Hamilton, Bermuda. Delivered at Tampa, Florida. Mar 24: Left for Vancouver. **1989** Sold to Naimo Shipping Corp., Monrovia. R/n *Naimo*. Managers: Ugland Bros., Monrovia.

1991 Still in service.

260 FORT CALGARY

Sister of *Fort Nelson* except: **B** 1976 **T** 21,893g, 13,609n, 35,974dwt.

1975 Dec 18: Launched for CP (Bermuda).

1976 March: Delivered.

1989 Jan: R/n *Calga* by Calga Shipping Ltd, Hong Kong, with BCP Ship Management as managers. She was transferred to Liberian registry. **1991** Still in service.

261 FORT KAMLOOPS

Details as *Fort Nelson* except: **B** 1976. **T** 17,281g, 10,743n, 28,317dwt.
D 534.9/163.02 x 83.3/25.4 x 47.25/14.41. **E** As *Fort Nelson*.
H Five mechanically ventilated holds, 5 hatches. Carried lumber as deck cargo. **C**:1,296,061/ 36,700cu g + 486,800/13,784.7 cu deck. Five x 15 tonne deck cranes + 2 derricks aft.

1976 The first of a class of three ships which were 36ft/11m shorter than the *Fort Nelson* class. As an insight into net tonnage, three are recorded for these ships: Net: 10,000, Suez Net: 14,100, Panama Net: 12,800. Oct 28: Delivered to Canadian Pacific (Bermuda) Ltd. Registered at Hong Kong.

1986 R/n *Kamloops Progress* by Addship Trading Co. Ltd, Hong Kong. This was a three ship purchase. The other two were *Fort Carleton* (267) and *Fort Hamilton* (268).

1988 Became *Kamo* of Kamo Shipping Corp., Monrovia. Operated by Singapore Ship Management Pte Ltd, Singapore. **1991** Still in service.

262 FORT VICTORIA

Sister of *Fort Kamloops* except: **B** 1977.

1977 Jan: Delivered to CP (Bermuda). Registered at Hong Kong.

1986 R/n *Victus* by Mill Reef Shipping Ltd, Hong Kong. BCP Ship Management as managers. **1988** R/n *Tusa* by Tusa Shipping Corp., Monrovia. Managers Fairmont Shipping (Hong Kong) Ltd. **1991** Still in service.

263 FORT YALE

As *Fort Kamloops* except: **B** 1977.

1977 May: Delivered to CP (Bermuda).

1981 Dec 27: During a storm in Lattakia Roads, Syria, *Bravo Neck* (Bravo Neck Shipping Corp) was in collision with *Wu Men* (China Ocean Shipping) and then slammed into *Fort Yale* causing considerable damage. *Bravo Neck* sank.

1990 Chartered to BHP Transport U.S.A., Inc. R/n *Copper Yale*. Operated by Fathom Management Corp, Oakland. Panama flag. **1991** Dec: Present CP fleet. For sale.

Drawing on page 133

264 PORT VANCOUVER

B 1977 Burmeister & Wain, Copenhagen. **T** 35,716g, 25,508n, 61,836dwt.
D 698.8/213.01 x 106/32.31 x 59.1/18.01.
E Sgl scr, oil. 7 cyl 2s.sa, Type 7K 80GF, 18,500 bhp at 126 rpm on 66 tpd oil. 15½ kts. By builder. **H** Steel. 1 dk. 7 holds, 7 hatches, centrally divided, side rolling hydraulically operated.

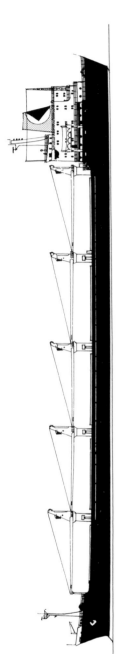

258/63 FORT NELSON, LEDA / FORT ST JOHN (I) / FORT NANAIMO,
FORT CALGARY, FORT KAMLOOPS, FORT VICTORIA, FORT YALE

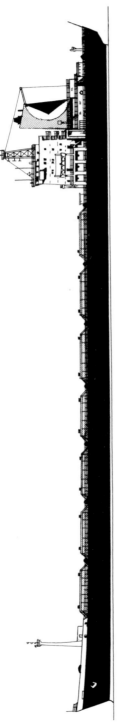

264/65 PORT VANCOUVER, PORT QUEBEC

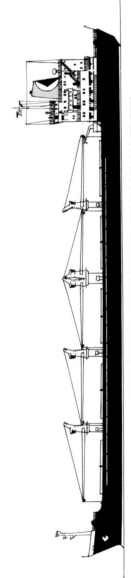

266/68 FORT WALSH, FORT CARLETON, FORT HAMILTON

C:2,789,885/79,001cu g. Had a 5 tonne overhead travelling crane aft + 2 davit cranes at the bunkering position aft.
1977 Jan 28: Entered service for CP (Bermuda). Bulk carrier.
1986 R/n *Vancouver* by Mill Reef Shipping Co., Hong Kong. They purchased both sisters for delivery at the end of current commitments.
1988 Became *Stacouver* of K/S Stamer Bulk Investments, Oslo. Owned by Helmer Staubo & Co., Oslo, whose ship names always commenced with 'Sta'.
1990 Sold to Novaton Pte Ltd, Singapore. R/n *Vancouver*. Still in service.

265 **PORT QUEBEC**
Sister of *Port Vancouver*.
1977 May 13: Completed for CP (Bermuda).
1986 Sold to Mill Reef Shipping Ltd., Hong Kong. R/n *Quebec*.
1989 R/n *Kali L* by Elprimero Inc., Piraeus. A subsidiary of the Livanos owned Ceres Hellenic group. **1991** Still in service.

Drawing on page 133
266 **FORT WALSH**
B 1978 Sanoyasu Dockyard Co., Osaka. **T** 14,088g, 8,753n, 22,450dwt.
D 527.95/160.91 obb x 75.4/22.99 x 44.25/13.49.
E Sgl scr, oil. 6 cyl 2s.sa, B & W type 6L55GF, 8,000 bhp at 150 rpm. 15½ kts. By Mitsui Zosen, Tamano. **H** Steel. 1 dk. **F** 42/13.4. **P** 95/29. Five holds/hatches, 3 single and one twin electro-hydraulic Nikko-Hagglung deck cranes.
1977 July 27: Launched for CP (Bermuda).
1978 Jan 17: Entered service. Registered at Hong Kong but ownership still Canadian Pacific (Bermuda) Ltd. but one of five managed by Canadian Pacific Steamships Ltd., London. Self trimming bulk carrier with a deck capacity for 126 containers. The first of a class of three slightly smaller versions of the *Fort Kamloops* trio.
1984 Nov: Sold to Guyana Timbers Ltd, Bahamas, and thence to Guybulk Shipping Ltd, Bahamas. R/n *Manaka*. **1991** Still in service.

267 **FORT CARLETON**
As *Fort Walsh*.
1977 Oct 14: Launched for CP (Bermuda).
1978 Mar 15: Delivered. Managed by CP Steamships, London.
1987 Sold to Addship Trading Co., Hong Kong. R/n *Carleton Progress*.
1991 Still in service.

268 **FORT HAMILTON**
Sister of *Fort Walsh*.
1977 Dec 23: Launched for CP (Bermuda).
1978 Mar 27: Entered service. Managed by CP Steamships, London.
1987 Sold to Addship Trading Co., Hong Kong. R/n *Hamilton Progress*.
1991 Still in service.

269 **FORT NORMAN**
B 1968 Eriksberg M/V A/B, Gothenburg. **T** 29,304g, 21,855n, 55,120dwt.
D 713.84/217.58 obb, 688.61/209.89 x 97.18/29.62 x 57.8/17.61.
E Sgl scr, oil. 8 cyl 2s.sa, B & W type, 12,000 bhp, 15½ kts on 40 tpd oil. By builder.
H Steel. 1 dk. 7 holds/hatches, strengthened for heavy cargoes with alternate holds empty. C:2,476,180/70,118cu g.
1967 Dec 21: Launched as *Rona* for Einar Saanum, Mandal, Norway.
1968 May: Operated by the subsidiary Skibs A/S Agnes.
1978 R/n *Pilot Trader* by Owen Corporation, Monrovia.
1979 Sold to Pacheia Shipping Corp., Monrovia. R/n *Norman Trader*. Nov: Acquired by

Canadian Pacific (Bermuda) and r/n *Fort Norman*.
1984 Feb 6: Arrived at Kaohsiung for scrapping by Shyeh Sheng Huat Steel Corp.

Drawing on page 136
270 FORT FRASER

B 1967 Mitsui Zosen, Tamano. **T** 42,446g, 28,872n, 74,422dwt.
D 825.1.251.48 obb, 796/242.62 x 105.7/32.21 x 61/18.59.
E Sgl scr oil, 9 cyl 2s.sa, B & W type, 20,700 bhp, 16 kts. By builder.
H Steel. 1 dk. F 74/22.56. 9 holds, 9 side opening centre-divided hatches. C: 3,072,359.3/87,000cu. 2 x 10 tonne derrick.
1967 Jan 9: Launched for the P & O subsidiary Trident Tankers. Jun 21: Delivered as *Fernie* with Hain-Nourse as managers. **1971** Oct 1: Transferred to the P & O Bulk Shipping Division.
1979 Jan: Sold to Alcyone Shipping Co., Monrovia. R/n *Alcyone*.
1980 Feb: Acquired by Canadian Pacific (Bermuda) Ltd., r/n *Fort Fraser*, Hong Kong.
1985 Jan 17: Arrived at Kaohsiung for demolition by Chien Yung Enterprise Co.

Appearance as *Fort Fraser* but no Fscle

271 FORT DOUGLAS

B 1968 Ishikawajima-Harima Heavy Industries, Kure. **T** 52,706g, 39,200n, 107,131dwt.
D 820.21/250 obb, 790.68/241 x 134.1/40.87 x 66.44/20.35.
E Sgl scr, oil. 10 cyl 2s.sa, Sulzer type, 23,000 bhp, 15½ kts. By builder at Aio works.
H Steel. 1 dk. Ore-bulk-oil carrier. 11 holds, 11 hatches (five alternate ones were 35ft/10.7; the other six varied. All were 65.6/20m wide) C:4,044,602.1/114,531cu. Strengthened for heavy cargoes with the smaller holds empty. Crew 35.
1968 Launched as *Sidney Spiro* for General Ore International Corporation & International Marine Owners Co. Ltd., Monrovia. General charter work.
1979 Aug: Owned by Docynia Shipping Corp., Monrovia. R/n *Docynia* (in 1980).
1980 Feb: Acquired by Canadian Pacific (Bermuda) Ltd. R/n *Fort Douglas*.
1982 June: Sold to Daeyang Shipping Corp. Ltd, South Korea. R/n *Daeyang Glory*.
1991 Still in service.

Drawing on page 136
272 FORT ERIE

B 1967 Nippon Kokan K.K., Tsurumi. **T** 33,586g, 22,373n, 57,567dwt.
D 742.1/226.5 oa, 712.3/217.1 x 102.2/31.15 x 57.5/17.53.
E Sgl scr, oil. 8 cyl 2s.sa, Sulzer, 17,600 bhp, 16½ kts. By Uraga Heavy Industries, Tamashima.
H Steel. 1 dk. F 62/18.89 B 30/9.14 on P 135/41.15 aft. 7 holds, 12 hatches C:2,422,595/68,600.6cu. Strengthened for heavy cargoes, deck top curved inwards from bulwark end to superstructure. Her bow was round with no stem.
1967 Feb: Launched as *Jasaka* for A/S Kosmos, Anders Jahre, Sandefjord, Norway. Had a docking television camera mounted on the fore mast.
1978 Sold to Arion Shipping Corp., Monrovia. R/n *Nemesis*.
1979 Owned by the Nemesis Shipping Corp.
1980 Acquired by Canadian Pacific (Bermuda) Ltd. R/n *Fort Erie*. Registered at Hong Kong.
1981 Sold to Orient Rose Shipping Inc., Monrovia, Liberia. R/n *Orient Rose*.
1986 May 15: Arrived at Kaohsiung for demolition by Tong Hing Steel & Iron Works Co. Ltd.

Drawing on page 136
273 FORT ASSINIBOINE

B 1980 Sanoyasu Dockyard Co., Mizushima. **T** 19,982g, 11,923n, 31,766dwt.
D 556.1/169.5 obb, 524.9/160 x 89.57/27.3 x 48.26/14.71.
E Sgl scr, oil. 6 cyl 2s.sa, B & W type, 11,200 bhp, 15 kts. By Mitsui Eng & SB Co., Tamano.
H Steel. 1 dk. F 53.15/16.2. P 111.2/33.9. C: 1,437,299/40,700cu liquid in 24 tanks. Chemicals in the centre holds and other defined chemicals in the wing tanks. The lattice radio masts are port side only. Square transom stern. Island funnel box.
1979 Dec 7: Launched for CP (Bermuda). Chemical carrier
1980 Jun 15: Delivered. Registered at London. Her agents were CPS.
1991 Sold to Ceres Hellenic Enterprises Ltd, Piraeus. R/n *Conquestventure L.*.

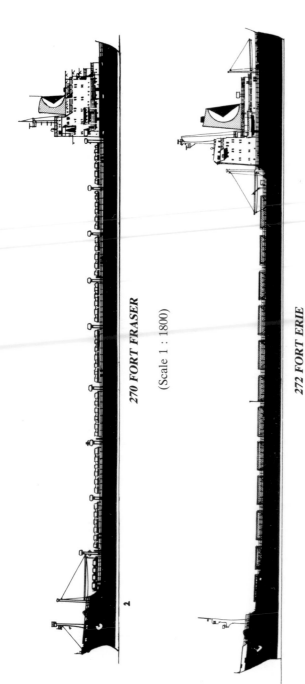

270 FORT FRASER

(Scale 1 : 1800)

272 FORT ERIE

273/76 FORT ASSINIBOINE, FORT GARRY, FORT ROUGE, FORT TORONTO

274 FORT GARRY
Sister of *Fort Assiniboine*.
1980 Mar 14: Launched for CP (Bermuda). Sept: Entered service. Registered at London.
1989 Sold to Ceres Hellenic Shipping Enterprises Ltd. R/n *Crystalventure L*. Owned by Elcrystal Inc. They were all single ship companies. **1991** Present Fleet.

275 FORT ROUGE
Sister of *Fort Assiniboine*.
1980 May 29: Launched for CP (Bermuda). Dec: Delivered. London registry.
1882 Aug 8: Chartered by the North Atlantic Treaty Organisation, via the Royal Navy, as a replenishment oiler for their Atlantic exercises. It underlined the fact that all the naval vessels taking part did not use the same types of oil fuel and were, therefore, not strictly interchangeable.
1989 R/n *Courageventure L* by Elconcept Inc. with Ceres Hellenic Shipping Enterprises Ltd as managers. **1991** Still in commission.

276 FORT TORONTO
Sister of *Fort Assiniboine* except **B** 1981.
1980 Aug 28: Launched for CP (Bermuda).
1981 Feb: Delivered. London registry. CPS as agents, but not managers.
1991 Became *Clipperventure L* of Ceres Hellenic Shipping Enterprises Ltd., Piraeus. Owned by the Livanos group. Present fleet.

TWO CHARTERED SHIPS GIVEN C P NAMES

277 C P HUNTER
B 1979 N.V. Boelwef S.A., Tamise. **T** 13,384g, 9,669n, 19,775dwt.
D 536.4 /163.5 obb, 75.26/22.94 x 45.34/13.82.
E Sgl scr, oil, 6 cyl, 2s.sa, 12,400 bhp, 16 kts. BY MAN, Ghent.
H Steel. 2 dks. F 88.25/26.9. P 106.3/32.4. 4 holds. 697 TEU's.
1979 Built as *E.R. Brussel* for Ahlers & Partners, Antwerp, Belgium, for the spot charter market.
1980 Jan: Chartered to Canadian Pacific Steamships. R/n *C P Hunter* for the duration. (Note: There was a *C.P. Hunter*, a person's name, for a brief spell; she became *Covadonga*.)
1981 Owned by Algemene Scheepsvaartmij Temse N.V., Antwerp. R/n *Cast Walrus* on charter to the Cast consortium. **1982** Reverted to *E.R. Brussel*; same owner.
1984 R/n *Hapag-Lloyd Kiel* on charter to Hapag-Lloyd. She became *Hodeidah Crown* for the second charter of the year. Reverted to *E.R. Brussel*.
1985 Again on charter. R/n *Nedlloyd Brussel* by the Nedlloyd Group. Reverted to *E.R. Brussel* by the year end. **1990** Sold to Chester Shipping Co. Ltd., Limassol. R/n *Patraikos II*.
1991 R/n *Kwangsi*; same owners. Still in service.

Drawing on page 139

278 C P AMBASSADOR (II)
B 1971 Swan Hunter Shipbuilders Ltd, Walker Yard, Newcastle. **T** 31,036g, 17,658n, 28,488dwt. **D** 759.67/231.55 obb, 719.19/219.21 x 100.52/30.64 x 51.18/15.6.
E Sgl scr, oil. 10 cyl 2s.sa, Sulzer, 29,000 bhp, 23 kts. By G. Clark & N.E.M. Ltd., Wallsend. Bow water jet thruster.
H Steel. 1 dk. F & B 692.25/211. 34 hatches. Container ship for 1,535 TEU's. Carried 40ft/12.19 size in holds with 20ft/6.09 on deck. 1 x 5 tonne crane.
1970 Oct 14: Launched for the Dart Container Line Ltd. Owned by the Bristol City Line.
1971 May: Entered service as *Dart Atlantic* (red hull) for the Dart Container Consortium, formed by Bristol City Line, Bibby Bros, Cie Maritime Belge and Canadian Clarke Traffic Services of Montreal (in which Canadian Pacific held substantial equity). Chartered to Dart.

Her sister was *Dart America.*

1972 Bristol City Line was taken over by Bibby Bros., Liverpool, together with four ships and their share in the unprofitable Dart consortium.

1980 Sold to Furness Withy. Same name and service.

1981 Dart re-organisation farmed the container fleet out. *Dart Atlantic* was r/n *C P Ambassador* on demise charter to CP and owned by Tricity Finance Ltd. Continent-UK-Montreal all year round service.

1985 R/n *Canmar Ambassador.* Same owner. Now operated by 'Canmar' = Canadian Marine Drilling Ltd., Calgary but still on CP demise charter.

1988 Her owner became Channel Ltd., London. Managed by BCP Ship Management Ltd.

1991 Still in service.

Drawing on page 139

279 **FORT PROVIDENCE**

B 1982 Hyundai Heavy Industries, Ulsan, South Korea. **T** 36,391g, 26,372n, 64,584dwt.
D 736.1/224.37 obb, 705.35/214.99 x 105.94/32.29 x 59.09/18.01.
E Sgl scr, oil. 7 cyl 2s.sa, 15,200 bhp, 15½ kts. By builder.
H Steel 1 dk. F 58/17.7. 7 holds/hatches.
1982 April 3: Launched for CP (Bermuda). July: Delivered. Registered at Hong Kong. Managed by Canadian Pacific Steamships, London.
1988 R/n *Stena Africa* on charter to Stena Line. Same owner. Then sold to El Seguro Inc, Piraeus. R/n *Captain George L..* Managers: Ceres Hellenic Shipping Enterprises Ltd.
1991 Still in service.

280 **FORT RESOLUTION**

Details as *Fort Providence* except: **B** 1983. **T** 36,284g, 24,044n, 64,413dwt.
1982 July 17: Launched. Registered at Hong Kong. Same operators as her sister.
1989 Sold to Elmotores Inc., Piraeus. R/n *Captain John L.*
1991 Still in service.

Drawing on page 139

281 **FORT DUFFERIN**

B 1983 Burmeister & Wain, Copenhagen. **T** 35,008g, 22,197n, 64,000dwt.
D 738.28/225.03 obb, 701.34/213.77 x 106/32.31 x 59.09/18.01.
E Sgl scr, oil. 4 cyl 2s.sa, 12,330 bhp, 16 kts. By builder.
H Steel. 1 dk. Bulk carrier. 7 holds/hatches. 853 TEU's. C:2,782,427/78,790cu. Round nosed hull. Island funnel structure with an athwartship crane. Sideways rolling hatches.
1983 June 10: Launched for CP (Bermuda). Registered at Hong Kong.
1989 Sold to La Fontana Blanca Ltd., Greece. R/n *Annitsa L.*
1991 Still in service.

282 **FORT FRONTENAC**

1983 Sept 30: Launched for CP (Bermuda). Registered at Hong Kong.
1989 Sold to La Fontana Clara Ltd., Greece. R/n *Peter L.*
1991 Still in service.

WARTIME SHIPS MANAGED BY CANADIAN PACIFIC
WORLD WAR I

Other than those acquired no ships were bare boat managed. However, from time to time, a number were chartered especially after the sinking of a CPS vessel left a gap in the committed sailings.

Two standard ships were purchased *War Peridot* (164) and *War Pearl* (165).

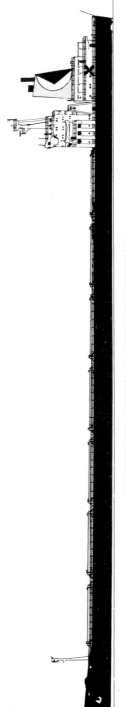

278 C P AMBASSADOR

279/280 FORT PROVIDENCE, FORT RESOLUTION

281/82 FORT DUFFERIN, FORT FRONTENAC

WORLD WAR II

EMPIRE CUTLASS, EMPIRE LANCE

283 EMPIRE CUTLASS

B 1943 Consolidated Steel Corp., Wilmington, Cal. **T** 7,117g, 4,823n, 11,650disp.
D 417.8/127.34 oa, 396.5/120.85 x 60.1/18.32 x 35/10.67.
E Sgl scr, 2 drg stm turbs, 4,400 shp, 2 wt blrs, 14 kts max. **H** Steel. 2 dks. Crew 43.
1943 July 27: Launched as *Cape Compass*. US standard ship type CI-S-AY1. 'S' = full scantling. AY1 = Landing Ship Infantry Large. Nov: Completed as *Empire Cutlass* on Lend/Lease to Ministry of War Transport. Operated as a mercantile manned LSI (L).
1944 Taken over by the Royal Navy (one of 12 sisters). R/n HMS *Sansovino* (F 162). 1 x 4 in, 1 x 12 pdr, 24 Anti-aircraft. Crew 250.
1946 June: Reverted to *Empire Cutlass*, Ministry of War Transport, with CPS as managers. The ship made only three voyages for them; mostly repatriating troops.
1947 Late: Returned to the United States Maritime Commission. Reverted to *Cape Compass*.
1948 R/n *Empire Cutlass* for her sale to the Nationalist Republic of China but the transfer was postponed due to a lack of dollars. Owned by the United States Department of Commerce. Traded to Taiwan. **1960** R/n *Hai Ou*; China Merchants S.N. Co., Keelung, Taiwan. Black funnel.
1970 Oct: Broken up at Kaohsiung.

284 EMPIRE LANCE

Sister of *Empire Cutlass*.
1943 Aug 28: Launched as *Cape Pine*. Dec: Completed as *Empire Lance*.
1944 After D-day the ship was used as a troop shuttle Southampton-Le Havre.
1945 May 9: When the Channel Islands were re-taken she was used on this route to rush supplies to the isolated and malnourished islanders. July: Transferred to the Royal Navy. R/n *Sir Hugo* and used as a troop shuttle Hull-Cuxhaven; operated by the army with an R.N. Volunteer Reserve crew - hence the Royal Fleet Auxiliary 'Sir' name. Blue Ensign.
1946 Returned to M.O.W.T. and *Empire Lance*. CPS as managers.
1949 Having been earlier returned to the USMC she now reverted to *Cape Pine*. Owned by the US Department of Commerce. **1965** Broken up.

EMPIRE KITCHENER See 208 *Beaverford* (II)

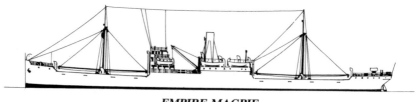

EMPIRE MAGPIE

285 EMPIRE MAGPIE

B 1919 Federal SB Co., Kearny, New Jersey. **T** 6,211g, 3,837n.
D 395.5/120.55 x 55.2/16.82 x 31.4/9.57.
E Sgl scr, 2 drg stm turbs, 12 kts. By Mid West Engine Co., Indianapolis, Indiana.
H Steel. 1 + shelter dk. F 38/11.58. B 110/33.53. P 45/13.72.
1919 Oct: Completed as *Bellemina* for the US Shipping Board. One of 43 standard sister ships built by Federal.
1941 Transferred under Lend/lease to M.O.W.T. R/n *Empire Magpie* with CPS as managers.
1948 R/n *Jui Hsin* by Zui Kong S.S Co., Shanghai with Chinese Maritime Trust Ltd as managers. **1950** Became *Oriental Dragon* of Pacific Union Marine Corporation, Panama.
1955 R/n *Atlantic Unity* by Atlantic Bulk Carriers Inc., Panama. **1960** Broken up.

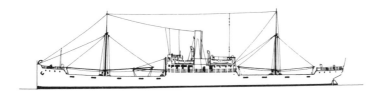

286 EMPIRE MOUFLON

B 1921 Hanlon DD & SB Co., Oakland, Cal. **T** 3,234g, 1,976n.
D 320.8/97.78 x 46.2/14.08 x 24.4/7.44.
E Sgl scr, tpl exp, 2 sgl blrs, 10 kts. By Allis Chalmers Manufacturing Co., Milwaukee.
H Steel. 1 dk. F 33/10.06. B 79/24.08. P 26/7.92.
1921 Feb: Completed as *Memnon* for the US Shipping Board, San Francisco.
1926 Sold to Fred Barker, Astoria. Transferred to the Columbia River Packers Association Inc., Astoria. **1940** R/n *Empire Mouflon* by M.O.W.T., Sir R. Ropner & Co. managers.
1944 Canadian Pacific were the managers for 7 voyages before returning her to Ropner.
1946 Acquired by Preston Shipping Co. with Sir R. Ropner & Co. managers. R/n *Preston* (III). As drawn. **1951** Sold to Avance Cia Maritima S.A., Panama. R/n *Avance*.
1958 R/n *Avlis* by Avlis Shipping Co. S.A. Greece.
1962 June: Broken up by Elbes Ltd at Ambelaki, Greece.

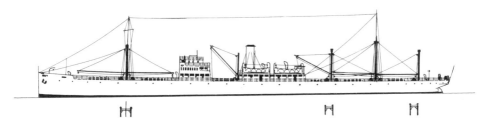

287 EMPIRE SAILOR

B 1926 Stabilimento Technico., Trieste. **T** 6,140g, 3,691n.
D 430/131.06 x 55.5/16.92 x 27.6/8.41.
E Sgl scr, oil. 6 cyl, 2s.sa, direct acting, 1,323 nhp. 12½ kts. By Fiat, Turin.
H Steel. 2 + shelter dk. Flush. P 40.
1926 Apr 29: Launched as *Cellina* for Naviera Libera Triestino, Trieste. One of a class of four. Italy-Vancouver service. **1936** Dec 17: Transferred to 'Italia' with ten of the fleet.
1937 Re-engined at Monfalcone. Fiat 6,000 bhp. 13.5 kts.
1940 June 10: Captured off Gibraltar the day Italy entered the war. R/n *Empire Sailor* with CPS as managers.

1942 Nov 21: Torpedoed off Cape Race by *U-518*. She was in convoy ON 145 (ON = UK-America fast; pre-July 1941 OB). *U-518* sank two tankers, *British Renown* and *British Promise* plus *Empire Sailor* in one 7 minute spread of torpedoes; two of which, 4 minutes apart, struck the freighter.

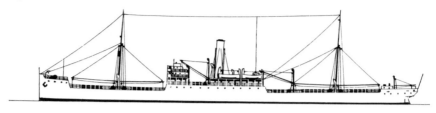

288 EMPIRE UNION

B 1924 Stabilimento Technico, Trieste. **T** 5,952g, 4,068n.
D 390.8/119.1 x 54/16.46 x 29/8.84.
E Sgl scr, tpl exp, 465 nhp, 3 sgl blrs, 12½ kts. By builder.
H Steel. 1 + shelter dk. F 36/10.97. B 128/39.
1924 Launched as *Salvore* but, May 1, delivered as *Sistiana* to Navegazione Libera Triestino. One of five general cargo sisters. Served mainly on the African routes.
1936 Dec 17: Transferred with 18 others to Lloyd Triestino. **P** 40.
1940 June 10: Seized at Cape Town when Italy entered the war. R/n *Myrica* by South African Government. **1941** Transferred to the M.O.W.T. R/n *Empire Union*, CPS as managers.
1942 Dec 27: One of 4 ships torpedoed by *U-356* in convoy ONS 154 (=UK-America slow).

289 EMPIRE WOODLARK

B 1913 New York SB Co., Camden, N.J. **T** 7,793g, 4,448n.
D 423.8/129.17 x 54.9/16.73 x 17.7/5.39
E Tw scr, 2 x 3 cyl tpl exp, 2 dbl blrs. 12 kts. By builder.
H Steel. 4 + shelter dk. C: Refrigerated. **P** 250
1913 Built as *Congress* for the Pacific Coast Company Inc., New York. Pacific coast passenger services. **1916** Caught fire and burned out at Coos Bay. No lives lost.
1917 Rebuilt. R/n *Nanking*, China Mail S.S. Co, New York.
1923 Became *Emma Alexander* of H.F. Alexander's Pacific S.S. Co., Seattle which had taken over the Pacific Coast Co.'s coastal service to San Francisco. Traded as the Admiral Line.
1936 Jan: After the final passenger sailing Seattle-San Francisco laid up.
1942 Acquired under Lease/lend by M.O.W.T. R/n *Empire Woodlark*. CPS as managers. Used for trooping. Her machinery gave trouble and the accommodation caused such complaint that she was only used for short sea movements. Later used as an accommodation ship.
1946 Scuttled in the Atlantic with a cargo of gas bombs and chemical weapons.

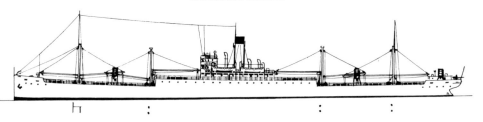

290 EMPIRE YUKON

B 1921 Stabilimento Technico, Trieste. **T** 7,651g, 4.464n.
D 450.8/137.4 x 57.4/17.49 x 32.2/9.81.
E Sgl scr, tpl exp, 680 nhp, 4 sgl blrs, 180 psi, 13.4 kts max, service 11½ kts. By builder.
H Steel. 3 + shelter dk. **B** 168/51.21. **P** 40 1st.
1916 Laid down as *Zrmanja* but unfinished during the war being launched on Oct 11, 1919.
1921 May 31: Completed as *Duchessa d'Aosta* for Navigazione Libera Triestino, Trieste, with extraordinary four strut latticework goal post masts and cross trees. Trieste-New York service.
1923 Chartered to Lloyd Triestino for two years. Far East route.
1929 Again with Lloyd Triestino; same name. Registered at Venice. Trieste-Kobe route.
1930 Modernised. **T** 7,872. Oil burning. **P** 48 Cabin, 12 3rd. Given an extra passenger deck. Refrigeration fitted. North Pacific run. **1932** Laid up during the depression.
1935 May: Used as an air force transport to Eritrea during the Abyssinian war.
1936 Dec 17: Transferred to Lloyd Triestino with 19 of the fleet (ten others went to Italia). Round Africa service.
1940 June: At Santa Isabel, Fernando Po when Italy entered the war.
1942 Feb 14: Broke out but captured at sea by Free French naval forces. Taken into Calabar. Became a war prize. R/n *Empire Yukon* by M.O.W.T. CPS as managers. Cut down to cargo only by the removal of the upper passenger deck. Wartime masting and rig as shown on the drawing. The foremast was starboard side and the mainmast port side of the posts.
1945 CPS declined the offer by M.O.T. to purchase her.
1946 Sold to Petrinovic S.S. Co., London. R/n *Petconnie*. Black funnel, white band, blue 'P'. Altered by having a goal post-cross tree added to the after bridge-deck posts with conventional masting on this and the fore goal posts.
1951 Sold to the Italian flag COSCA S.A., managers Cia Nav 'Odero' S.A. R/n *Liu O.*
1952 Broken up in Italy.

Note:
When, in 1942, the Canadian Government formed the Park Steamship Co. Ltd they built, between 1943 and 1945, 176 standard ships costing a total of $270 million. 114 of these were 10,000dwt 'Park' ships, the remainder being tankers or smaller cargo types. During hostilities the ships were managed by a number of Canadian concerns including Canadian Pacific. CPS were allocated 22. Many for the single loaded delivery voyage to Europe. The vessels were crewed from pool and not by CPS. Post war the fleet was sold off and all had gone by 1947. Canadian Pacific purchased none.

CANADIAN AUSTRALASIAN LINE

History

1893 James Huddart, whose shipowning dated back to 1876, formed the Canadian-Australian Steamship Co. and placed two ships *Miowera* and *Warrimoo* on the mail carrying route: Sydney-Brisbane-Fiji-Honolulu-Victoria-Vancouver. May 18 being the first sailing. At the time it was known as the 'Imperial Route'. Huddart next unsuccessfully put a proposal to the Canadian Government for a transatlantic mail link to provide an 'All Red Route' from the UK to Australia (British colonies and Dominions were coloured red on maps).

1897 When the New Zealand Shipping Co's *Aorangi* (bt 1883) was refitted for the service a new concern the Canadian-Australian Royal Mail Shipping Co. was formed but this matched a time when the fortunes of James Huddart were in decline.

1898 Feb: The company was wound up and, unwillingly, the New Zealand Shipping Co. kept the services going at Auckland. Canadian Pacific took over the Canadian and European agencies and Burn, Philp & Co. those in Australia.

1899 The mail contract expired and had to be renegotiated. The Union S.S. Co. of New Zealand already served Auckland-San Francisco and, being the only ones interested in the service, negotiations with them commenced.

1901 Apr: The Union S.S. Co. accepted all existing contracts and assumed control of the Canadian-Australian Line's service. They used ships from their own existing fleet.

1903 The Canadian Pacific Railway Co. inaugurated a cargo service from Vancouver to Australia and New Zealand.

1908 *Makura* was the first ship specially to be built for the service and was the largest ship in the Union fleet until the arrival of *Niagara*.

1910 Union S.S. Co took over all outstanding aspects of the Canadian-Australian Royal Mail S.P. Co. and decided to modernise the route. This obtained for them the renewal of the mail contract worth a subsidy of £20,000 annually for five years.

1913 *Niagara* was delivered and ran in consort with *Makura* and *Marama*.
To link Australia with Canada as a part of the 'All Red' route from Great Britain via Canada to Australia and New Zealand. To protect their interests CPR took a minor part of the equity of the reformed Canadian-Australian R.M.S.P. Co. This gave them the sole Canadian representation and a network of offices and agents in Europe.

1924 *Aorangi* was commissioned.

1931 The route was hit by the recession but also by the intended fierce competition of the Matson Line out of San Francisco. The further assistance of Canadian Pacific was sought and this resulted, in July, in the formation of the jointly owned Canadian-Australasian Line Ltd. *Niagara* and *Aorangi* were transferred on charter to the company although Union S.S. Co. remained as managers and supplied the relief steamers as needed. In effect CPR, who stood to gain most from the 'All Red Route', shared any future profit but also the current losses.

1941 The war caused the cessation of the service until 1948.

144

1950 July: The Company announced the cessation of the services with effect from the January 4 1951 sailing.

1951 January: A storm of protest led to the granting of a subsidy by the three route Governments concerned which ended up as $250,000. Apr 5: The service recommenced but air had taken the mail contract as well as the passengers. The 'All Red Route' was doomed, although the subsidy was extended for another year.

1953 May: *Aorangi* was laid up at Sydney. From there she left for breaking up at Dalmuir and with her going the Canadian-Australasian Line Ltd was wound up. The route itself, obviously an essential one, has lingered on and still exists.

LIVERY

The ships carried the Union S.S. Co. of New Zealand passenger livery of the period:
Hull: Bottle green with a yellow band (except for *Aorangi*'s white hull of four months duration) and brown-red waterline, white uppers with brown masts and black funnel area vents; white elsewhere.

Funnels: The Union S.S. Co's red funnels, black tops and two pin-stripe bands.

Houseflag: White, red diagonal cross with the blue letters C A S Co in each segment, the 'A' top centre, 'Co' bottom (note that the letters do not match the owners title; the flag came from the earlier company).

FLEET LIST

Drawing on page 146

Drawing on page 146

291 NIAGARA
B 1913 John Brown & Co., Clydebank. **T** 13,415g, 7,582n.
D 524.7/159.93 x 66.3/20.21 x 34.5/10.51. Dft 28.1/8.56.
E Tpl scr, 2 x 4 cyl tpl exp (2 lp), wing shafts, + lp turb, centre shaft, 2 dbl + 6 sgl blrs, 220 psi. 17 kts. By builder
H Steel. 3 + shelter dk. **C**: Mostly ref. **P** 281 1st, 210 2nd, 176 3rd. Crew 205.
1912 Aug 17: Launched for the Union Steam Ship Co. of New Zealand for the Canadian-Australasian service with Union S.S. Co. as managers.
1913 Apr: M/v to Auckland-Sydney; the first passengership to have a Board of Trade certificate to burn oil fuel. She was, in fact, never to visit UK waters again.
1914-18 Normal service. This continued right up to her loss.
1931 July: Transferred, with *Aorangi*, on wet boat charter to the new Canadian-Australasian Line. Owners as managers.
1935 July: Collided with the steamer *King Egbert* (King Line, Dodd, Thompson) in the Juan de Fuca Strait off Victoria.
1940 June 18: Left Auckland. Her cargo contained rifle ammunition plus, secretly, £2½ million in gold ingots. These were loaded in 295 boxes of two bars each.
June 19: 03.00. Entering Hauraki Gulf, the vessel struck a mine on a calm night off Bream Head, Whangarei, and all aboard took to the boats. The ship settled by the head and at 05.30 hrs sank in 430ft/131.06m of water. This was the first intimation that the German raider *Orion* (ex-*Kurmark*, Hapag, British: Raider A) was active in New Zealand waters. Her mines had been laid across the main shipping lane and after the warning caused by the sinking of *Niagara* only two ships, *Port Bowen* (Port Line) and *Baltanic* (United Baltic) were lost although three of the minesweeping force were also sunk.
The gold was important and salvage was decided upon, although 439 feet was deeper than any previous attempt The previous record was in 1930 when *Artiglio* (Soc. Recupari Marittimi) salvaged gold at 396 feet from P & O's *Egypt*.

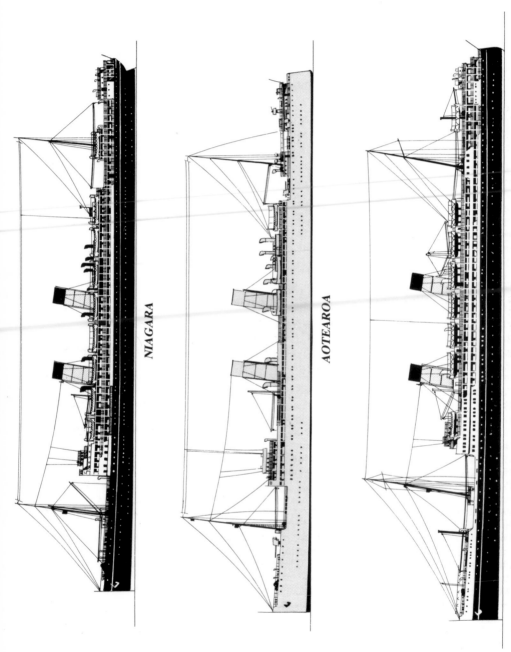

NIAGARA

AOTEAROA

AORANGI

1941 Feb 2: The wreck was finally located, laying on its side in 438ft off Whangarei, by the specially fitted out coaster *Claymore* (Northern S.S. Co., Auckland) which had been equipped with a remotely controlled grab and a specially constructed diving bell from which the grab operation could be monitored. Next the salvage ship was specially moored to hold its precise position over the wreck and divers blasted a hole in the hull to give access to the strong room. Apr: Recovery work commenced. The debris had to be removed and the access passage within the hull shored up. Work could only be carried out in calm weather and mainly at the twice daily slack of the tide when the water was still. In October the first gold was brought to the surface and by December 4th 277 out of 295 boxes plus one loose bar had been recovered. The problem of the remainder had to be left because the task was made dangerous by the settling of the whole hull. *Claymore* returned to Whangarei to be greeted with the news of the Japanese attack on Pearl Harbor. Further salvage was abandoned.
1953 Aug: Risdon Beazley's *Foremost 17* returned to the site and recovered a further 30 bars leaving only five unaccounted for.

292 **AOTEAROA**

This ship was ordered as a sister to join *Niagara* on the Canada route for Union S.S. Co. of NZ Co. In appearance she was to have been similar except for a cruiser stern.
1913 Laid down. **1915** June 30: Launched, having been taken over by the Admiralty. Completed as the auxiliary cruiser HMS *Avenger*. The upper accommodation deck being omitted but she had a weather fcsle added.
1917 Jun 14: Torpedoed and sunk by *U-69* enroute to Scapa Flow off her northern patrol duties. One dead.

293 **AORANGI**

B 1924 Fairfield SB & E Co., Glasgow. **T** 17,491g, 10,773n.
D 580.1/176.81 x 72.2/22 x 43.4/13.22. Dft 29.9/9.11.
E Quad scr, oil. 4 x 6 cyl 2s.sa, Sulzer diesel, 3,177 nhp. 17 kts. By builder.
H Steel. 4 dks. **F** 93/28.34. Prom 419/127.71. **P** 440 1st, 300 2nd, 230 3rd.
1922 Ordered as a motor ship; the first on the Pacific. To obtain the necessary horse power she had to have 4 sets of machinery and this led to her four shafts.
1924 Jun 17: Launched. Dec 16: Completed. Owned by the Union Steam Ship Co. of New Zealand.
1925 Jan 3: M/v Southampton-Vancouver and placed in the Vancouver-Sydney service. Feb 6: First sailing Vancouver-Sydney.
1931 Transferred to the Canadian-Australasian Line when it was jointly formed. Same route and with Union S.S. Co. as managers.
1938 Refitted at Sydney. **P** 248 1st, 266 Cabin, 125 3rd.
1940 After a spell on normal service, Feb 10, entered service as a New Zealand troop ship.
1941 Taken over by the Ministry of War Transport for trooping. Assisted in the evacuation of Singapore.
1944 Fitted out as the mothership for the 150 tugs to be used to tow caissons etc during the Normandy invasion.
1945 Converted into the flagship for the Pacific squadron of the Royal Fleet Auxiliary. July: Far East accommodation and depot ship at Manus.
1946 Apr: Returned to he owners at Hong Kong where she had been latterly based. Reconditioned at Sydney being much delayed by strikes and shortages.
1948 Aug 19: First post war sailing Sydney-Auckland-Fiji-Honolulu-Victoria-Vancouver with a white hull and thin green band - this much photographed innovation lasted for only two round voyages. **P** 212 1st, 170 cabin, 104 3rd.
1950 The service was only continued after the respective governments had agreed to a subsidy. However money for a replacement ship was not to be forthcoming.
1951 The route limped along with, at one time, *Aorangi* laid up while funding was argued.
1953 June 8: Arrived at Sydney for the last time. June 9: Purchased by BISCO. June 19: Left Sydney for the Clyde. July 27: Arrived at Dalmuir for breaking up by W.H. Arnott Young.

CANADIAN PACIFIC CAR & PASSENGER TRANSFER COMPANY

History

1863 May: A ferry service was started across the St Lawrence River between Prescott, Ontario, Grand Trunk Rly, and Ogdensburg, New York, The Northern Railroad Co., with the jointly owned six-car *St Lawrence*.
The route did not really prosper because the two lines had differing rail track gauges.

1873 *St Lawrence* was condemned; her hull was rotting. Because both lines were now standard gauge (5ft 8½ins) the local coal merchant Isaac D. Purkis replaced her with his single tracked, 3 car ferry *Transit*. Purkis built four more steamers for St Lawrence summer work some of which were used on the ferry service.

1881 CPR took over the St Lawrence & Ottawa Railway Co. as part of the absorption of the South-Eastern Railway on which the lending banks had foreclosed due to the non payment of its mortgage. This take over, into the Canada Central Railway's system, was valuable to CPR in that it completed the through route Saint John, New Brunswick-Boston, Mass.

1882 The St Lawrence & Ottawa Rly also used a ferry service between Brockville, Ontario and Morristown, N.Y. (12 miles upstream) operated by David H. Lyon with his ferry *William Armstrong*. He called his firm the **Car Ferry Company**

1885 The Canada Central Railway and its numerous adjuncts was integrated into CPR and their separate names disappeared. Both ferries were now 'CPR' fed.

1888 Mar 17: Captain Lyons combined both ferries and the service was renamed the **Canadian Pacific Car & Passenger Transfer Company**. The important thing was that CPR did not own it. When asked to explain Capt Lyons said all the railway cars carried were, since 1885, CPR but the passengers were not all CPR. So if the name was correctly read it defined the service precisely. CPR agreed.

1896 The older subsidiary service between Brockville, Ontario, and Morristown, N.Y., dating from 1886, was discontinued being displaced by the Prescott crossing.

1908 *Charles Lyon* entered service.

1929 Sept 1: Canadian Pacific took over control of the Company.

1930 The New York Central Railroad acquired an interest and *Prescotont* and *Ogdensburg* replaced *Charles Lyons*.

1970 The passenger portion of the service ended when a bridge was built to connect Prescott with Ogdensburg. Freight continued.

1972 The Ogdensburg terminal was destroyed by fire and deemed not worth rebuilding. The freight service was therefore terminated and the two vessels were put up for disposal.

FLEET LIST

294 TRANSIT

B 1874 Clayton SB Co., New York. **T** 141 reg. **D** 108/32.92 x 21/6.4 x 6/1.83.
E Tw scr, 2 sgl cyl engines, 60 hp. By John King, Oswego, N.Y. **H** Wood. 1 dk.
1873 Built for Isaac D. Purkis. One track, 3 wagons.
1886 Taken over by Canadian Pacific Car & Passenger Transfer Co. **1901** Scrapped.

WILLIAM ARMSTRONG   **CITY OF BELLEVILLE**

295 WILLIAM ARMSTRONG

B 1876 A & J.W. Wood, Ogdensburg. **T** 181g. **D** 100/30.48 x 30/9.14 x 6/1.83.
E Sgl scr, 2 cyl comp, 349 hp, 2 sgl blrs. By John King, Oswego, N.Y. **H** Wood. 1 dk.
1876 Nov 23: Launched for David H. Lyons, owner and captain. Operated on CPR's Brockville crossing. One track, 3 wagons. Twin funnels, split superstructure with a platform wheel house on struts.
1889 June 20: Left Morristown with three loaded coal wagons. The chief engineer came up on deck (for a smoke) and saw the ship was unduly weighed down by the stern. Then he noticed that one engine room exhaust vent was under water. Sure enough the river was flooding into the engine room. He got everyone on deck just as the ship foundered but one passenger drowned. Raised and returned to service.
1910 Sold to the dredging contractor Robert Weddell, Trenton, Ontario. Became the drilling barge *Mons Meg*. **1938** Dismantled.

296 CITY OF BELLEVILLE

B 1878 at St Catherines, Ontario. **T** 101g, 69n. **D** 89.7/27.34 x 15.4/4.69 x 7/2.13.
E Sgl scr, 1 cyl, 60 rhp. **H** Wood. 1 dk.
1878 Passenger steamer, built for Isaac D. Purkis. She towed a 3 rail car barge named *Jumbo* on the Prescott-Ogdensburg crossing. Her sisters were *Caribou* and, the drawing, *Henry Plumb*.
1881 Bought by the South-Eastern Rly Co. for use as a St Lawrence ferry Brockville-Morristown. **1886** Operated by the Car Ferry Co.
1888 Owners renamed Canadian Pacific Car & Passenger Transfer Co.
1896 Transferred to the Prescott-Ogdensburg route. Acted as relief vessel, too small for the growth of traffic.
1908 Replaced by *Charles Lyon*. Transferred to the new Prescott & Ogdensburg Ferry Company.

297 INTERNATIONAL

B 1881 A. Cantin, Montreal. **T** 395g, 269n. **D** 182/55.47 x 30/9.14 x 10/3.05.
E Tw scr, 2 x 2 cyl comp, 150 rhp. By E. Gilbert & Sons, Montreal. **H** Wood. 1 dk.
1881 Completed as *South-Eastern* for the Longeuil Navigation Co., Montreal. Operated for the South-Eastern Rly Co. between Longueil and Hochelaga until the Lachine Bridge was built.
1886 Oct 4: Sold to the Richelieu & Ontario Navigation Co.
1890 Apr 14: Acquired by Canadian Pacific Car & Passenger Transfer Co.
1909 Replaced by *Charles Lyon*.
1910 Sold to Sincennes-McNaughton and reduced to a sand barge.
1912 Sold to Touzin Sand Co., Montreal. Lasted only two years before being scrapped.

298 CHARLES LYON
B 1908 Polson Iron Works Co., Toronto. **T** 1,658g, 1,127n.
D 280/85.34 x 40/12.19 x 19.9/6.06.
E Tw scr, 2 x 2 cyl inclined comp, 212 nhp, 4 sgl Scotch blrs, 130 psi. By builder.
H Steel. 1 dk.
1907 Ordered as *Ogdensburg*. Dec 7: Launched. Named after the owner's father. Split superstructure, twin funnels, 4 masts (2 x 2 pairs), 2 wheel houses on a 4 strut platform.
1908 Jan: Delivered. Rail car ferry with 3 tracks, 14 wagons. Noted for her humped backed appearance.
1909 Acquired by Canadian Pacific Car & Passenger Transfer Co. to replace the two older ferries. **1935** Sold to J.P. Porter & Sons, Montreal. Reduced to a barge.
1941 Broken up at Hamilton, Ont.

OGDENSBURG   PRESCOTONT

299 OGDENSBURG
B 1930 American SB Co., Lorain, Ohio. **T** 1,405g. **D** 290/88.39 x 45/13.72 x 12/3.66.
E Nil. One auxiliary power diesel generator. **H** Steel. 1 dk. 2 rudders.
1930 Rail car ferry barge for *Prestcotont*, three tracks amidships converging to two at bow and stern. 17 rail cars.
1970 The service ended when Ogdensburg dock was destroyed by fire.
1972 Oct 1: Sold to the Windsor Detroit Barge Line, Detroit, Michigan. Container carrier.

300 PRESCOTONT
B 1930 Davie SB Co., Lauzon, Quebec. **T** 302g. **D** 110.1/33.55 x 28.3/8.64 x 12.6/3.84.
E Sgl scr, oil. 12 cyl, 4s.sa, connected to electric drive, 264 nhp. 11 kts. By Winton Eng'g Co., Cleveland, Ohio.
H Steel. 1 dk. Strengthened for ice. Fire float.
1930 Tug for the rail barge *Ogdensburg* which is controlled from her tug. The rudders of both synchronise from the bridge of the tug. During the winter the tug also acts as an icebreaker to keep the channel open between the two terminals.
1970 The freight service was withdrawn.
1972 Oct 1: Sold with her charge and still used as her chaperon.

PENNSYLVANIA-ONTARIO TRANSPORTATION COMPANY

1906 Feb 16: Founded as a joint venture between John W. Ellsworth, CPR and the Pennsylvania Railroad Company to operate the 81 miles from Ashtabula to Port Burwell, CPR's main port on Lake Erie. Initially the firm was named Ellsworth Transportation Co., after the Ashtabula coal merchant who set up the deal. His northbound coal traffic predominated.

1954-58 The Company made only one profit, in 1956, and this was only $9,190. The 1957 loss was $40,000.

1961 Sept 29: The Company was wound up.

ASHTABULA, MAITLAND 1

301 **ASHTABULA**
B 1906 Great Lakes Engineering Works, St Claire, Michigan. **T** 2,670g, 1,525n.
D 338/103.02 x 56/17.07 x 17.5/5.33.
E Tw scr, 2 x tpl exp, 324 nhp, 12 kts. By builder.
H Steel. 2 dks. 4 track railway ferry. 6 wagons on the outer tracks and 7 on the inner pair. 26 total. Crew 32.
1906 May: Launched for the Ellsworth Transportation Co.
July: Entered service for Ellsworth Transportation Co. but within weeks Ellsworth withdrew.
Aug: The Company name was changed with CPR and the Pennsylvania RR Co. owning half each. The normal cargo from the United States was coal for CPR locomotives returning with Canadian wheat or meat vans.
1909 Dec 12: Grounded during a storm off Port Burwell. Came off on Dec 28.
1933 Feb 10: Became stuck in ice off Port Burwell. Came off, with the aid of icebreakers, the following day. There after she went into winter lay ups from Jan 10-Apr 10 each year.
1939 Sept: The outbreak of war involving Canada postponed the decision to sell the ship. She had spent much time in lay up - due to diesel locomotives displacing coal fired steam. Now she carried supplies that Canada needed.
1955 Oct: Celebrated round trip number 12,000. Sailing Monday to Friday each week the ship still averaged 250 such trips per year.
1958 Sept 18: Sank in shallow water on an even keel, with her superstructure above water, after being hit just behind the bridge by the Great Laker *Ben Moreell* (Wilson Transit Co.). *Ashtabula*, which was trying to avoid the other ship, was found guilty of crossing the bow of the oncoming vessel and underestimating her speed. *Ashtabula*'s Captain, Louis Sabo, committed suicide the evening before the Disciplinary Court convened. *Ashtabula* was raised but, because of her age, broken up by the Acme Scrap Metal & Iron Co. at Port Burwell. *Ben Moreell* was also scrapped.

Note: CPR had a 27.1% interest in the **Toronto, Hamilton & Buffalo Navigation Company** which owned *Maitland 1*. She was a sister to *Ashtabula* and came from the same yard in 1916, except that the after pair of lifeboats were on deck right aft. Sixteen years in service followed by 10 years in lay up at Ashtabula she ended as a wood barge.

QUEBEC SALVAGE
& WRECKING COMPANY

1914 Formed by CPR and George T. Davie for tug and salvage work out of Quebec. The first two vessels were the tugs *Gopher* (106) and *Musquash* (105) which were transferred from Liverpool. (My other names George Davie derive from this Haws-Davie family relationship).

1944 Sept 30: The company and its two vessels were sold to Foundation Maritime Co., Halifax.

---

302 **GTD**
B 1891 T.A. Wilson, Bridgewater, Nova Scotia. **T** 333g, 154n.
D 123/37.49 x 30/9.14 x 12/3.66. **H** Wood. 1 dk. 3 masted schooner. Fcsle and poop.
1891 Built as *Tyree*.
1907 Purchased by George T Davie & Sons, Lauzon. R/n *GTD* = George Taylor Davie.
1914 Sold to the Quebec Salvage & Wrecking Co. as a diver and wreck equipment store ship.
1930 Broken up.

303 **LORD STRATHCONA (I)**
B 1902 J.P. Rennoldson & Sons, South Shields. **T** 495g, 201n.
D 160/48.77 x 27.2/8.28 x 13.6/4.14.
E Tw scr, 2 x tpl exp, 268 nhp, 180 psi, 2 sgl blrs, 10 kts. By builder.
H Sttel. 1 dk. F 16/4.88. B 62/18.9.
1902 Built for G.T. Davie & Sons, Lauzon.
1914 Transferred to the Quebec Salvage & Wrecking Co. Same name.
1944 Sept 30: Sold to Foundation Maritime Co., Halifax, N.S. Salvage vessel.
1947 Broken up.

---

304 **TRAVERSE**
B 1930 G. Brown & Co., Clydebank. **T** 317g, 152n. **D** 130/39.62 x 26/7.92 x 10/3.05.
E Sgl scr, oil, 4 cyl 2s.sa. By Worthington, Simpson & Co., Newark.
H Steel. 1 dl. F 26/7.92. Q 40/12.19. Mchy aft.
1930 May 12: Launched. June 23: Left Greenock for Quebec. Was QS & W Co's wreck attendant. **1944** Sept 30: Sold to Foundation Maritime Co., Halifax.
1952 Sold to Levis Shipping Co. R/n *Fort Levis*.
1958 Owned by R.L. Leclerc. Same name. **1961** Sold to B. Dufour.
1964 Mar 20: Crushed by ice off Magdalen Island. Salved but broken up.

INCAN SHIPS LTD

1973 Incan Marine Ltd was formed by Canadian Pacific, holding 40%, and Inchcape (Canada) Ltd, (60%) a member of the Inchcape Group. Its function was purely research orientated. May: A further subsidiary was formed called Incan Ships Ltd with a capital of $6,000,000. In this concern CP subscribed 43% and Inchcape 57%. A long term contract was obtained for a new rail and road car route from CP's rail head at McKellar Island, Thunder Bay, Ontario, across Lake Superior to Superior, Wisconsin with a round trip time of 36 hours. The principal cargo was newsprint and wood pulp from The Great Lakes Paper Company, Thunder Bay. Initially one ship was ordered, *Incan Superior* but a second ship was soon added for a second service between Quebec City and Baie Commeau which failed to materialise and the ship was sold.
1991 The Company still trades with the one vessel.

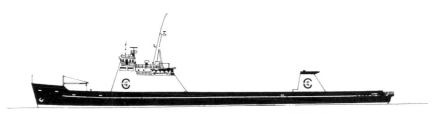

INCAN SUPERIOR, INCAN ST LAURENT

305 **INCAN SUPERIOR**
B 1974 Burrard DD Co., Vancouver. **T** 3,838g, 1,733n.
D 382/116.44 oa x 66.34/22.22 x 24/7.32.
E Tw scr, oil. 2 x 12 cyl 2s.sa, 900 rpm srg to 225 rpm, 4,300 bhp, 14 kts. By General Motors, La Grange, Illinois.
H Steel. 1 dk. Twin rudders + bow thruster. Ro-ro cargo ferry for 32 40ft/12.19m rail or 26 50ft/15.24 vehicles. 1,800 tons newsprint.
1974 Feb 28: Launched, un-named. May 3: Delivered and named at Vancouver. June: Entered service Thunder Bay-Superior. Owned by Incan Superior Ltd.
1991 Still in service on the route.

306 **INCAN ST LAURENT**
Sister to *Incan Superior* except **B** 1976.
1976 Built for an intended new down river service Quebec City-Baie Commeau. When this failed to operate, because the rail service via Tadoussac made the scheme non-viable, the vessel remained at Vancouver.
1975 June: Chartered to the Alaska Trainship Corp. for their service between Whittier, Alaska, and New Westminster. This too ran into the problem of insufficient traffic.
1976 Laid up at Vancouver.
1977 Jan 4: Sold to CN Marine, Canadian National Railway Co., Montreal. R/n *Georges Alexandre Lebel*. Placed on a rail car service directly across the St Lawrence between Matane, Gaspe Peninsular and Baie Commeau. Tonnage remeasured to 7,908g, 4,574.
1991 Still in service on the route.

OZMILLION SHIPPING CORPORATION

1986 Canadian Pacific still had their on-going china clay and newsprint trade. With the decline in the conventional fleets well under way they acquired *Canada Maritime* and converted her. She was then registered under the above owners and chartered into the trade.

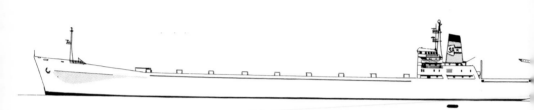

307 REPAP ENTERPRISE

B 1972 O/Y Wartsila, Turku, Finland. **T** 10,999g, 6,806n.
D 532.7/162.36 oa, 483.4 /147.35 bp x 63.8/19.44 x 23.62/7.2 dft.
E Tw scr, variable pitch, 2 x 8 cyl 4s.sa, Pielstick, 8,000 nhp, 15 kts. by builder.
H Steel. 2 dks. F /18.9. ro-ro, 542 TEU, 4 hatches/holds, stern ramp. Bow thruster.
1972 March: Built as *Mont Royal* for A/B Svenska Amerika Linien, Gothenburg.
1978 Lengthened and converted to ro-ro as above by Nobiskrug. Her name was now spelt *Mount Royal* when her owners name was anglicised. (As drawn).
1984 R/n *Atlantic Premier* by Swedish American Lines Ltd, Gothenburg.
1985 Became *Incotrans Premier* on charter then reverted to *Atlantic Premier*. The third name which she carried during the year was *Atlantic Star*, also on charter. Acquired by Bore Line (Singapore) Pte and r/n *Canada Maritime*.
1986 Acquired by Canadian Pacific. Aug 6: Arrived at Boele's yard at Dordrecht for conversion into a china clay and paper carrier. R/n *Repap Enterprise*. Registered as owned by Ozmillion Shipping Corp., Monrovia.
1991 Dec: Confirmed by CPR Montreal as still owned by Canadian Pacific but under their withdrawal policy the ship is up for sale. Technically the last vessel owned by them.

INDEX

CHANGES OF NAME ARE ALSO INDEXED BUT NOT SHIPS
MENTIONED IN THE TEXT

Nike	252	Preston	286	Queen Anna Maria	221
Niki	88	Prince Albert	114	Queen City	56
Ningchow	62	Prince Arthur	113	Queen of the North	190
Nitinat	131	Prince Edward	116A		
Nootka	183	Prince George	112	R.A. Emerson	248
Nootka Prince	218	Prince Rupert	115	R.B. Angus	229
Norman Trader	269	Princess Adelaide	102	R.P. Rithet	57
		Princess Alice	103	Rangol	79
Oakleaf	80	Princess Beatrice	82	Red Sea Pioneer	239
Ocean Crown	218	Princess Charlotte	97	Repap Enterprise	307
Ocean King	106	Princess Elaine	191	Rey Alfonso	72
Ocean Monarch	222	Princess Elizabeth	198	Robert Bornhofen	165
Ogdensburg	299	Princess Ena	94	Roga	226
Ogilvie	37	Princess Helene	200	Romanic	147
Okanagan (I) 1907	93	Princess Irene	122	Romanza	211
Okanagan (II) 1947	210	Princess Joan	199	Rona	269
Olympia	55	Princess Kathleen	180	Rosebery (I) 1928	192
Ontario	13	Princess Louise (I)		Rosebery (II) 1943	202
Orient Rose	272	1869	55	Rosita	214
Oriental Dragon	285	Princess Louise (II)		Rossland	30
Osco Edmo	251	1921	170	Ruthenia	68
Osco Macle	249	Princess Maquinna	121		
Ottawa Parapet	214	Princess Margaret	123	St Florence	179
Otter (I) 1900	54	Princess Marguerite		St George	124
Otter (II) 1887	66	(I) 1924	181	St Hugo	132
		Princess Marguerite		St Mellons	166
Patriakos II	277	(II) 1949	212	Salvage Chief	131
Pacific Logger	236	Princess Mary	104	Salvage Queen	59
Panther	65	Princess May	62	Salvor	51
Parthia	6	Princess Norah	190	Salvore	288
Pedoulas	230	Princess of Acadia		San Lorenzo	243
Pegasus	198	(I) 1950	215	Sandon	41
Pender Queen	178	Princess of Acadia		Sansovino	283
Perseus	158	(II) 1971	245	Sardinian	146
Petconnie	290	Princess of Alberni	218	Saxol	67
Peter L	282	Princess of Nanaimo	216	Scandinavian	147
Philippine Commander	256	Princess of Nova	245	Schwatka	25
Piemonte	157	Princess of Vancouver	220	Scotian	148
Pilot Trader	269	Princess Patricia		Seaboss	237
Ping An	204	(I) 1902	101	Shang Ho	160
Polar Chief	72	Princess Patricia		Shanta Rohan	236
Pomare	218	(II) 1949	213	Shikotan Maru	7
Pomeranian	144	Princess Royal	95	Shin−en Maru	240
Port Hawkesbury	239	Princess Sophia	110	Shining Star	240
Port Quebec	265	Princess Victoria	63	Shinzan Maru	77
Port Vancouver	264	Prinz Friedrich		Sicamous	130
Porthmeus	239	Wilhelm	171	Sicilian	140
Powerful	64	Proctor	44	Sidney Spiro	271
Prairie Cock	134	Prygona	67	Silvana	207
Pratincole	238			Sir Hugo	284
Premier	50	Qualicum	109	Sir W.T. Lewis	66
Prescotont	300	Quebec	265	Sistiana	288
Pretorian	145	Queen Alexandra	101	Skuzzy (I)	9

NOTES